Understanding Drugs

of related interest

Group Work with Children and Adolescents
A Handbook
Edited by Kedar Nath Dwivedi
ISBN 1 85302 157 1

Arts Approaches to Conflict
Edited by Marian Liebmann
ISBN 1 85302 293 4

Art Therapy with Offenders
Edited by Marian Liebmann
ISBN 1 85302 171 7

Mental Health in Your School
A Guide for Teachers and Others Working in Schools
Young Minds
ISBN 1 853-2 407 4

Raising Responsible Teenagers
Bob Myers
ISBN 1 85302 429 5

Understanding Drugs

A Handbook for Parents, Teachers and Other Professionals

David Emmett and Graeme Nice

Jessica Kingsley Publishers
London and Bristol, Pennsylvania

Special Note

The reader will appreciate that we are unable in this one volume to give details of the current prices for the various drugs and their legal status in all countries, and therefore those quoted are for Britain alone. Similarly, the drug slang quoted is restricted to that commonly used in Britain, but much of it has become universally accepted.

First published in the United Kingdom in 1996 by
Jessica Kingsley Publishers Ltd
116 Pentonville Road
London N1 9JB, England
and
1900 Frost Road, Suite 101
Bristol, PA 19007, U S A

Copyright © 1996 David Emmett and Graeme Nice

Library of Congress Cataloging in Publication Data
A CIP catalogue record for this book is available from the Library of Congress

British Library Cataloguing in Publication Data
Emmett, David
Understanding drugs: a handbook for parents, teachers, and
other professionals
1. Drug abuse 2. Narcotics 3. Drug abuse – Treatment
I. Title II. Nice, Graham
362.2'93

ISBN 1 85302 400 7

Printed and Bound in Great Britain by
Biddles Ltd, Guildford and King's Lynn

*Human history becomes more and
more a race between education and
catastrophe.*

H G Wells
The Outline of History (1920)

**With special thanks to Jean
Emmett and Alan 'Deano' Dent**

Contents

CHAPTER I

Introduction

A senior officer from the New York Police Department was recently quoted as saying in an interview, 'The war against drugs in New York is over, it has been won, drugs won'. We would like to say very firmly right at the outset that drugs have not won yet in the UK and, if we all work together, we can ensure that they never do.

One of the questions that is often asked of us during our work with young people is whether we have ever taken any illegal drugs. Indeed it is often thrown out as a sort of challenge, 'How can you talk about drugs, have you ever tried them?' The short answer to the question of whether we have ever taken any illegal drugs is a simple 'No, never'. But that is not because we have ever made any conscious choice about it, but simply that no one ever offered us anything so we have never had to choose. We suspect that this experience is common to most adults of our age. We were lucky enough to grow up at a time and in a place where they simply were not about. We never spoke of it with our friends, never thought about it and knew no one who did. Drugs were simply not part of our world picture.

Young people today are not growing up in the world that we did; their world is very different. Most young people will have to make a choice. They will be making that choice because someone will ask them to; someone is likely to offer them something. It is difficult enough, as all adults know, to understand the mind of an adolescent. How much more difficult it is to understand the mind of an adolescent who is making a decision that most of us were never challenged to make at that age, and now are very unlikely to be.

No one is going to come up to us in a pub or a club and offer us drugs and let's face it very few of us will ever be welcome at a rave. We are protected by our age and will never be called upon to choose; we are too old; we are past it. We are no longer a member of the customer generation, it is our children who are.

Our personal experience of illegal drugs therefore does not come from ever having tried any but comes from our work over many years with the subject in all its forms. That work has taught us countless things about this subject and it is worth outlining a few of them.

It is our view that the problem of illegal drugs represents the biggest single danger that faces our society today, bar none. We believe that this problem is potentially going to do more damage to our society in the next twenty years or so than anything ever has in our national history or that of most other countries. If you think that is overstated or an exaggeration then look around the world at what is happening in the field of drugs. Look in particular at what is happening in the United States. There are large parts of many American cities that are uninhabitable to non drug taking people. There are areas where the ordinary things of life do not go on, where you can not get a taxi or a bus, where it is impossible to get someone to come and fix your television or your heating, even areas where the United States mail service does not operate. None of these things are possible because no one will venture in there. To do so is simply not safe. If one of us blundered in to such a place, perhaps on holiday or on business, it would not be a matter of the inconvenience of being lost, it would be a matter of survival. We would be lucky to get out alive. We could be killed for the shoes on our feet or simply to be seen to fall down. The biggest single cause of death for American males under the age of twenty-five is being shot in a drug-related murder. What happens in the United States often happens here a few years on. It does not have to, but often does and is perhaps beginning to. One only has to keep an eye on the newspapers and the television news reports to see stories almost daily of the deaths of young people, the destruction of families, the turning of estates into no go areas, of crime, of shootings and so on, all related to drugs.

These are mostly problems that belong to today's young people and not just to us, as adults. Most adults have no problem around drugs, but many young and some not quite so young people do. The decisions that adults make about drugs are of little importance and have limited effect. It is the decisions that our young people make that count. They are in charge of the drug scene, not us. They are deciding what role they want illegal drugs to occupy in the society that they are rapidly inheriting.

The current problem of drugs is one that adults have given to today's young people. When we were young the whole scene was almost insignificant, but as the sixties, seventies and eighties have gone by, we have just let it slowly develop and grow around us and have done nothing about it, nothing effective at least. We have done nothing, either because we were unaware that we had a problem, we had no idea what to do about it or perhaps we didn't care. Maybe we had ill-conceived ideas about what should be allowed and what should not, and now we have handed over the problem to the younger generation. They have it now and we are seemingly safe. Our greatest fear is that our young people will do just what we did, nothing, and just let it go on growing around them. If they do that then they will pass it on to their children in due time. By then it may have become a problem of such a magnitude that their children will inherit a society the like of which we can hardly imagine and one that they will not thank us for.

As well as having the problem we believe very strongly that our young people have the power to do something about it, because they have something that most adults have very little of. They have influence over each other. We learned a long time ago that the influence of parents, teachers, indeed of all adults over young people is nothing, compared to the influence that they wield over each other. Surveys of young people taken across the UK today will show that the majority of young people state that they have not and do not intend to take drugs. Indeed if we pushed them a little further a good majority would state that they are opposed to drugs. We would like to pose some questions to those anti-drug youngsters, 'What are you doing about it? What have you done about it today?' It is the anti-drug young people who have the real power to change things, not those who want to take drugs and see them as being fashionable and desirable. Their influence does not count. Let us try and illustrate this point by looking at two different examples, the first an adult example and the second a young person's example. Let us look first at the subject of adult cigarette smoking, which is now regarded by most people as being anti-social and unacceptable. Cigarette smokers are looked down upon as being somewhat socially inferior creatures. A few years ago if you had held a party in your house, even as a non smoker, you would have felt obliged to put ashtrays out for your guests and then, after they had gone home, opened all the doors and windows and complained about the smell. Now it is different, for if someone lights up a cigarette in a non smoker's house without permission, they are liable to find themselves ejected into the garden. Light one in someone's car and you might find yourself walking for the rest of your journey. Most work places are now non smoking environments and every day we see groups of people huddled on the pavement outside office blocks to have their smoke, because they are banned from doing so inside. As a result of this public disapproval, this peer pressure, the number of adult smokers is dropping very rapidly. It was not the influence of smokers that brought this about, it was the influence of the non smokers. Smokers did not go around saying that smoking was unacceptable, that it polluted the air and so on, it was the non smoker who felt liberated to have their say and what a difference they have made.

Now let us look at a young person's example. At the beginning of the 1980s we were involved in dealing with a major outbreak of the sniffing of solvent glues, by children on a large housing estate. The craze lasted for three years and during that time five young people died as result of their sniffing. If you had paid a visit to the estate during that period you would have got the impression that the problem was out of control, with young people, some as young as nine years of age, sniffing everywhere. But then, during the summer of 1983, something very remarkable happened. In the space of a few short weeks the problem disappeared, it simply faded away. It did not go away as a result of the efforts of the many teachers and other adults who became involved in trying to deal with it, but went away simply because it went out of fashion. What had been in favour was now outmoded. If you talk with the majority of young people on that estate now about glue sniffing they will answer that this practice is for losers, but in the early 1980s it had been cool. If you were not sniffing then, you had no street credibility, but by the end of 1983 you had none if you were. It was not the influence of the sniffers that brought this about; they did not go around telling people that glue sniffing was for losers. It was the non sniffers who did that; they brought about the change and as a result the problem passed into history, and to date has not returned to that estate as a visible problem. Everything that we do in drugs education must be geared towards unlocking this weapon of positive influence, a weapon that can change the world.

We have become used in recent years to thinking that young people's influence over their peers is mostly bad, mostly negative. Perhaps it is time we started to recognize the immense power of positive influence. We need to be reinforcing the decisions of non drug taking young people and to strengthen and empower them in the use of that influence. It is after all their society that drug taking is likely to damage. It sometimes seems that we are beating our heads against an enormous and unstoppable object that is slowly overwhelming us, but drugs can be overcome. There is a light at the end of the tunnel. We cannot see it yet as it is around the corner, and there may be more corners after this one, but it is there waiting for us. It is there because many people who are concerned about the problem are starting to work together. Parents are beginning to get themselves educated about drugs, when previously they felt helpless and unable to have any sensible and useful discussion of the subject with their children. They are starting to acquire the necessary knowledge to make a real contribution.

Teachers similarly are beginning to receive the training necessary to enable them to work with this subject, and schools are putting together good, integrated, drugs policies and education programmes for pupils. These programmes not only deliver information, but also lead to an understanding of the issues that go along with drug use. The police too are getting involved in the schools drug education programmes and bringing their unique experience of the subject into lessons and discussions. In addition, health authorities are also putting a great deal of effort and well trained personnel into prevention, education and treatment, as is the prison service.

In 1995 the UK Government funded the setting up of local Drug Action Teams and Drug Reference Groups under its 'Tackling Drugs Together' initiative. It is also funding well conceived and expertly presented awareness raising campaigns as well as supporting the efforts made by a whole range of other agencies.

Only by working together can we enable young people to begin to solve the problem. We as adults cannot solve it, only they can. Our job is to help them do it.

At the end of the battle of El Alamein, the first major allied victory of the second world war, Winston Churchill said, 'This is not the end of the war, it is not even the beginning of the end, but it is perhaps the end of the beginning'. We believe that this is where we are currently in the war against drug abuse. The beginning is over and we have engaged the enemy. A few short years ago the majority of people did not even know there was a war to be fought, much less become personally involved. But now we can all be involved, and because of this we need not fail, we must not, for to even contemplate failure is to think the unthinkable.

CHAPTER 2

A Brief History of Drug Use and a Snapshot of the Current Drugs Situation

Western Europe has very little history of drug use. It is only necessary to look at its geographical position to see why. The climate brings little in the way of hot weather or bright sunlight, and therefore none of the major drug supplying plants have evolved. No opium poppies occur naturally, no coca bushes and no mescaline cacti. Similarly, cannabis of drug producing quality does not occur naturally, but has been introduced illicitly in recent years on a small scale.

In historical times the only drug that occurred naturally was based on the hallucinogenic mushroom. Only in certain parts of Scandinavia and northern Russia was there substantial usage of these fungi for recreational and religious purposes. Whilst there is little doubt that early residents of the remainder of Europe knew of the properties of the various 'magic mushrooms', their use remained largely restricted to a few pagan religious leaders and soothsayers. The Romans had knowledge of opium through their dealings with the Middle and Far East, and used several different preparations of the drug for pain relief. They undoubtedly brought supplies of these with them during their occupation of other countries, but there is no evidence at all of its use as a mind altering substance by the indigenous population. When the Roman occupation ended as their empire retreated, the use and knowledge of opium was lost for many hundreds of years.

It was not until the European nations began to create their own empires and sent their forces around the globe that their populations began to come into contact with the major plant based drugs. Opium and cannabis reached Europe through contacts with Africa and Asia, and then coca from the new world. Non medical use of these drugs was largely restricted to sailors, travellers and to a small number of wealthy people who were able to afford their importation. The use of such drugs by ordinary people and in particular by young people was to remain almost unknown until after

World War II. In the years following that war, people's incomes began slowly to rise and to provide them with a little more in the way of disposable funds that could be used to have a good time. Simultaneously young people throughout the world began to seek for their own particular cultures and identities. It has often been said that until the 1950s there was no such thing as a 'youth culture' or a 'youth market'. Young people began to have money in their pockets to spend, and others began to provide commodities for them to spend it on. The same thing had been happening for some years in the USA and drugs had become one of the specific commodities that young people had taken to. This soon spread throughout Western Europe and the other developed countries, and by the beginning of the 1960s we began to see an increase amongst certain sectors of young populations in the use of cannabis, which was followed inevitably by the other drugs of abuse. Many people have the idea that drugs, and particularly cannabis, were in use by the majority of young people during the 1960s. The authors were both young men during the 1960s and can say, from their own experience, that nothing could be further from the truth. The vast majority of young people had no contact with drugs of any kind. This picture remained static throughout the 1970s and indeed many countries even saw a decline in the use of certain drugs, but all that has now sadly changed.

Within the past 10 to 15 years, the world-wide drug culture has evolved in dramatic and alarming ways. The reasons for these worrying changes stem from two developments. First, the major customer generation has shifted sharply towards the young, especially adolescent and young adult males, and second, the availability of drugs has become very widespread indeed, to the point where whole nations, from inner city areas to suburban towns and even sleepy country areas seem to have become affected.

Prices, especially of the more popular substances, have become much more affordable and well within the reach of greater numbers of people who may wish to try them. Add to this scenario the advent of the designer dance drugs which have permeated the commercial social scene, such as raves, clubs and bars, and which appear to have become accepted by many young people as an integral part of relaxation and pleasure, and you will appreciate that drug taking is no longer viewed as an anti-social activity carried out by a small number of 'losers'.

Nowadays, drugs supply is a major international business, which nets vast sums of money each year for the producers, importers, suppliers and dealers. For these people, the name of the game is money and power, and their greed feeds upon the exploitation of the vulnerability and weakness of others. They will not lose sleep by worrying about the misery they cause, or potentially destructive nature of the goods that they peddle. There will always be new recruits to replace those who escape their clutches or who sadly lose their lives.

Despite the falling prices, the development of a tolerance and dependency by users towards their drugs will lead many of them to turn to crime to fund their increasingly expensive habits. In the UK alone it has been estimated that three to four billion pounds worth of property crime is committed each year for this reason alone. Add to this the legally available funds and goods used to buy drugs, and you can appreciate the very lucrative nature of this multinational industry. Many users are tempted to take risks in order to make quick and easy money by supplying street drugs. Several court cases in recent years have even involved drug dealers who were above their country's state retirement age.

Certain of these street drugs can even be produced in private homes, especially cannabis and amphetamine, although by far the greater proportion are imported. Many of the countries in Western Europe, Asia, the Middle and Far East and South America have become major producers and exporters of various illegal drugs, and there is growing evidence that suppliers in some former Eastern Bloc countries are now cashing in on the trade in order to attract much sought after foreign currency.

Street drugs today are not so much pushed as pulled. Dealers no longer have to put themselves at risk by trading on the streets, many hiding behind the geographic anonymity offered by the mobile phone. Users will now seek them out to provide supplies of their chosen drug. At an even more basic level, some users themselves may supply drugs to their friends and social acquaintances in order to pay for their own drug habit. They will buy in bulk and then sell on the drugs in smaller quantities at a good profit.

For many younger people today, the way is open for more freedom of choice, opportunity and experience. Consequently, illegal drug use has infiltrated their world in order to increase that choice of experience.

One of the most notable of these drugs, a drug which receives a great deal of media attention from time to time, is ecstasy. The drug itself is not new, it being available in the early part of this century for use in the treatment of certain psychiatric disorders. It has merely been repackaged and relaunched as a relatively harmless substance that, due to its stimulant and hallucinogenic properties, will enable the user to dance for hours, make friends easily, and have heightened sensory experiences. It is mostly used by the young in commercial social settings, such as raves or parties, and in Britain for example it is used by an estimated 250 to 500 thousand people on a fairly regular basis, most use being concentrated at the weekends.

We have also seen in recent times the re-emergence of LSD, another hallucinogenic drug formerly used in certain psychiatric treatment regimes, with its origins in the early part of the century. LSD which found much favour in the 'flower power' days of the 1960s and 1970s, is now marketed as 'acid' or 'trips', and is very much associated, along with ecstasy, with the 'acid house' music and rave scene. It is now more widely available and at a cheaper price than ever before, with a similar number of young people using it on a regular basis as ecstasy. Both ecstasy and LSD were removed from use in psychiatric medicine due to their associated harmful effects on patients, and yet today we see it being sold in forms that would be attractive to children.

A third drug associated mostly with young people and the rave/dance scene is amphetamine, known in some drug slang as 'speed', 'billy' or 'whiz'. This powerful stimulant drug is cheap and easy to produce, and because of its street appearance as an off-white powder, is easy to adulterate with other substances in order to increase sales profits. For its users it seemingly gives confidence, energy and stamina, and suppresses their appetites. It can, however, cause a real depletion of the body's reserves of strength and, more worryingly, it can also induce paranoia, temporary or permanent psychosis, depression and insomnia, together with an adverse effect on the immune system. Put simply, what goes up must come down, and apart from the above, users may well experience other unpleasant withdrawal effects. All of these facts are of course not good selling points for amphetamine dealers and so are never mentioned to their many young customers. Amphetamine is now a very popular illegal substance in use by young people world-wide, with millions of regular users. There is a growing trend towards the injecting of amphetamine, even by young people, thus exposing such users to even greater harm.

Ecstasy, LSD and amphetamine are today closely linked with young people's social scenes. Thankfully only a small percentage of users will ever suffer any permanent or discernible harm, such is the resilience of the human body.

The effects of long term regular use over a period of years are not clearly understood, however, and it could be considered that all those using these drugs on that basis are taking part in one of the largest drugs trials the world has ever seen.

Along with these three street drugs there is another, this time a depressant with mild hallucinogenic properties, that is in regular use across the world by an even greater number of people of all ages. This drug is cannabis, and a conservative estimate based on a recent national survey in Britain indicates that it is in use on an occasional to regular basis by more than six per cent of the adult population, some three million plus individuals, thus making it the most popular illegal drug of abuse in this country.

Due to the high level of international demand for cannabis, the bulk of its supply comes from countries with a climate more favourable for intensive cultivation of the plant from which it is produced. Increasingly, however, it is being cultivated on a semi-commercial basis in the countries where it is in demand. An ever increasing quantity of cannabis is being produced with the use of highly sophisticated hydroponic growing methods and artificial sunlight, under factory-like conditions in converted rooms, or in some cases whole houses or other premises totally devoted to the process.

Individuals too grow their own plants for personal use on window ledges at home, in gardens, sometimes at work, and in the case of one innovative user, alongside a busy motorway, until put out of business by a sharp eyed traffic policeman.

Home growing of cannabis has increased simply to help fulfil the heavy demand. The cannabis seeds are easily obtainable from other growers or from centres such as Amsterdam, where visitors can see whole shops devoted to the cultivation and use of the plant. It is likely that the popularity of cannabis will continue to rise in the years to come and the legalization debate is now being considered in many countries, even in government circles. This debate is being promoted and influenced by the pro-cannabis lobbies which have sprung up in various countries. Their ultimate aim is to see cannabis made legal or, at the very least de-criminalized, as it is in Holland. We have no doubts that the real reason behind the actions of many who wish to see the drug legalized is that they stand to make a great deal of money cultivating and marketing the drug to an ever increasing customer population.

The wide acceptance of cannabis use can also be noted from some of the many logos and slogans that can be found on a wide range of young people's fashion garments. Caps, jeans, jackets and T-shirts are all available from markets and even many leading stores with a variety of pro-cannabis symbols.

Apart from these four drugs, which many would wish to have us consider as 'soft' drugs, and which seem to have become an integral part of international mass youth culture, we still have to contend with the menace of other substances such as heroin, cocaine and 'crack' cocaine, usually considered as 'hard' drugs. It is our view that no drug should be considered as hard or soft, as all have the ability to cause many problems for the user and for society as a whole.

Most heroin, cocaine and crack cocaine originates from outside of the main user countries, and despite record seizures by customs and police officers each year, enough slips through the defences to fulfil the requirements of the countless users throughout the world. Happily, the number of users of these substances is much smaller than those who favour cannabis. Despite only a small percentage of adult populations using these drugs, the social problems and crime associated with them, especially heroin, easily outweigh those created by any other illegal drug.

Addiction to heroin and cocaine, which can occur very quickly is, in Britain, a condition notifiable to the Home Office Drugs Branch, and the number of notified addicts has been steadily increasing over the past six years. Notifications for the year 1993, for example, showed an increase of 13 per cent over the previous year and the current proportion of such addicts under the age of 21 years has risen to 75 per cent of the total. It perhaps indicates that the 'power of the powder' is finding a foothold amongst young people. The power of heroin must never be underestimated. One 20-year-old addict recently related to us his experience of heroin as 'living under water and having to buy air to breathe', outlining his total dependence on the drug simply to feel normal and to be able to carry out his everyday functions.

Of those who succumb to heroin, few can ever give up their need for the drug. Relapse amongst former users can almost be considered normal behaviour. The psychological attraction to its use, even after years of abstinence, can be overwhelming, even though its users' expectations may never be fulfilled by actual use of the drug. Many of the notifications of heroin users to the British Home Office are classified as re-notifications.

Addiction to heroin is the root cause of much property crime today. Most of these crimes are daylight robbery and opportunist theft, but much worse deeds may be perpetrated to fund habits which in extreme cases may cost a British user as much as £100 per day, £35,000 per year. It is accepted that much of the property stolen may only realize as little as ten per cent of its true value, and that a heavy user may therefore be faced with obtaining property to the value of £350,000 every year. Note that this figure is for just one user and for just one drug.

On top of all of this must be added the further costs to society in providing social and medical intervention services and substitute drugs, such as methadone, to existing and former heroin users.

By contrast to heroin, fewer cases of addiction to cocaine are reported. Its much talked about derivative, crack cocaine, does not seem to have swept other countries as it has in some parts of the USA, and was feared and predicted to do world-wide. Currently, pockets of high crack usage are mostly confined to inner cities and areas of high social deprivation.

We must at this point introduce a degree of perspective amongst all this doom and gloom and state quite categorically that there is evidence to show that most people will never use any illegal drugs, and of those who choose to, only a small number will ever become permanently dependent or suffer irreversible adverse effects. Most young people will make the decision that drugs are not going to form a significant part of their lives, and if we could only harness the power of this non-using majority we may be in a position to firmly reject and to eject illegal drugs from our societies.

To complete this snapshot picture of drug use today, we must now concentrate on three other types of substance in common usage that are currently all available from legal sources.

The sniffing and inhaling of volatile substances has been with us for many years, and there are some indications that the habit has experienced something of a resurgence in popularity amongst some young people in recent times. The use of solvents is constantly changing, and today it seems that a wider and much more dangerous variety of products are being used. The use of solvent glues for inhalation has in many countries given way to the spraying of liquid petroleum gas and other lighter fuels directly into the mouth and throat. As a consequence there are still many instances of death through asphyxiation and associated problems due to this type of substance misuse. More deaths occur amongst young people from these practices than from the use of any other single street drug.

Tranquillizers and sleeping pills and tablets are still much misused. Millions of genuine prescriptions for these are written by doctors every year, and a proportion of these, together with those obtained by fraud and theft or by importation, form the basis of a thriving street trade. Many users of other drugs will seek them out in order to cope with the adverse effects of their more usual drug, or to alleviate the comedown effects they experience when their usual drug is unavailable to them. Others will use them simply for the numbing, stress relieving and sleep inducing effects for which they were designed. The sleeping pill Temazepam, for example, is misused by many, and has proved to be a particular problem within some communities in Scotland where, in its gel capsule form, it has been used intravenously. This practice will, however, soon cease, as new government restrictions will prevent or curtail its distribution in this form in Britain. However, tablet forms of temazepam will remain available and these can easily be crushed and mixed with water in order to be injected. The majority of doctors are much more aware nowadays that certain prescription drugs can be misused, and are now more reluctant to supply them, favouring alternative treatments or alternative drugs that do not cause dependencies, and that cannot be so easily misused.

The final group of drugs that we need to be aware of, because of their increasing popularity, especially amongst some young males, are the steroid drugs that are manufactured for oral use or for injection. The anabolic type of steroids are used in conjunction with regular heavy exercise and certain diets to build muscle bulk. They should only ever be used under strict medical supervision as incorrect use can lead to potentially dangerous side effects. Despite the dangers, many young people involved in weight training and body building, together with many of those in the rave and dance club scene, use them to re-sculpt their bodies. This is done in order to raise their self-esteem by having a body that they perceive as being sexually attractive to potential partners. As in all areas of drug use, there are of course unscrupulous suppliers. Many of the so called steroids available on the streets are of spurious quality or not even steroids at all, whilst others come from very questionable sources such as veterinary surgeries, and are intended solely for use with animals such as horses.

Many countries operate needle and syringe schemes, originally set up to combat the spread of HIV infection amongst injecting drug users. Many of these are now reporting a steady increase in the numbers of young steroid users who are making use of their services. Here they can obtain clean injecting equipment, together with correct information and advice concerning steroid use. Again it is expected that some governments will shortly introduce controls to try to stem the improper supply and use of these very dangerous drugs, but it remains to be seen whether these proposed controls will merely drive the problem further underground.

To conclude and summarize this snapshot picture of drug use and availability today, it must be realized that the whole range of drugs and other substances, both legal and illegal, that can be misused are readily available throughout many countries. There are some national, local and regional variations in the range of available drugs, due to preference, financial circumstances and the age range of the using populations, but the 'fab four' favoured especially by young users – cannabis, amphetamine, ecstasy and LSD – appear universally and readily available. Due to their sheer popularity, a vast international network of manufacturers and suppliers has grown up to service this great demand.

If societies are unwilling or unable to halt the illegal supply of substances on the streets, then they only have education to resort to as a means of averting a further escalation of the problems that we already face as a result of drug misuse.

Part I

CHAPTER 3

Cannabis
Delta 9 Tetrahydrocannabinol

Cannabis
Delta 9 Tetrahydrocannabinol

Cannabis: Quick Reference Guide

Source

Plants of the genus Cannabis, particularly Cannabis Sativa.

Forms and appearance

Herbal – dried plant material, similar to a coarse cut tobacco like mixture, usually a greenish brown in colour, sometimes the mixture has been compressed into blocks and occasionally is seen wound with thread around a thin stick.

Resin – dried and compressed resinous sap, found in blocks of various size and shapes, ranging in colour from black or grey, through every shade of brown, russet brown, and greenish brown to a golden pine colour and in consistency from hard and brittle, hard and dense, soft and oily to dry and crumbly.

Oil – extracted from the resin form by the use of a chemical solvent, seen as a thick, heavy oil ranging in colour from dark green or dark brown to jet black with a distinctive smell like rotting vegetation.

Marketing

Sold by the ounce or as a fraction of an ounce in a variety of packaging and sometimes with no packaging at all. Available in every town and village in the country, in most public houses, clubs, on the street, outside schools; indeed anywhere that young people in particular gather.

Cost

Between £80.00 and £150.00 per ounce for both the herbal and resin forms. There is no fixed price for the much rarer oil.

Legal position

A Class B, schedule one, controlled substance under the Misuse of Drugs Act 1971.

Methods of use

Commonly smoked in a variety of ways, can be put into cooking or made into a drink; occasionally eaten on its own.

Effects of use

Relaxation, happiness, congeniality, increased powers of concentration, sexual arousal, loss of inhibitions, warmth, increased appetite, talkativeness.

Adverse effects

Loss of short-term memory, impaired judgement, impaired driving skills, dry mouth, lethargy, decreased blood pressure, dizziness, confusion, anxiety, panic, paranoia, bloodshot eyes, together with a potential for cancers and breathing disorders.

Tolerance potential

Tolerance rapidly develops with continued use.

Habituation potential

A true physical habituation is rare but most users will develop a strong psychological habituation with continued use.

Withdrawal effects

Disturbed sleep patterns, anxiety, panic, restlessness.

Overdose potential

It is not thought possible to fatally overdose with cannabis.

Cannabis: In Depth Guide

Introduction

Cannabis is without any doubt the most commonly abused illegal drug in use anywhere in the world, particularly the developed world. It is imported into the UK in vast quantities, so vast that the amounts seized by the police and customs are officially recorded in metric tonnes.

Source

Cannabis plants

All plants of the genus Cannabis produce within them a complex chemical called Delta 9 Tetrahydrocannabinol, known as THC. Three varieties of the plant produce THC in significant amounts, Cannabis Sativa, Cannabis Indica and Cannabis Ruderalis. Of these, Sativa produces THC in the highest concentrations and is therefore the preferred source of the drug. Sativa occurs wild in countries that lie on either side of the tropics and is extensively cultivated in many of those countries for export to the rest of the world. It is grown in the UK but does not flourish unless artificially provided with the high light levels, extended daylight hours and warm temperatures that it is used to. Indica and Ruderalis produce lower levels of THC but are more tolerant of the climatic conditions of northern Europe and are grown both under artificial conditions and in the open. In recent years all three varieties have been hybridized to produce varieties that will provide high THC levels and grow well in this country. The plant has two distinct forms, a male and a female, both of which produce THC within them, the female producing higher levels than the male.

Forms and appearance

Herbal

Examples of cannabis in herbal and resin form

Herbal or vegetable cannabis is, by a small margin, the commonest form of the drug in use in the UK. It is produced by drying and chopping the leaves of the Cannabis plant into a coarse cut tobacco-like mixture. The finest quality herbal cannabis is produced by drying and chopping the flower, known as the bud, of the female cannabis plant. This preparation, known on the streets as *Sinsemilla* or *Sinsy*, contains the highest levels of THC in herbal form but is rare and relatively expensive.

Drug producers are more interested in the quantity of drugs that they can produce rather than quality and so the vast majority of herbal cannabis that finds its way onto the streets of the UK is of generally poor quality. It consists of a mixture of chopped leaves of all sizes from both the female and male plant, thin stems, small quantities of flower bud and some seeds.

Most samples of herbal cannabis are a greenish brown in colour, although on rare occasions samples are seen that are pale green or golden.

Herbal cannabis can easily be mistaken for various forms of tobacco due to its similar appearance and many parents and teachers have had the embarrassing experience of accusing a young person of illegal possession of cannabis only to find later that it was nothing of the sort. Close examination of the sample should eliminate that mistake. Most samples of tobacco have been produced by chopping dried plugs of tobacco leaves that have been formed from several leaves from different tobacco varieties layered together and cured. This layering can be seen in the form of strata of differing colours in the small shreds of tobacco. Cannabis has no such layering. Round seeds, approximately 5mm in diameter, are often found in herbal cannabis whereas tobacco contains no such seeds. Tobacco often has a strong, aromatic smell, whereas herbal cannabis simply smells a little musty.

Resin

The leaves and stems of both the male and the female cannabis plant are covered in a coating of fine hairs. In bright sunlight, as the plant approaches maturity, each hair begins to exude a sticky resinous sap from its end. This exudate is collected and then dried and compressed to produce the finest forms of cannabis resin. As with the herbal variety, modern producers are intent upon producing the drug in large quantities without being concerned about quality and so, rather than wait for the plant to exude its own resin, will crush the sap from the whole plant in commercial sized crushing machines.

Cannabis resin is only a little less common than the herbal variety in the amount in use in the UK. We produce no cannabis resin in the UK; all of the resin that we see is imported from countries with generally warmer climates than our own. Countries such as Morocco, Lebanon, Pakistan, Turkey, India and Afghanistan are major producers.

Cannabis resin is seen in a wide variety of colours, consistencies and forms. The variations in colour and consistencies are mostly a result of climatic differences between the various producing countries together with differing production methods.

The colour can vary between the deepest black down through every shade of brown that you can imagine to a pale golden pine. Some black forms are hard, shiny and brittle and can be snapped like old fashioned liquorice. Dark brown resins tend to be very hard and dense and very difficult to break up. The user normally has to heat the block with a match or a cigarette lighter before being able to crumble it. This process of heating is called *roasting* or *toasting*. Many of the paler coloured resins are soft and dry and crumble easily in the fingers.

Oil

Cannabis oil is produced by dissolving cannabis resin in a powerful commercial solvent, filtering out the fibre content and then evaporating off the solvent leaving behind a viscous, heavy oil that contains a very high level of THC. The oil varies in colour from dark green or dark brown to

Cannabis oil

black and has a very powerful smell similar to rotting vegetation. Anyone who has smelled a rotting cabbage or a bag of brussel sprouts will have smelled something similar. This oil is either dribbled onto hand rolling cigarette tobacco or smeared with a matchstick onto the sides of commercially made cigarettes.

Special note

It is worth making the point very strongly that despite the differences between the various forms of cannabis it is all in essence simply THC. Whatever it is called and whatever it looks like, it is all the same. Many users claim that they only use one sort or another and never touch the other forms. All of that is nonsense, for whatever form they use it is THC that they are taking into their bodies.

Marketing

Cannabis is smuggled into the UK, for example, through a wide variety of entry points and by a vast range of methods. The majority of imported cannabis enters in huge consignments, weighing many tons each, through entry ports and across isolated beaches all around the country. It also enters in medium to small consignments in the thousands of cars and goods vehicles that constantly criss-cross the English Channel and North Sea on holiday and on business. If you add to that the not inconsiderable quantities that are individually smuggled, in small amounts, in the pockets and baggage of travellers and tourists you have a picture of smuggling on a vast scale. It is impossible to give any accurate figure for the amount of cannabis that enters this country; the best estimates from HM Customs and Excise would suggest that in excess of 500 metric tonnes of cannabis in all its forms is smuggled into the UK every year.

Much of the cannabis that enters the UK is packed in individual amounts that weigh many pounds and it therefore needs to be broken down through the distribution chain into smaller and smaller quantities so that it reaches the streets in amounts that are convenient to the distributor and user in terms both of size and price.

Curiously, cannabis is the only one of the many street drugs in use in the UK to be sold by the ounce or fractions of an ounce, all other street drugs being sold in metric measures.

Herbal cannabis is sold at street level in small bags, commonly those issued by banks for holding coins.

Resinous cannabis is sold in blocks of various size, often wrapped in clear plastic film. The resin will have been cut up by the dealer to suit the particular market that he is supplying. A sixteenth of an ounce, known on the streets as a *Louis* or a *teenth*, or an eighth of an ounce, known as a *Henry* or simply as an *eighth* are common when selling to young people, although other sizes will be available. As with most commodities there are savings to be made by buying in bulk and young people will often pool their resources in order to buy in larger amounts and get a cheaper deal.

Cannabis oil is usually sold in small bottles by fractions of a fluid ounce, or sometimes contained inside a condom, although this is rare. Oil is still a rare drug on the streets being a very specialist article. It is unlikely that young people will be offered it but it will be available 'by special order' from many dealers.

Cost

The price of both herbal cannabis and resin cannabis fluctuates wildly according to the amount available in any one location. It follows the laws of supply and demand closely and when cannabis is in good supply the price will fall dramatically; in time of shortage, what users call 'droughts', the price will move rapidly upwards. A price of between £80.00 to £150.00 per ounce is common. An average user would require around £2.00 worth of herbal or resin cannabis to provide one smoke of good strength. However, special prices are often agreed when suppliers are opening up a new market, particularly amongst young people. We have seen low grade cannabis sold to school pupils for as little as 50 pence for sufficient to provide one smoke.

Cannabis oil is still so rare and difficult to obtain that no fixed price exists. The supplier is able to ask almost any price for it and many users will be willing to pay a high price just for the experience of trying it before returning to their more usual forms of the drug.

Legal position

Cannabis in its various forms is a class B, schedule one, controlled substance under the Misuse of Drugs Act 1971. Its inclusion in Schedule one means that cannabis has no legally recognized medical uses.

All drugs under class B carry the same penalties.

Simple possession

Maximum penalty on indictment, five years imprisonment plus an unlimited fine.

Possession with intent to supply to another

Maximum sentence on indictment, 14 years plus an unlimited fine plus the seizure of drug related assets.

Supplying to another

As immediately above.

Cultivation of cannabis plants

As above.

Another offence that is worth mentioning is one that concerns persons in control of premises in which cannabis is smoked. Any person who is in control of any premises and allows those premises to be used for the smoking of cannabis commits an offence that is punishable on indictment by a maximum of 14 years imprisonment. There are many thousands of parents up and down this country, who are either conned or intimidated by their children into allowing them to smoke cannabis at home, and who run the risk of prosecution for this offence. In the eyes of the law the controller of any premises has to take all steps possible to prevent cannabis being smoked there. It is not sufficient for that person to say that they forbade their children to smoke cannabis there. They have to positively prevent it, even to the point of calling the police. It is worth noting that the young person who is using runs the risk of a five year sentence while their parents run the risk of 14 years.

The full rigour of the law is rarely applied by police forces in the UK to the offence of possession of small amounts of cannabis for personal use. Persons so found would almost always qualify for a police drugs caution. A caution is not a criminal conviction and so does not result in a criminal record. The possession of a criminal record for a drugs offence is still an immensely powerful conviction and would be an insuperable bar to entry into a career in most government services, the armed forces with the recent exemption of the army, the police services and so on. Many countries operate a ban on the issuing of residential or work permits to persons with such convictions. Such restrictions could have an extreme effect on a young person's life and prospects and can perhaps be viewed as being too severe for an act of rashness carried out in adolescence. The use of the police drugs caution allows young people in particular to be given a second chance, a chance to learn that possession of drugs is not a game and can bring very serious consequences. In deciding whether a person qualifies for a caution the police have to be satisfied that the amount of cannabis found in that person's possession can rightly be called a small amount for personal use. No fixed figure is used, it is the circumstances that count. A person who lives in a place where there is a ready supply of cannabis can buy whenever they want and so the amount would need to be small, whereas a person living in a place where cannabis is difficult to obtain would only be able to buy at more irregular intervals and would need to purchase larger amounts each time. Young people often have the idea that possession of amounts such as an eighth of an ounce will qualify for a caution, while larger amounts would result in a prosecution. This is dangerous nonsense, for it is the circumstances of the offence that are important, not just the amount of drugs found.

Methods of use

Cannabis joints

Cannabis is most commonly smoked, with the lungs carrying the active ingredient, THC, into the bloodstream. It can be smoked in many ways but whatever way is chosen, there are several practical problems for the user to overcome. First, herbal cannabis is a dry and short stranded product unlike tobacco which is moist and long stranded. It does not cling together in the way tobacco does and is therefore not an easy substance to roll into cigarettes. Second, it burns at a very high temperature, much hotter than tobacco, and if the user does not take some measures to deal with that degree of heat then it will burn the lips and the tongue. Third, it contains much higher levels of tar than tobacco. The average street sample of cannabis contains some three to five times the amount of tar as the highest tar rated commercially available tobacco.

The commonest method used to smoke cannabis is to roll it in a hand-rolled cigarette called a *joint* or a *spliff* or *splith*. If the smoker is using herbal cannabis then this will be rolled without the addition of tobacco but if the resin is used then it will be crumbled and a little added to tobacco before rolling. The tobacco for mixing with cannabis is often obtained by splitting open commercially made cigarettes. The remains of such cigarettes, usually in the form of a clean unused filter attached to some strands of paper are a good indicator of cannabis smoking. The smoker will often use one of the commercially produced 'king sized' cigarette rolling papers to 'build a joint'. Many thousands of packets of these papers are sold in the UK every week, allegedly for the hand rolling tobacco smoker, but we have yet to meet one who uses such papers. All of the users of 'king size' papers that we have come across use them for cannabis. If the smoker does not use such papers then a number of the normal, smaller, papers are used together. Three papers is a common number – two laid side by side with the third across the top. The smoking mixture is added and, before sealing, a small cylinder, called a *roach* or *roach end*, is inserted at the mouth end. This cylinder is made from a small piece of cardboard, usually torn from the cigarette paper packet cover, that is rolled up tight and then allowed to relax. It forms into a spiral which serves two purposes. First, it acts like a mesh to keep the smoking mixture inside the cigarette and stop it coming out into the mouth of the smoker, and second, it places the burning end of the cigarette a little further away from the smoker's mouth and thus alleviates the heat problems. It is doubtful whether the short length of most roaches can have any real effect on the temperature of the smoke and it seems likely that it is more a question of fashion with most users.

The use of a roach end is perceived to be the correct way to construct such a cigarette and gives the smoker status as someone who is familiar with the drug. The opposite end of the joint is twisted together to prevent the contents spilling out. The cigarette paper packet cover is only capable of providing a small number of roaches before coming apart. There will normally be several cigarette papers left in the packet at this stage and they are often to be found, still interleaved together, spilled on the floor. The presence of such spilled papers is a good indicator of the use of the area by cannabis smokers.

There is a fashion amongst many smokers for making their joints in all sorts of extravagant shapes and sizes. Large joints are built using five or even seven papers. Some are as large as a corona cigar and are used as 'party joints', being intended for several people to share. Some smokers stain their cigarette papers with colouring agents first; cold tea is often used to give a yellowish brown colour. Curious shapes are sometimes constructed, often with more than one burning end. There are a number of freely available

Examples of home made 'bhongs'

Examples of home made 'bhongs' (continued)

publications which give instructions to users in building such strange creations.

A traditional way of smoking cannabis using a water pipe has in recent years enjoyed a great revival. The hand crafted and decorative hookah pipe is still used but more commonly a crude version called a *bhong* is constructed using a wide assortment of different water-tight objects. At its simplest, such a pipe will be constructed from a plastic drinks bottle of around one litre size. A hole is pieced in the side of the bottle about half way up from the bottom and a tube inserted at a downwards angle until its end reaches close to the bottom. A waterproof seal is then made between the side of the bottle and the tube with chewing gum or something similar. This tube can be made from plastic, glass, wood, rubber or metal. At the other end of the tube a smoking bowl will be constructed using tin foil with holes punctured at the bottom and fixed to the tube end. A bottle top is often used, although more robust smoking bowls are often made from mechanics sockets which have had a hole drilled through the base of them. Water is poured into the bottle until the lower end of the tube is covered and the bhong is ready for use. The smoking bowl is filled with cannabis and is lit while the smoker inhales through the neck of the bottle. By doing so the smoker creates a depression over the water and smoke is drawn from the burning cannabis down the tube to bubble up through the water to the smoker's mouth. This is the basic design of the bhong but there are many variations on this theme. We have seen bhongs made from all sorts of bottles and containers, including brandy bottles, chemical retorts, ball valve floats, buckets and on one occasion a dustbin.

Bhongs are often abandoned by users when smoking is finished. It is not uncommon to find numbers of them in places where young people gather and they provide good evidence of the use of cannabis in that area.

Users of bhongs claim that this is a healthier way of smoking cannabis as the water cools the smoke and removes from it most of the tar that it contains. The tar is certainly removed; the water in the vessel goes a dark brown during use and tar is condensed in large quantities on the inside of

Carved wooden 'chillum' pipe

the bhong. Their claim to healthier smoking is, however, unfounded. By cooling the cannabis smoke and removing a lot of the tar, bhong users make the smoke much less irritating to the lungs and so are able to inhale it much more deeply and to retain it in their lungs for much longer. They thus absorb much higher levels of THC than they would smoking it in a joint. They may well avoid the dry mouth and burnt throat but the higher levels of THC will lead them on to much more serious problems.

Bhongs made in the Far East from poor quality materials are sold legally and at very low cost on stalls at many markets and in certain shops.

Many smokers of cannabis have taken to using a special pipe called a *chillum* to smoke their drug. Chillum pipes are usually purchased ready made but can be home made. The main feature of a chillum is a drilling made straight through the stem from the mouth piece under the bowl to open at the front of the pipe. The bowl has an opening at its base which leads directly to this drilling. The smoker places a finger over the front opening of the drilling and is thus able to close or open this hole to allow air to be drawn into the smoke coming from the bowl to both cool and dilute it. Chillum pipes are also sold openly in the same way as bhongs.

Toke cans

Another form of pipe used for the smoking of cannabis is the *Toke* or *Toke Can*. These are becoming very popular with many young people as they take only a few seconds to prepare. The user takes an empty drinks can and uses the thumb to make a depression in the side of the can near to the base. This depression is made in line with the ring pull opening and on the same side of the can. A few holes are punctured in the base of the depression and the pipe is complete. The user places a small quantity of herbal or resin cannabis in the depression and lights it whilst sucking at the ring pull opening. The body of the can being metal and large enough provides sufficient cooling of the smoke. When finished the can is simply thrown away and a new one made when required. Most people see discarded drink cans as mere litter but a careful look at such discards will often provide a clue as to whether a place is being used for the smoking of cannabis. As with bhongs and chillums, toke cans are available ready made with hand painted cannabis leaves decorating the sides and with a reinforced smoking bowl from similar sources.

'Lung' filled with smoke

Another form of cannabis pipe, known as a *lung*, has recently become popular amongst young people in some areas. A lung is manufactured from a small plastic drinks bottle. The bottom is cut off and a plastic bag is fixed over the bottom with sticky tape. A simple smoking bowl is constructed at the open top of the bottle with metal foil which has a number of holes punctured in it. Herbal or resin cannabis is added to the bowl and lit. The plastic bag is pumped up and down to draw the smoke down into the bottle and bag. The smoking bowl is then removed and the user then pumps the plastic bag to drive the smoke back out of the bottle into the mouth. The lung may be passed round a group until all the smoke has been used up and the process repeated.

Cannabis smokers are ingenious people and all sorts of other ways have been found to indulge in their pastime.

Another way of smoking cannabis is called *hot knifing*. In this method a knife is heated with a match or cigarette lighter until it is very hot and then pressed against some herbal cannabis or a piece of resin, which will immediately begin to smoke. The smoke is then collected with a cupped hand or using a funnel made from the top of a lemonade bottle and breathed in. Sometimes the sleeve from a box of matches is used to collect the smoke, the matchbox sleeve is known as a *mouth organ*, and using it in this way is called *playing the mouth organ*. Another variation is to use two hot knives and to pick up a piece of cannabis resin between the blades, collecting the smoke as before. The possession of a knife with a blade stained by heating is a good indicator that the owner is smoking cannabis. There is almost no other reason to burn a knife blade, for such treatment spoils the sharpness of the edge.

A further variation is known as *spotting*. A small piece of resin is impaled on the end of a pin; sometimes the pin at the back of a badge is used. The resin is then ignited with a match or lighter and the smoke allowed to fill a glass, often a beer glass. When full, the glass is passed around a group with each member 'drinking' some of the smoke.

Whilst smoking cannabis is by far the most popular method of using the drug, cannabis can be taken by mouth. Herbal or resinous cannabis can be eaten on its own but is more usually used as an ingredient in various forms of cooking. The drug can be introduced into all sorts of food items. Pies, stews, pizzas and quiches are very popular. Cakes containing the drug and called *hash cakes* or *space cakes* are regular fare at certain parties. A drink can be prepared by infusing herbal cannabis in boiling water to make a form of tea, also popular at parties. Taking the drug by eating or drinking introduces the THC into the body via the stomach, this method being slower than through smoking but with much the same effect.

It raises an important point for young people who attend parties. They need to take care about what they eat and who prepares the food. Many cases exist of young people being badly effected by cannabis taken inadvertently by eating food prepared by someone who sees the *spiking* of it as some sort of joke – one that could have disastrous consequences.

Effects of use

The effects of using cannabis and the duration of those effects vary greatly from person to person and according to the strength used and the expectations and mental state of the user. An inexperienced or irregular user can expect one cannabis cigarette of medium strength to produce effects that will last for between two and four hours with a tapering off of the effects after that.

Most users will experience a feeling of bodily warmth, which is a purely physical reaction to the drug. The small blood vessels close to the surface of the skin dilate and suffuse with blood. This gives the skin a flushed appearance and makes it warm to the touch. It also leads to the characteristic cannabis user's blood shot eyes known as 'cannabis red eye'.

Users often report a feeling of relaxation, happiness and congeniality, with them taking a great deal of pleasure from the company of the people around them. If these people are also using cannabis then there is the potential for very pleasurable experiences. Many cannabis users make use of the drug in order to give themselves confidence in social situations and they find that it helps them to mix with others and to make friends. Cannabis users often become very talkative and report that the drug has so opened their minds and given them such insights that they are able to have wonderful conversations with other cannabis users about all sorts of subjects including all of the big questions of life, love, religion, death and so on. The objective experience of this is very different. Non-cannabis users listening to these conversations find them to be utter drivel and to make no sense at all.

In some users cannabis in low doses apparently temporarily increases the powers of concentration and many young people use it as an aid to studying and revision. They feel that the drug enables them to study for longer periods without fatigue.

Most users will lose their inhibitions and do things that they would never dream of doing whilst sober. In some users cannabis raises their sexual awareness and this together with the loss of inhibitions may lead them to have unprotected sex, possibly leading to pregnancy or the transmission of various diseases.

Adverse effects

Short term effects

At low and infrequent doses the adverse effects of cannabis are fairly mild and many users report few if any at all. Some users will suffer from dryness of the mouth and throat if the cannabis has been smoked and some will suffer bouts of nausea and dizziness. An increase in appetite is also seen in most users. Many will experience what users call the '*munchies*' during which they will consume large quantities of food, often stripping the refrigerator on their return home of anything edible, even things that they would not normally touch.

At comparatively low levels of use most users will suffer from short-term memory loss with no retention of any clear memory of events occurring during and immediately following their use of the drug. This makes a nonsense of the use of the drug as an aid to studying. Such users may well have the powers of concentration that study requires but the drug prevents them retaining much of what they have been studying. Even at low levels cannabis has a powerful effect on the judgement and information process-ing skills required to perform complex tasks such a driving a car or even riding a bike. Its effect on such skills has been likened to the effect that alcohol has, but there is a difference. The user's own perception of their return to a 'sober' state occurs much earlier than it does with alcohol. Their real return to sobriety, however, can take just as long as it does with alcohol and so they may embark on tasks such as car driving long before they are fit to do so.

Many cannabis users who make regular use of the drug report that time appears to run at a different rate than normal. This 'cannabis time' runs much more slowly, with minutes feeling more like hours. Some report that they feel that they are walking in slow motion when under the influence of the drug.

As the dose increases many users will begin to suffer the onset of many of the more unpleasant side effects of cannabis. THC is a moderately powerful hallucinogenic substance and users will begin to experience an altering of their perception of the world around them. Their hearing may be enhanced and low level sounds may be exaggerated until they reach unpleasant or even frightening proportions. Light levels and colours may change causing confusion, disorientation and nausea. The initially pleasant feeling of relaxation and happiness may be replaced by anxiety, panic and eventually paranoia. Many users report that they feel trapped inside what they are still able to recognize is a false reality created by the drug and feel that it is never going to end.

Although rare, full scale hallucinations are possible with high doses of cannabis. These 'trips', unlike those induced by some other hallucinogenic drugs, are almost without exception unpleasant and can be positively terrifying.

If the dose of cannabis used is high enough, then very unpleasant psychological effects can occur with the user becoming deeply confused and disorganized and even clinically psychotic.

Cannabis can cause a worsening of symptoms in users with schizophrenia and may contribute to the development of the disease in some high dose users.

Long term effects

Trying to make sense of all of the available information about the long term effects of regular cannabis use is very difficult. Our current state of knowledge can be likened to the position society was in some years ago with our knowledge of the health problems associated with the smoking of tobacco. Research had revealed some very serious problems, such as lung cancer and heart disease, but as time went on further research was to reveal much more. Medical research of a similar nature into cannabis use is still in the early stages but it too is beginning to reveal some worrying evidence.

Perhaps the most worrying effect of regular cannabis use by young people is that their use of it as a way of dealing with the ups and downs and the stresses and strains of modern life means that they fail to learn the necessary coping skills to deal with such problems in the real world. Such coping skills can only be learnt properly when a person is young; trying to learn them effectively during adulthood is difficult, if not impossible. If a young person fails to learn those skills then they will have great difficulty in dealing with adult life and many will find that they can only cope with the pressures of life by the use of drugs, often much more potentially dangerous drugs than cannabis.

Many regular users of cannabis suffer a loss of basic motivation. It is not uncommon for such users to drop out of school or college, to give up any form of work and to opt out of life in general. They will have no goals and see no point in having any. Their life will be characterized by drift and will be built entirely around their drug use.

Cannabis is certainly cancer causing. The smoke produced by burning it contains about fifty per cent more known carcinogens than the same volume of cigarette tobacco smoke. This is not as straightforward as it seems at first glance. Most people who smoke only tobacco consume much greater amounts of their chosen drug than do people whose choice is cannabis. Having said that, it is not so unusual now as it once was to find people who use amounts of cannabis that approach the amounts of tobacco consumed by many cigarette smokers. There are also differences in the way users smoke cannabis that are important. Most users of cannabis will inhale very much more deeply than do most tobacco smokers and will, in order to extract the maximum effect from it, retain the cannabis smoke in their lungs for much longer. This means that the smoke will be in contact with the membranes of the throat and lungs for a greater period of time than is usual with cigarette smokers. The picture is further confused by the fact that most cannabis is smoked mixed with tobacco and most cannabis smokers also smoke tobacco cigarettes. What is clear is that there are a growing number of documented cases of throat, mouth and lung cancers that appear to be directly connected to the smoking of cannabis.

There can be very serious problems for the foetus growing in a womb of a woman who uses cannabis. Cannabis crosses the placental barrier and enters the bloodstream of the unborn infant, who will be affected in the same way as the mother but to a much greater extent. Without in any way making light of this, it is worth saying that when a pregnant woman is stoned then so is her child. The developing foetus is very delicate and susceptible to damage caused by the actions of drugs taken by its mother. Evidence from recent research suggests that there is a very strong link between the use of cannabis by pregnant women and the incidence of spontaneous abortions, still births, deaths in the first few days after birth, together with physical and mental abnormalities. This is a serious picture and not to be taken lightly.

Cannabis has an effect on the level of the hormone testosterone in males. This is the hormone that provides the masculine characteristics of the male. As soon as a male begins to use the drug his testosterone level begins to reduce. If he then stops using, the level will quickly return to normal. The real problems occur for males who continue to use cannabis on a regular basis and over an extended period. Research indicates that in some, the reduction in testosterone levels becomes permanent and becomes so low that problems are then experienced in achieving or maintaining an erection and performing the act of sexual intercourse. It would seem to us that these things are of some importance with most young males and something that they ought to consider.

All of this research is ongoing and it appears likely that much more will be revealed. What can be said with certainty at this stage is that cannabis is not a harmless herb, as some would have young people believe, but is a powerful drug that no one should underestimate.

Tolerance potential

As with the majority of drugs, cannabis users can quickly develop a tolerance. The usual pattern is that they require larger doses to achieve the same effect. The pattern of tolerance is somewhat confused in new users by another of the drug's characteristics. THC is very persistent and is absorbed by the fatty tissues around many of the bodies soft organs and by the brain. From there it leeches back out into the bloodstream over a long period. This steady leeching maintains a level of THC in the bloodstream all the time and if further doses of the drug are then taken they 'add on' to the drug already there and the user appears to experience a sort of reverse tolerance with the full effects of the drug being reached with lower doses. This phase soon passes as bodily tolerance grows until a more normal pattern is reached with ever increasing doses required to achieve what the user is seeking.

Habituation potential

When considering this aspect of any drug we need to be clear as to what terms such as addiction and habituation mean. A true addiction is normally taken to mean some form of chemical dependence on the substance being taken. The addicted person requires further doses of the substance to stave off physical symptoms of withdrawal. Their bodies have adapted physically and require the substance to continue to operate. Drugs such as heroin, cocaine and nicotine are powerful producers of chemical addictions in their users. Habituation, on the other hand, is more often a purely psychological thing. The user becomes dependent mentally on their substance. It can best be likened to the habit of biting one's nails. Is the nail biter addicted to the calcium in their nails or maybe the uncertain substances under them? No, this is a purely mental thing. The nail biter chews away out of boredom, to relieve stress or merely to derive some comfort from it. This is a psychological habituation but no less difficult to deal with. Anyone who has tried to break a child of the habit of nail biting will know how difficult it can be. Sometimes parents put thick gloves on their child and fix them with tape or paint evil tasting products on their nails, but the child carries on biting until the nails and fingers are often left bleeding and very painful.

Many users of cannabis will claim that the drug is not addictive and for the vast majority of its users this will be true. It is very rare for anyone to become chemically dependent on the drug in the same way that users of other drugs such as heroin or cocaine often become. Cannabis produces in many of its users a very powerful psychological habituation. This dependence is purely mental, and users become to rely on the drug to deal with the everyday processes of their lives. We know of many users who feel totally unable to get out of bed in the morning without first using the drug and who then go on to use regularly throughout the day to enable them to cope.

Withdrawal effects

There are very few purely physical symptoms from the cessation of use of cannabis, most of which are psychological. The symptoms that any particular user will experience are dependent upon the amount that they have been using and the period over which they have been using it. A person who has only used on an occasional basis or over a short period will experience very little in the way of withdrawal symptoms but as the amount used increases or the period of use becomes extended then some users will experience great difficulty in giving up.

Some will experience problems with sleep, becoming restless and suffering insomnia. Sleep deprivation can be difficult to handle and the temptation to fall back into use of the drug will be very powerful. Others may suffer panic attacks and the feeling that they are unable to cope alone with the ordinary trials of day to day life.

All of these symptoms can be overcome by giving the user support, counselling, and in some cases medication, but it is often a difficult and rocky road to be overcome before the user is truly able to operate without the substance.

Overdose Potential

It is not thought possible to overdose fatally on cannabis. It is possible to take such a high dose that the user will fall into a stupor during which they may be at risk of being sick and inhaling their own vomit or being at risk of accident.

Street Names

- Herbal – **grass, marijuana, puff, blow, wacky baccy, herb.**
- Resin – **pot, hash, shit, black, gold, squidgy.**
- Oil – **oil, hash oil, diesel, honey.**

Slang associated with use

- **Joint** or **spliff** – hand rolled cannabis cigarette.
- **Bhong** – water pipe for smoking cannabis.
- **Chillum** – clay or wooden pipe for cannabis smoking.
- **Skinning up** or **building** – making a cannabis cigarette.
- **Henry** or **an eighth** – an eighth of an ounce of cannabis.
- **Louis** or **a teenth** – a sixteenth of an ounce of cannabis.
- **Toking** – smoking cannabis.
- **Toke can** – a pipe made from a drinks can for smoking cannabis.
- **Hash cakes** – cakes made from cannabis.

Cannabis

Reasons for use   Problems

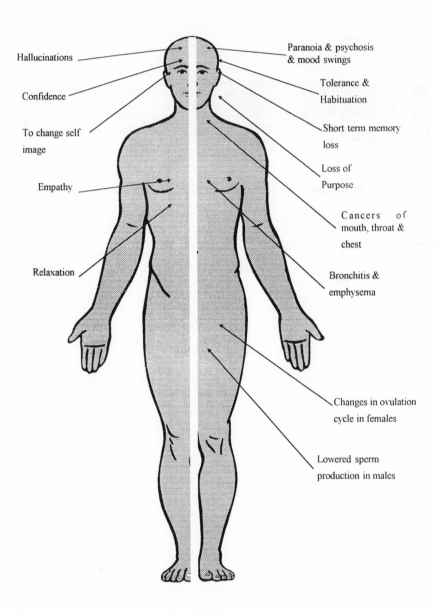

Hallucinations

Paranoia & psychosis
& mood swings

Confidence

Tolerance &
Habituation

To change self
image

Short term memory
loss

Loss of
Purpose

Empathy

Cancers of
mouth, throat &
chest

Relaxation

Bronchitis &
emphysema

Changes in ovulation
cycle in females

Lowered sperm
production in males

CHAPTER 4

Stimulants

Amphetamine
Amphetamine Sulphate

Amphetamine: Quick Reference Guide

Source

A totally synthetic product.

Forms and appearance

In powder form seen in various colours, off-white, yellow and pink being the most common.

In tablets and capsules of various colours, sizes and shapes.

Marketing

Sold as a powder by the gram or half gram, commonly wrapped in paper packets made from a small square of carefully folded paper, or in small press seal plastic bags.

Tablet forms of the drug are sold loose and priced by the tablet.

Amphetamine is available all over the UK in public houses, night clubs, dances and raves, on the street and from local, small time drug suppliers.

Cost

Amphetamine is currently selling in the UK for between £6.00 and £10.00 per gram with no fixed price for individual tablets or capsules, but commonly the price varies between £2.00 to £15.00 per tablet.

Legal position

A class B, Schedule 2, controlled substance under the Misuse of Drugs Act 1971.

Methods of use

The powder form is most commonly taken orally by dissolving in a drink or by licking off the finger, or more rarely by rubbing the powder into the gums. It can be sniffed up the nose or mixed with tobacco or cannabis for smoking, or smoked straight off tin foil. It is also used by dissolving in water for injecting.

Effects of Use

Increase in energy, strength and powers of concentration, feelings of euphoria and elation. Increase in confidence, suppression of appetite and reduction in the need for sleep.

Adverse effects

Increase in blood pressure with increased risk of stroke, dry mouth, diarrhoea and increased urination, disturbance of sleep patterns, tiredness, loss of appetite and consequent weight loss, restlessness, mood swings and agitation, depression, delusions, panic, paranoia and psychosis.

Tolerance potential

Tolerance develops rapidly with continued use.

Habituation potential

Physical dependence is rare but psychological dependence develops quickly in most regular users.

Withdrawal effects

No physical symptoms. Mental agitation, depression, panic and feelings of being unable to cope.

Overdose potential

Fatal overdose is possible with amphetamine. This could occur at low doses with inexperienced users.

Amphetamine: In depth guide

Source

Amphetamine Sulphate is a synthetic manufactured product. It was first produced in Germany in the 1880s and used medically as a stimulant and tonic. Its value as a powerful stimulant and appetite suppressant was quickly recognized by military authorities all over the world, and the drug was regularly given in tablet form to troops engaged in battle or when long periods of physical activity without pauses for rest or food were required. Indeed, during World War II some 72 million amphetamine tablets were issued to British troops. From the 1950s onwards as more people became weight conscious, and with the increasing fashion for slimming, large quantities of amphetamine were prescribed as an aid to weight loss. Its use for these purposes was not without its risks, and such use has now largely ceased. Some varieties of amphetamine are still used medically in the treatment of certain sleeping disorders, for chronic bed wetting, and hyperactivity in children, but this is becoming rare.

The manufacture of illicit amphetamine is not a difficult process. It requires only a basic knowledge of chemistry and very little in the way of equipment to produce the drug in substantial quantities.

Form and appearance

Most commonly, amphetamine is seen in the form of a coarse crystalline powder. This will usually be a rather dirty off white to cream colour, very coarse in constituency, containing crystals of different sizes and small lumps of coagulated powder. This form will be only between six and eight per cent pure amphetamine sulphate, with the remainder being made up with all sorts of other substances. If the user is lucky, these mixing or 'cutting' agents may be caffeine, milk powder, glucose, vitamin C powder or bicarbonate of soda. If the user is less lucky the adulterants may be chalk or talcum powder, and if they are very unlucky their amphetamine may well be 'cut' with a rat poison such as strychnine, or even bath scouring powders.

Powder forms are sometimes seen in different colours. These coloured varieties are usually pink or yellow and have normally been produced by crushing pharmaceutical amphetamine tablets. Amphetamine powder produced in this way is usually more pure, and of a much higher strength.

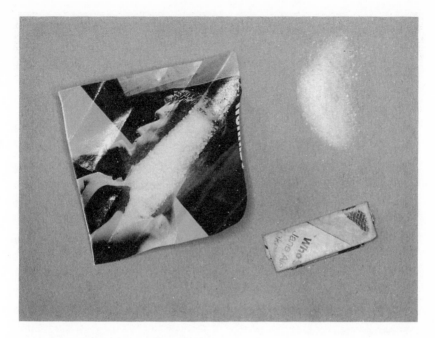

Amphetamine with open and folded 'wrap'

However, it is not unknown for ordinary, crudely produced amphetamine to be mixed with coloured powders to attract a higher price.

There are many varieties of amphetamine produced by the pharmaceutical industry for medical use in tablet and capsule form. The tablets are most commonly pink, white or yellow in colour with the capsules available in a wide range of different colours and colour combinations. Small quantities of home made tablets are also available on the streets from time to time. The amphetamine used in the manufacture of such tablets is usually of a reasonably high grade and is coloured to imitate the commercially produced varieties.

Marketing

Amphetamine powder is dealt on the streets in individual doses of half a gram or one gram. Each dose is usually contained in a carefully folded paper envelope called a *wrap* or a *deal*. These envelopes are made from a square piece of paper of around five centimetres by five centimetres. The paper is commonly from glossy magazines, often with German or Dutch printing on it. The glossy paper is preferred because it repels moisture a little better than plain paper, but damp proofing is sometimes reinforced by adding a layer of clear plastic film around the paper wrap. Once folded a half gram paper wrap will measure approximately one centimetre by two and a half centimetres. It is a very efficient container for powder drugs such as amphetamine, is virtually leak proof and can be easily concealed. Users will often hide them under the tongue when being searched by the police and will even conceal them by inserting the wrap into their anus or vagina. When unfolded the paper wrap has a characteristic pattern of criss-cross fold lines across it, making it instantly recognizable. The finding of such pieces of paper is a very good indicator of the use of amphetamine or other powder drugs. Numbers of individual wraps are sometimes seen bundled together in small packages of twenty or so, secured with an elastic band. These bundles are commonly called *decks* or *bindles*, and two such bundles will fit easily inside a twenty cigarette packet.

Drug suppliers will also make use of more modern packaging when dealing amphetamine. The drug is often seen in small plastic bags, each approximately three centimetres square, with a press seal opening, larger such bags being used for bulk supplies.

Amphetamine in tablet form is commonly sold one tablet at a time with no wrapping.

Cost

The street price of amphetamine varies considerably dependent upon the availability of supplies in any one area, and also what the supplier believes that any particular market will bear. Low grade amphetamine in powder form will sell for between £6.00 and £10.00 per gram. As with all drugs there is discount available for purchases in quantity and penalties to be paid for smaller purchases. A beginner buying perhaps half a gram to try out the drug will expect to pay at least £5.00. Many users will pay higher prices for pink and yellow amphetamine in the belief that they are buying a purer and stronger form of the drug, and prices as high as £20.00 per gram for such a product are not unusual.

Amphetamine in tablet form is sold at prices that vary to an even greater extent. Single tablets will sell for anything from £2.00 to £15.00 depending upon the circumstances of the sale. Tablets bought on the street will be cheaper than the same product bought in a pub and even higher prices will be achieved for tablets sold at parties and raves.

Legal position

Amphetamine sulphate is a class B, Schedule two, controlled substance within the Misuse of Drugs Act 1971. As a class B drug, offences concerning amphetamine carry the following penalties.

Simple possession

Possession of amphetamine for personal use carries a maximum penalty on indictment of five years imprisonment together with an unlimited fine. If the amphetamine has been prepared for injection the maximum penalty increases to 14 years plus the fine.

Possession with intent to supply

Possessing the drug with the intention of supplying it, either by sale of by gift, to another person carries a maximum penalty on indictment of fourteen years imprisonment plus an unlimited fine, and the seizure of drug related assets. Injectable amphetamine in the same circumstances increases the maximum imprisonment term to life.

Supplying to another

As for possession with intent to supply.

Importation or manufacture

As for possession with intent to supply.

Its inclusion in schedule two of the act recognizes that there are some limited medical uses for the drug and its use by doctors is therefore permitted but under very strict controls.

Methods of use

Most amphetamine is taken orally. The powder is usually dissolved in a soft or alcoholic drink and swallowed. We have seen users who prefer their amphetamine in a cup of tea and others who take it mixed with neat spirits. Dosage may vary from as little as half a gram to several grams at a time, depending on tolerance levels.

Another common method of taking the drug is known as *dabbing*, using a wet finger to pick it up and transfer it to the mouth.

Some users will use the same wet finger technique to pick up the drug but will then rub it into the teeth and gums. This method is called *washing*, and some users will employ it as a way of checking the quality of what they have bought. Good quality amphetamine will produce a tingling sensation in the teeth when rubbed in, and the degree of sensation will tell an experienced user the approximate strength of the sample.

Less commonly amphetamine is *snorted* or inhaled through the nose. The powder can be snorted directly from the paper wrap or placed in the hand or in a spoon held up to the nose. The practice of snorting amphetamine is less common than it once was. The poor quality of present street samples and the uncertainty of what has been used to cut or dilute the product has put many users off, as many of the cutting agents used can cause a great deal of painful damage to the nasal membranes.

Amphetamine is sometimes sprinkled onto cannabis or tobacco and smoked in hand rolled cigarettes, or in *bhongs*. It burns readily and the smoke produced carries the drug into the body through the lungs. Heating amphetamine powder up on a piece of tin foil by applying a match, candle or lighter underneath it will also cause the drug to burn, and produce a light coloured smoke with a harsh acrid smell. The smoke is then inhaled through a rolled piece of card or a match box sleeve.

The powder can also be dissolved and injected. A common agent for dissolving amphetamine is water to which has been added a few drops of lemon juice. There is a belief amongst some users that the addition of lemon juice enhances the effect of the drug. Certainly injecting any drug will increase the immediacy of the *hit* or *rush* that it produces.

Tablet forms of the drug are usually taken orally but good quality pharmaceutical products are often crushed between two spoons and dissolved for injection.

Effects of use

The time interval between the taking of the drug and the onset of its effects is very short. If injected, the effects will be almost instant, the *rush* occurring within a few seconds of the drug entering the blood stream. If the drug has been taken orally it will have to pass through the stomach wall in order to reach the blood stream, and then on to the brain, which can take between ten and twenty minutes, according to the contents of the stomach. The rush produced will be slower to build and be less pronounced. The short term effects of the drug may last for several hours. The exact duration will vary greatly from person to person and will depend on the amount taken and on how much experience the user has of the drug. Each person's physical make up is different and there are many factors that will have an influence on the drug's effects, such as body weight and gender. An inexperienced or irregular user can expect effects that will last between three and four hours from a single medium strength dose.

The rush that amphetamine produces will give its users a great feeling of well being and even euphoria. Feelings of fatigue, stress, anxiety and fear will be swept from the mind. Most users will experience a considerable increase in energy and a feeling of strength. Along with the energy will come an increase in the ability to concentrate and a substantial increase in self-confidence. Many users who are normally shy and feel socially awkward by nature will use amphetamine to give themselves the necessary self-confidence to enable them to mix with others and 'have a good time'. Amphetamine, like most stimulants provides no energy of its own. Its action is to increase the user's metabolic rate so that they consume their own blood sugar levels at a faster rate. The more of the drug that is taken, then the faster that consumption will occur. When the blood sugar levels drop to a point at which the user can not sustain the activity they are engaged in, they will *crash*, and experience great fatigue and loss of strength.

Amphetamine suppresses the body's need for sleep and so users are able to keep going for long periods. As a result it is often used for this purpose by young people attending all night parties and raves.

It is also a very powerful appetite suppressant and many users will take the drug as an aid to slimming. The increase in energy burns off calories at a high rate, and in combination with the loss of appetite, rapid weight loss is inevitable.

Adverse effects

Amphetamine sulphate is a very powerful drug whose position in class B of the Misuse of Drugs Act 1971 belies its potential for causing real harm to its users.

The physical problems that it causes for users are few but can be significant, but of much more importance for all to understand is amphetamine's real potential for causing profound psychological problems. It is not an exaggeration to say that it is a drug that has the power to destroy a person mentally in a very real way.

Physical effects

Amphetamine increases blood pressure and raises the temperature of the body. The energy produced by using the drug may result in strenuous physical activity which will also have the effect of further raising the blood pressure and body temperature. If the user has any underlying and perhaps unknown defect or weakness within their blood circulatory system, then this increase in pressure will find it out, and there are many documented cases of stroke and heart failure being suffered by users, often first time users. Most users will experience dryness of the mouth and an increased thirst, and if not satisfied, then the user will run the risk of dehydration and collapse.

The sudden onset of tiredness and loss of strength experienced when the stimulating effects of the drug wear off can be very unpleasant and can only be dealt with by allowing the body to rest and to regain its strength naturally. The temptation is to take more of the drug in order to be able to keep going. This has the effect of burning up what little reserves of blood sugars remain and will result in an ever greater crash at the end. The powerful sleep suppressing effects of the drug may prevent its user obtaining the rest that is needed to refresh the body and rebuild reserves of strength; as a result general bodily condition will be reduced. The appetite suppression effects may well mean that the body is prevented from taking in the necessary fuel it needs to return the blood sugar levels to normal. These two effects taken together mean that many users lose a great deal of weight and their general health and bodily condition will become very poor. The immune system in some users may be damaged, leaving them prone to a whole range of illnesses.

Psychological effects

It is in this area that amphetamine causes its most profound and distressing problems. Most people can understand and feel able to cope with a physical illness or infirmity but a mental illness is a different thing. It is perhaps the fear of the unknown that makes it so frightening but all users of amphetamine should clearly understand that they are taking a drug that has a real potential for releasing latent mental illnesses, that may be very difficult if not impossible to treat successfully.

It is very rare for people to suffer adverse psychological effects at their first experience of the drug or if their use is only occasional. The potential for mental problems become more apparent with continued or heavy use. Many such users will become very depressed when not actually under the influence of the drug and feel that life without the drug is simply not worth while. This depression can move very easily into paranoia with the sufferer feeling that everyone – and life in general – is against them. Very complicated and well constructed delusions can result with the user believing that people around are all part of a complex plot that is being hatched against them. Long term and heavy users can move into a drug induced psychosis where these delusions become the basis of their lives.

These can be very deep seated and difficult to treat and can result in the sufferer requiring inpatient treatment is a psychiatric hospital.

Tolerance potential

Most users of amphetamine rapidly develop a tolerance. The body becomes familiar with the drug and adapts to its effects, so that the usual dose rapidly becomes insufficient to achieve the effects that they are looking for, and much larger doses are required. It is not uncommon for users of amphetamine who have been involved with the drug for any length of time to be using as much as two or three grams at a time, several times a day.

Habituation potential

Without doubt, amphetamine has a real potential for the development in its users of a powerful dependence. There is little evidence of users developing a true physical addiction to the drug. The major risk lies in the development of a profound psychological dependence. Amphetamine pushes away the problems of life, makes the user feel good and provides the energy and confidence to face up to all the problems and stresses that life can produce. As the user comes down from the drug they will experience physical tiredness and loss of strength, typical of the use of stimulants and therefore feel even less able to cope than they did before using the drug. There is clearly a temptation to continue use in order to cope. With the added complication of the onset of amphetamine induced mental illness, such as psychosis, users may become terrified to give up use of the drug. This habituation can be so intense that it becomes very difficult to deal with and the user may require very expert professional treatment by a regime of medical drugs and supportive counselling if they are to have any real hope of recovery.

Withdrawal effects

The withdrawal effects of amphetamine use will vary according to amount that the user has been taking and the duration and regularity of the use. Most inexperienced users who have only taken a small to moderate amount of amphetamine will experience a period of tiredness and loss of strength. This can be dealt with by allowing the body to rest, sleep being the best way of doing so. If the use of the drug has been at a much higher level or over an extended period the withdrawal effects will be much more severe. Many such users will find it extremely difficult to cope with the feelings of anxiety, panic, paranoia and insomnia that such withdrawal will bring.

Anyone attempting to give up the use of amphetamine after heavy or prolonged use is well advised to seek the advice and guidance of a professional drug service.

Overdose potential

There is a real possibility of overdosing on amphetamine. The dose will be high in most users but an inexperienced person could reach overdose at quite low levels of the drug. The main risks lie in pushing the body temperature up to such a high level that the brain is unable to cope and suffers convulsions. In some cases these convulsions can lead to the death of the user.

Street names

- **Speed, Buzz, Whiz, Billy Whiz, Amphet, Sulph, Dexie**

Slang associated with use

- **Wraps** or **deals** – folded paper packets containing the drug
- **Decks** or **Bindles** – bundles of wraps secured with an elastic band.
- **Snorting** – sniffing the powder up the nose.
- **Rubbing** or **washing** – rubbing the powder into the teeth or gums.
- **Dabbing** – licking from a finger.
- **Hit** or **rush** – the effects felt as the drug reaches the brain.
- **Crash** – sudden onset of tiredness experienced when the effect of the drug wears of.

Amphetamine

Reasons for use   Problems

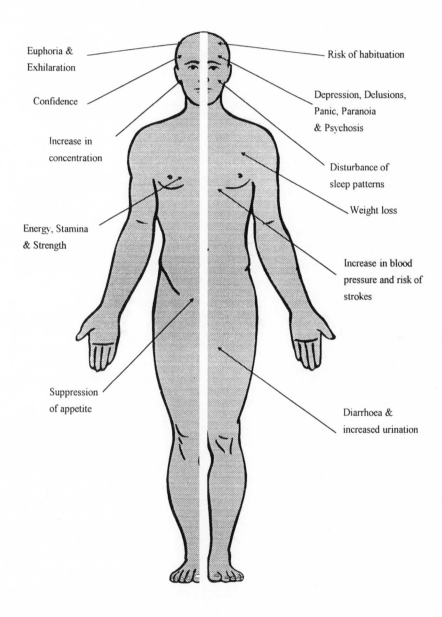

Euphoria & Exhilaration

Confidence

Increase in concentration

Energy, Stamina & Strength

Suppression of appetite

Risk of habituation

Depression, Delusions, Panic, Paranoia & Psychosis

Disturbance of sleep patterns

Weight loss

Increase in blood pressure and risk of strokes

Diarrhoea & increased urination

Methylamphetamine
Methylamphetamine Hydrochloride

Methylamphetamine: Quick Reference Guide

Source

A totally synthetic drug, closely related to amphetamine sulphate.

Forms and appearance

Most commonly, the drug is seen in the form of large clear crystals of various sizes, the largest being approximately two centimetres across, and having the appearance of clear ice or glass.

It is occasionally seen as tablets or in the form of crystalline powders of various colours, white, yellow and light brown being the most common.

Marketing

Methylamphetamine in powder form is sold on the streets in the same half and one gram packaging as amphetamine sulphate. The crystal form is sold by the gram or fractions of a gram or sometimes by the crystal. Tablets are sold loose, without packaging.

Cost

The tablet and powder forms have no regular price due to their rarity but the crystal form is currently selling for around £200 per gram and £15.00 to £30.00 per crystal, depending on size.

Legal position

A class B, schedule two, controlled substance under the Misuse of Drugs Act 1971.

Methods of use

Methylamphetamine is used in similar ways to amphetamine. The powder and tablet forms can be taken orally in a drink. The powder can also be taken from a wet finger or by sniffing into the nose or by burning and inhaling the fumes, or by injection. The crystal form is almost exclusively used by burning them in a special pipe and inhaling the fumes.

Effects of use

Feelings of euphoria, great strength and energy, the ability to sustain high levels of activity over extended periods without rest or food.

Adverse effects

Increase in blood pressure and body temperature with increased risk of stroke and heart failure, dehydration, dry mouth, diarrhoea and increased urination, severe disturbance of sleep patterns, lethargy, loss of appetite and consequent weight loss, restlessness, aggression, violent mood swings and agitation, visual and auditory hallucinations, depression, delusions, panic, paranoia, psychosis and bizarre psychotic behaviour.

Tolerance potential

Tolerance builds up very rapidly with continued use.

Habituation potential

Profound psychological dependence develops quickly in most users Physical dependence can also occur.

Withdrawal effects

Severe cravings for the drug may be experienced with high levels of mental agitation, depression, panic and feelings of being unable to cope.

Overdose potential

Serious risk of fatal overdose at very low levels in some people.

Methylamphetamine: In Depth Guide

Source

Methylamphetamine is a synthetically produced stimulant. It is similar in formulation to amphetamine sulphate and is produced commercially for use in certain pharmaceutical preparations. Very little of the legally produced drug reaches the street market. Most forms of the drug found on the streets are produced in illicit plants that are to be found all over Europe and the US.

It enjoyed a period of popularity in the early 1970s in its tablet and powder form but its high level of unpleasant side effects and the violence that is often associated with users of the drug made that period of popularity short lived. It has returned to the streets of the UK since the beginning of the 1990s in its crystal form and increasing amounts are becoming available.

Forms and appearance

The powder form of methylamphetamine is similar in appearance to amphetamine sulphate. The drug is often of a higher purity and the powder will have a more even appearance with greater uniformity of particle size. The colours available vary widely but creamy white, pale yellow and light brown varieties are by far the most common.

Tablets of the drug are still rare, although there has been some increase in their availability at certain raves and dance clubs. Some of these tablets are produced commercially by the pharmaceutical industry under various brand names and in a variety of shapes and colours, while home produced tablets are characterized by the crudeness of their manufacture and their uneven coloration. One particular tablet form that has been seen of late is white, with the words 'speed king' imprinted upon them.

Since the late 1980s a crystalline form of the drug has appeared on the streets of the UK. By processing the basic drug with other chemicals it has been possible to form it into clear, glass like, colourless crystals of various sizes. Most of these crystals are quite small and have the appearance of fine grade rock salt but many of them are of a much larger size with some individual crystals measuring as much as two centimetres across.

Marketing

The powder forms of the drug are sold in much the same way as ordinary amphetamine and are usually seen in paper wraps or plastic press seal bags containing half or one gram. The tablet forms, when available, are sold by the individual tablet with no particular packaging.

Crystal or 'ice' methylamphetamine is sold by weight or by individual crystal. The small crystals are sold in plastic bags containing a gram or fraction of a gram, while the larger crystals are sold individually with the price being set according to the weight. Users are prepared to pay a premium for the largest of the crystals in the belief that its use will achieve the most powerful effects. Individual crystals will usually be wrapped in a twist of clear plastic film or more rarely in a single cigarette paper. This type of packaging is sometimes called a *bomb* because of its shape.

Cost

Because of the irregular nature of the supply of methylamphetamine in powder and tablet form it has as yet not settled down to a regular pricing structure. Suppliers are able to ask what ever they think the market will bear. Many first time users will be prepared to pay very high prices to experience the drug. A more steady market price has become established for the crystal form of the drug. Many users believe that drug in crystalline forms are less likely to be adulterated with other substances, and these are preferred when available. Crystal methylamphetamine is slowly gaining in popularity at the wealthier end of the rave and dance club scene. Prices of around £200.00 per gram for the smaller crystals are common, with larger crystals achieving prices of between £15.00 and £30.00 each, according to size. A single £15.00 crystal would be enough for one 'hit'.

Legal position

Methylamphetamine is a class B, schedule two, controlled substance within the Misuse of Drugs Act 1971. As such it attracts the following penalties.

Simple possession

Possession of methylamphetamine for personal use carries a maximum penalty on indictment of five years imprisonment together with an unlimited fine. If the drug has been prepared for injection the maximum penalty increases to 14 years plus the fine.

Possession with intent to supply

Possessing the drug with the intention of supplying it, either by sale or by gift, to another person carries a maximum penalty on indictment of fourteen years imprisonment plus an unlimited fine and the seizure of all drug related assets. Methylamphetamine prepared for injection, in the same circumstances increases the maximum imprisonment term to life.

Supplying to another

As for possession with intent to supply

Importation or manufacture

As for possession with intent to supply

Its inclusion in schedule two of the act recognizes that there are some limited medical uses for the drug and its use by doctors is therefore permitted but under very strict controls.

Methods of use

Methylamphetamine is used in similar ways to amphetamine sulphate. The powder forms are mostly used orally, taken in a drink, dabbed from a wet finger or rubbed into the gums and teeth. Much smaller quantities of the drug are needed and users will experiment until they find the right quantity for them to achieve the effect that they desire. The powder can also be sniffed up the nose, but this is rare. The powder form or crushed tablets can be mixed with water and a mild acid such as lemon juice and injected intravenously. Injecting provides a much more instant and intense *hit* and an increasing number of users are favouring this method. Methylamphetamine powder can also be mixed with tobacco or cannabis and smoked in the same way as ordinary amphetamine. The smoking of methylamphetamine is not popular as the high temperatures reached in the burning cigarette, particularly in a cannabis cigarette, can damage the drug and reduce its effects. The crystal or 'ice' form of methylamphetamine is most commonly smoked on its own. In this form the high temperatures do not seriously reduce its effects and the ease of the method makes it very popular. A few small crystals or a single larger one is placed in the smoking bowl of a glass or metal pipe and heated with a match or cigarette lighter causing the drug to melt and slowly vaporize. The vapours are then deeply inhaled and the drug carried into the blood stream through the lungs. This is a very efficient way of using the drug, providing a hit whose speed of onset and intensity is second only to injecting.

Effects of use

The effects of methylamphetamine are similar to, but much more intense, than ordinary amphetamine. The user will experience feelings of supreme euphoria, great strength and energy. These feelings will be particularly intense if the drug has been injected or smoked. The *rush* felt by such users has been described by many of them as the most intense of any drug. The effect achieved is particularly long lived and can last anywhere between two and sixteen hours, depending upon the amount taken. The user will feel able to dance or take part in any other strenuous activity for very long periods without rest or food. Many users report that the drug also causes a tremendous increase in their sexual appetite and that, together with its energy giving properties, leads them to engage in long sexual sessions.

Adverse effects

As with the desired effects, the adverse effects of methylamphetamine are similar to ordinary amphetamine but to a more intense degree. The same feelings of great fatigue and physical weakness will be felt when the drug has run its course. The user's blood pressure, body temperature and heart rate is raised by the drug and can reach dangerous levels in some people. These physical effects are as nothing compared to the potential that the drug has for causing psychological problems or exacerbating existing mental conditions. Methylamphetamine users often report the experience of powerful visual and auditory hallucinations. Many of these hallucinations are of a frightening and unpleasant nature and can lead to the user becoming extremely violent to those around them, appearing to have little or no little control over their emotions. This aggression and lack of control, coupled with the increase in sexual appetite has lead to many male users becoming involved in serious acts of sexual assault and rape.

The onset of psychiatric problems can be very rapid. Regular use over the course of only a few weeks can lead to the exhibition of very bizarre behaviour, the development of deep paranoia, complex delusions and psychosis. It has been shown to worsen existing cases of schizophrenia and been identified as a factor in the development of new cases.

Tolerance potential

Tolerance to methylamphetamine develops very quickly with continued use. Most users will use only a very small amount of the drug at their first experience. Amounts of around a twentieth of a gram are not uncommon for beginners. This will very soon rise as the user feels they are not getting the sensations they are seeking. The individual dose will increase as well as the frequency of use until they may be using as much as half a gram or even more a day. They will very soon reach the position of having acquired a seriously expensive habit.

Habituation potential

Physical dependence on the drug can occur within a very short time with regular use, and severe cravings for the drug will result. Even more powerful will be the deep psychological dependence that soon develops. Most regular users will reach a point very quickly of being totally unable to face their lives without use of the drug.

Withdrawal effects

Along with the severe cravings for the drug, the regular user who is trying to withdraw will often experience high levels of mental agitation, depression, panic and feelings of being unable to cope. These feelings, together with the likelihood that the user will be suffering from a range of psychological problems, will make withdrawal a very fraught process. No one who has regularly used methylamphetamine should attempt to withdraw from use of the drug without professional help.

Overdose potential

It is impossible to say with any degree of accuracy what amount of methylamphetamine will lead to overdose. In certain people this level can be very low. Everyone is different and factors such as their physical size and previous experience will make a difference. A person taking an overdose of the drug can suffer severe convulsions leading to coma, with the possibility of respiratory and cardiac arrest leading to death.

Street names

- Crystal form – **Ice, meth, crystal, glass, ice-cream**
- Powder or tablet form – **Meth, methedrine**

Slang associated with use

- **Bomb** – clear plastic film or cigarette paper wrapping containing individual crystal
- **Hit** or **rush** – the effects felt as the drug reaches the brain.

Methylamphetamine

Reasons for use   Problems

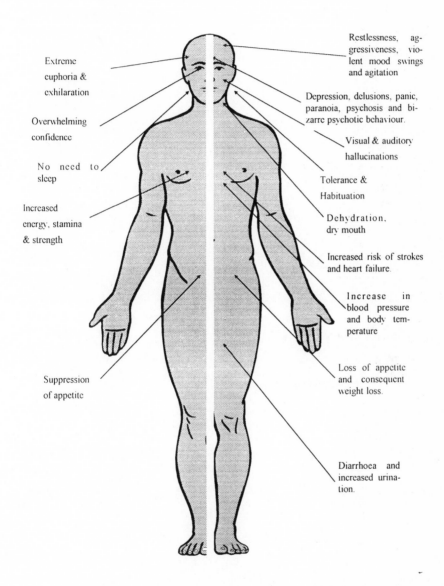

Extreme euphoria & exhilaration

Overwhelming confidence

No need to sleep

Increased energy, stamina & strength

Suppression of appetite

Restlessness, aggressiveness, violent mood swings and agitation

Depression, delusions, panic, paranoia, psychosis and bizarre psychotic behaviour.

Visual & auditory hallucinations

Tolerance & Habituation

Dehydration, dry mouth

Increased risk of strokes and heart failure.

Increase in blood pressure and body temperature

Loss of appetite and consequent weight loss.

Diarrhoea and increased urination.

Cocaine
Cocaine Hydrochloride

Cocaine: Quick Reference Guide

Source

Derived from the leaves of the coca bush, Erythroxylum Coca.

Form and appearance

Commonly seen as a white crystalline powder with a sparkling appearance. Very occasionally seen in its paste form.

Marketing

Sold by the gram or fractions of a gram. The usual form of packaging is a paper wrap similar to that used for amphetamine. Also seen in small plastic press seal bags. Coca paste is so rare that there is no recognized form of packaging. Cocaine is available in most large centres of population and on an irregular basis is many smaller ones.

Cost

Between £50.00 and £80.00 per gram for the powder form with no established street price for coca paste.

Legal position

Cocaine and coca paste are class 'A', schedule two, controlled substances under the Misuse of Drugs Act 1971. Cocaine addiction is a condition that must be notified to the Home Office under the Misuse of Drugs (notification and supply to addicts) Regulations 1973.

Methods of use

Cocaine powder is commonly used by being sniffed through the nose. The paste form can be smoked in pipes or, less commonly, mixed in hand rolled cigarettes with tobacco or cannabis. Both are sometimes dissolved in water and injected, either into veins or under the skin.

Effects of use

Feelings of energy, strength, exhilaration, euphoria, confidence and well being are often reported following cocaine use. Users often become very talkative.

Adverse effects

Agitation, panic and feelings of persecution or threat often follow cocaine use. Regular use can damage nasal passages and cause exhaustion and weight loss. Injection can lead to collapsed veins or skin ulcers at the injection site. Larger doses may lead to delusions and violent behaviour.

Tolerance potential

Tolerance rapidly develops with continued use.

Habituation potential

Cocaine users will often rapidly develop both a physical and psychological dependence on the drug.

Withdrawal effects

Feelings of anxiety, depression and panic, with a severe craving for continued use.

Overdose potential

It is possible to fatally overdose on cocaine.

Cocaine: In Depth Guide

Source

Street cocaine is derived from the leaves of the coca bush, Erythroxylum Coca, which grows both wild and under cultivation in high altitude areas of South America, especially in Columbia, Bolivia and Peru. It also occurs in parts of South East Asia, India and Africa, although these areas are not considered to be major sources for the cocaine trade.

The leaves of the coca bush have been chewed by native South American peoples for many thousands of years for its stimulating effects and to reduce the effects of hunger and cold that were often a feature of their high altitude existence. Statues and carvings dating from 3000 BC have been discovered that show the chewing of coca. Each leaf contains about two per cent of cocaine that is locked into chemical compounds within the structure of the leaf. Repeated mastication of the leaf with saliva is enough to release small amounts of the cocaine that can be absorbed by swallowing. The early users discovered that if you chewed the leaf with an alkaloid substance this released much more of the cocaine. The traditional alkaloid used in South America is lime that has been produced by burning the shells of marine crustaceans and then pulverising them. This fine powder was kept in a hollowed out gourd which hung from the waist band of the user together with a pouch used to keep the supply of coca leaves. The top of the gourd was plugged with a stick which reached down into the lime powder. The user would lick the stick, pick up a little lime with it and place it in the mouth with a handful of leaves. By chewing the two together cocaine was released from the mixture and absorbed by the tissues of the mouth, tongue and gullet. The addition of lime also helped to sweeten the normally bitter taste of coca leaf. So common was the habit that it was normal in some South American native cultures for a boy, on reaching his twelfth birthday, to be presented with his own coca pouch and lime gourd by his proud parents.

When the Spanish conquistadors reached South America they found the use of cocaine to be almost universal amongst the native peoples. Priests, who travelled with the conquistadors, saw that many of the users had become dependent upon the drug and sought to forbid its use. The Spanish authorities at first agreed but then the more commercially minded of them began to see that this was a trade they could take over profitably. The growing of coca was then solely a monopoly of the occupying forces and the plants produced were either sold to the locals or used as payment for manual work done for the Spanish. The chewing of coca leaf by indigenous peoples in most of the South America cocaine producing countries is still lawful and continues.

In 1859 the active ingredient of coca was isolated and shortly afterwards a technique invented to extract it. It involves putting the coca leaf through a series of processes which lead firstly to coca paste and then on to cocaine hydrochloride which is the compound that we know as cocaine.

The drug has useful properties as a local anaesthetic and its use provided the foundation of modern pain free dentistry. Its stimulant properties were recognized at an early stage and it was used in a wide range of tonic and energy providing medicines, food and drink. Coca-Cola when first marketed contained a very small dose of cocaine to give the drink its stimulating properties and there was even an invigorating wine which was awarded a medal of quality by the Pope which also contained cocaine. A form of cocaine hydrochloride tablets called 'forced march' were carried by the members of Sir Ernest Shakleton's expedition to the Antarctic in 1909 and used to provide energy and protection from the cold. It is reported that the drug was used openly during training by athletes taking part in major international events, including the Olympic Games, around the turn of the century. One of the teams that relied on cocaine as an essential part of their preparation was the Canadian ladies lacrosse team which won many international titles at that time.

Many European heroin and opium addicts were given cocaine by their doctors in order to help them stave off the debilitating effects of heroin and opium withdrawal. The technique was successful but often turned the heroin or opium addict into a cocaine addict.

These original uses of the drug as a stimulant were based on the belief that the drug could be used without danger. This proved to be false and many people became dependent on cocaine-containing products. No legal use is now made of cocaine for its stimulating properties although it continues to be used on a small scale as a local anaesthetic.

Forms and appearance

Almost all of the cocaine that reaches the streets of the UK is in the form of cocaine hydrochloride powder. This is a pure white crystalline powder. The crystals are very small and even and sparkle when exposed to the light. Cocaine is usually about 85 per cent pure at the end of the manufacturing process and it is in this form that it enters the UK. It is 'cut' or diluted

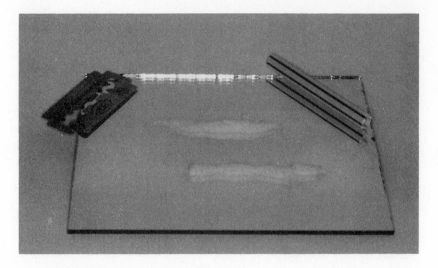

Lines of cocaine ready for 'snorting'

further, as it passes down the dealer network, before it reaches the streets, and may be reduced to as little as 30 per cent pure, although samples are seen that are still up to 60 per cent pure. The agents used to cut the imported cocaine are most commonly various forms of glucose or lactose, although on occasions other local anaesthetics are used such as lignocaine. The purpose of adding other local anaesthetics is that they will give the same numbing effect to the tongue of anyone testing the street drug as good quality cocaine.

Marketing

The production and distribution of cocaine from South America has become an enormous industry whose tentacles reach out into every country in the developed world. In countries such as Columbia and Bolivia the drug plays a significant part in the economy, and the growing of the coca bush has replaced the growing of food crops in a very big way. There are fantastic profits to be made through the production of the drug and this has led to a great deal of violence, often reaching warlike proportions, as the various growers fight with each other for control of the trade. The legitimate governments in those countries, acting under pressure from countries on the receiving end of cocaine distribution, are fighting a ceaseless and enormously expensive war on the industry, but those in control guard their empires with great ferocity and little impact is made. The drug is smuggled into the UK in a wide variety of ways. Very large consignments, often of many hundreds of kilograms at a time, enter the country through the sea ports. The smuggler uses a great deal of imagination and customs officers have to show the same degree of ingenuity. Cargo containers that have often arrived by very circuitous routes have been found with false bottoms or sides. Apparently innocent imports often conceal packages of compressed cocaine within them and so on. Another method of smuggling the drug into the UK is by light aircraft flying from airfields in continental Europe. There are hundreds of small, or disused, airfields in southern and eastern England where there are little in the way of controls over what arrives, and if no landing strip is available, the smugglers will drop consignments over open country for waiting accomplices to collect.

Significant amounts are smuggled in within the stomachs of couriers arriving by air. Fifty grams or so of cocaine can be placed in a condom and then swallowed just prior to departure. On arrival the traveller simply allows nature to take its course and the condom passes out of the body to be recovered. As many as 200 such condoms have been found in the stomachs of single couriers detected at airports. Such couriers are referred to as *mules* in the drug trade because they are acting as beasts of burden for the drug importers. Many mules are women and often come from very impoverished backgrounds. They are recruited to the trade with offers of large cash sums and are willing to take the risks. Several tragedies have occurred through condoms splitting within the courier's stomach causing a massive overdose of cocaine and almost certain death. It seems as though as soon as one smuggling method is detected and closed down then the distributors find another way, so lucrative is the trade.

Recently a case occurred in which in excess of six kilograms of cocaine had been dissolved and impregnated into the clothing contained in a single suitcase in the possession of a traveller.

Once safely in the UK the drug is divided into smaller and smaller amounts as it passes through the dealer chain that now exists nation-wide. As it does so it steadily increases in price until, by the time it reaches the streets, a lot of people have made very large sums of money from it. At street level it is normally sold in small paper *wraps* in the same way as amphetamine. The standard wrap will contain half a gram of cocaine but wraps of other sizes will be available. The drug is not as easily obtainable as drugs such as cannabis or amphetamine, but is not difficult to find in any of our major cities or larger towns. It will be available on a much more irregular basis in smaller towns and may only be supplied by special order in some small towns and villages. It is still one of our more expensive street drugs and this restricts its use to those with ready access to fairly large sums of money.

Cost

Cocaine powder currently costs between £50.00 and £80.00 per gram in the UK. The common half gram wrap would cost a user between £30.00 and £50.00. As with all drugs there are economies to be made by buying in larger quantities. Enough cocaine to provide one *hit* to an inexperienced user would cost around £15.00

Legal position

Cocaine and coca paste are class 'A', schedule two, controlled substances under the Misuse of Drugs Act 1971.

As with all class 'A' drugs, offences involving it carry the following penalties.

Possession for personal use

The possession of an amount of cocaine for personal use is punishable on indictment by a maximum sentence of 14 years imprisonment plus an unlimited fine.

Possession with intent to supply

Possession of cocaine with intent to supply the drug by sale or gift to another person is punishable on indictment with a maximum sentence of life imprisonment plus an unlimited fine and the seizure of all drug related assets.

Supplying

As for possession with intent to supply.

Importation

As for possession with intent to supply.

The position of cocaine within schedule two of the Misuse of Drugs Act 1971 means that it is permitted for doctors to use it for medical purposes but only under strictly controlled circumstances.

Any doctor treating a person who they have reason to believe is suffering from an addiction to the use of cocaine is obliged to inform the drugs branch of the Home Office within seven working days.

Methods of use

Most users of cocaine in its powder form use the drug by the practice known as snorting, involving the sniffing of the powder sharply into the nose and allowing the drug to be absorbed into the blood stream through the membranes inside the nose. The drug is placed on a smooth hard surface such as a mirror or a china plate and then arranged into a thin line by the use of a razor blade or a plastic credit card. The use of such a tool is also a very efficient way of dividing an amount of the drug into equal parts so that more than one person can share it. To divide a sample of powder into equal parts without scales is very difficult, but a high level of accuracy can be obtained by the use of such a device to create lines of equal thickness and length. Having arranged the powder into a line, the user then places a small tube into one nostril and closes off the other nostril with a finger. They then place the end of the tube at one end of the powder line and sniff sharply thus drawing the powder into the nose. As they do so they move the tube along the line sniffing up the powder. The tube may be a purpose made one constructed from glass, plastic or metal. It may even be shaped like the letter 'Y' so that it has two ends that can be placed in both nostrils at the same time. More commonly, a temporary device can be created by rolling a bank note or similar piece of paper into a tube and utilizing that. The inhaled powder adheres to the surface of the mucus membranes of the inner nose and is readily absorbed into the bloodstream.

In some circles there is a fashion for snorting cocaine from a small, specially shaped, spoon. This spoon is often very ornate and may well be made from solid silver, the bowl of which is set at right angles to the handle. It is filled with cocaine powder and held up to one nostril for snorting. When not in use the spoon is to be seen hanging from a silver chain around the neck of its owner, like a status symbol.

Some users of cocaine rub the drug into their gums with a finger. The cocaine is rapidly absorbed into the blood stream and for pure efficiency this method allows more of the drug to reach the brain than snorting it. However, the drug has a very bitter taste and this limits the popularity of the method.

Occasionally cocaine is used by dissolving it into a drink or placing it in cold food. This is not a particularly efficient way of getting the drug into the bloodstream and has few followers.

In recent years there has been a significant increase in the number of users who inject cocaine. This is done either by injecting into a vein or by a process known as 'skin popping' where a small amount of liquid is injected into the fat layer just below the surface of the skin. Injecting into the veins is the method that provides the most rapid 'hit' as the drug reaches the brain in high concentrations within a few seconds of injection. Skin popping is much slower as the drug has to find its way into the many minute blood vessels in the fatty layer beneath the skin and from them move into the main blood stream.

Coca paste is rarely available in the UK and when seen is treated by users almost as a curiosity. The normal method of using coca paste is to smoke it. The efficacy of cocaine in this form is easily damaged by high temperatures and so a normal tobacco pipe with its enclosed bowl is not favoured. The paste is normally smoked in small versions of the cannabis water pipe (bhongs) or in pipes with ventilation holes in them that provide a supply of cool air into the smoke (chillums). The few examples of coca paste that reach the UK are usually of a high purity level and contain around 60 per cent cocaine. This, together with the efficiency of smoking as a method of getting the drug into the bloodstream, make this a potent way of using cocaine.

Effects of use

The hit provided by cocaine is felt very rapidly. The brain takes up the drug very easily and the user will begin to feel the effects of its use within a few seconds of taking. The effects will be very short lived however and, dependent upon how much of the drug was used and the previous experience of the user, will vary from a few minutes up to two or three hours at the most.

Most users report powerful feelings of euphoria with overpowering feelings of well being, energy and strength. They will experience great clarity of mind and feel that they have been given deep insight into their lives. The drug will give users feelings of confidence and freedom from anxiety and stress. Cocaine users often become very excitable and talkative and will feel unable to keep still, wanting to be actively involved with other people.

In many users the drug increases the sexual appetite and desires and they may well become engaged in episodes of casual sex with other users who have been similarly affected.

Adverse effects

'What goes up must come down', and many users of cocaine pay for the energy and feelings of well being that it gives by equally powerful feelings of lethargy and depression. The user may well become very agitated and panicky and feel threatened by those around them. If the user has been taking very high doses of the drug this *coming down* period can lead to very bizarre and often violent behaviour.

Prolonged or heavy use of cocaine can lead to a loss of body condition and substantial weight loss. Some high dose users experience severe disruption to their normal sleep patterns and may suffer from chronic insomnia. Male users may become impotent and incapable of achieving or maintaining an erection. Some long-term heavy users will become extremely paranoid and may even exhibit symptoms of being clinically psychotic.

The practice of snorting cocaine powder into the nose can lead to real problems with the membranes and lining of the nasal passages. One of the immediate effects of cocaine is to cause a constriction of the blood vessel that it enters. This may lead, especially in the case of the minute blood vessels such as are found in the nose, to them closing down completely. This shutting down of the blood vessels leads to the tissues that they feed becoming starved of the blood supply necessary to keep them alive. The tissues begin to die, and cannot be replaced by normal processes at a fast enough rate, to keep up with continued use of the drug. The membranes often perforate causing ulcers to form within the nasal passages and it is not uncommon for the septum, the membrane that separates the right and left nasal passages, to perforate completely. Infections within these nasal ulcers are very common and the user may require a great deal of medical treatment to deal with the damage.

Injection of cocaine can also cause physical problems for the user. The drug causes constriction of the veins into which it is injected. The intravenous injector runs real risks of causing those veins to collapse and block. Such a blockage can lead to the blood supply being cut of to tissues normally fed by that vein which can lead to disorders such as gangrene, which if left untreated can cause septicaemia, the loss of limbs and even death. Because of this danger many injecting users prefer to inject subcutaneously, that is just beneath the skin, by the process known as skin popping, with small amounts of liquids being injected into the layer of fat that lies just below the skin. The thighs and the upper side of the forearm are favourite sites for this. The amount injected into any one site is between half and one millilitre of liquid. If larger amounts are being administered then several sites are used. The liquid causes a small bubble to form just under the skin which disappears as the drug is absorbed into the tissues. Because of the vein constricting properties of the drug, these sites often become ulcerated and very painful. Infections at the injection sites are common and can lead to serious problems unless treated medically.

People who are sharing needles and syringes with other users, who are infected, run the very real risk of acquiring the same infection. Diseases such as HIV, septicaemia and hepatitis are regularly passed from one person to another by such sharing.

The use of cocaine by women during pregnancy is extremely dangerous for the developing foetus. The blood flow to the infant is restricted causing a reduction in the supply of oxygen. This can lead to spontaneous abortion, still birth and, where the child is born alive, to both physical or neurological damage. The infant is also at risk of being born with a severe dependence upon cocaine which can badly affect its healthy development in the first weeks of its life.

Tolerance potential

Some level of tolerance will develop with continued use of cocaine. Regular use of the drug can lead to a point where the effects or their duration become noticeably reduced and the user has to increase the amount of each dose or the frequency of use.

Habituation potential

Very few users become physically dependent upon cocaine. The major risk lies in acquiring a psychological dependence upon it. This dependence can be very deep seated and difficult to treat. The short duration of effect, that is a feature of this drug, encourages the user to keep using. If users wish to be under the influence of cocaine for the duration of a party or other social event, they will need to take several doses spaced at regular intervals. The adverse effects of withdrawal are thus put off, but as with all such reactions, they can not be put off indefinitely and the *crash*, when it finally arrives, will be even greater. The feelings of weakness, anxiety and lack of confidence are very powerful and can be extremely unpleasant providing a further impetus to the desire to keep on using the drug.

Withdrawal effects

If the use of cocaine has been light and on an irregular basis then most users will be able to cease their use of the drug without any great difficulty. It is the regular and heavy user, particularly if that use has been over a prolonged period, that may have very real problems. The feelings of anxiety, depression and panic that may result from ceasing to use the drug will be very difficult to cope with and will result in a severe craving for continued use. Many cases of suicide have resulted from the torment that such withdrawal can bring. No one who has used cocaine on a regular basis over a long period should attempt to come off the drug without professional help.

Overdose potential

Overdoses can occur with cocaine at relatively low levels. Because of the uncertainty that exists over the strength of any particular sample of street cocaine it is very easy to take too much. The precise level of an overdose for any one person can not be predicted with any accuracy and regular users should always be aware of the risks that they run. An overdose of cocaine can lead to the heart rate and body temperature rising to dangerous levels and may result in convulsions and even cardiac or respiratory failure leading to coma and death.

Street names

Cocaine powder – **coke, snow, snowflake, bernice, charlie, charge, Bolivian marching powder, white lady**

Slang associated with use

- **Snorting** – inhaling through the nose
- **Line** – a line of cocaine on a flat surface ready for snorting
- **Mixing the gravy** – smoking cocaine mixed with other drugs
- **Flying** – the feeling after cocaine use
- **Speed balling** – mixing cocaine with heroin for smoking
- **Skin popping** – injecting cocaine just under the skin
- **Mule** – courier who smuggles cocaine inside their bodies
- **Wraps** – folded paper packets containing the drug
- **Coming down** or **crashing** – feelings of lethargy and depression as effect of drug wears off

Cocaine

Reasons for use

Problems

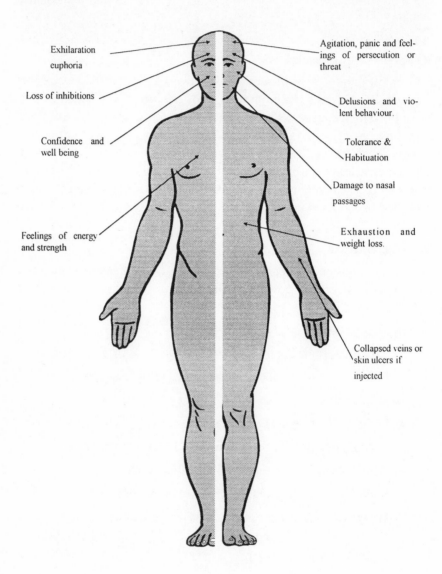

Exhilaration euphoria

Loss of inhibitions

Confidence and well being

Feelings of energy and strength

Agitation, panic and feelings of persecution or threat

Delusions and violent behaviour.

Tolerance & Habituation

Damage to nasal passages

Exhaustion and weight loss.

Collapsed veins or skin ulcers if injected

Crack & Freebase Cocaine

Crack and Freebase Cocaine: Quick Reference Guide

Source

Derived from cocaine hydrochloride by chemical process.

Forms and appearance

Crack cocaine is seen in crystals of varying sizes and colours that range from a clear yellow or pinkish yellow to a waxy white colour.

Freebase is normally a white powder.

Marketing

Freebase and the smaller crystals of crack are normally sold by the gram or fraction of a gram. Larger crystals are often sold singly. There is no established packaging for crack. The smaller crystals are commonly seen in small press seal bags while the larger crystals are often wrapped separately in clear plastic film or a cigarette paper.

Cost

Freebase and the smaller crack crystals sell for around £100.00 per gram with larger crystals being priced according to individual weight.

Legal position

Both freebase and crack are simply forms of cocaine and as such are classified in the same way. They are class 'A', schedule two, controlled substances under the Misuse of Drugs Act 1971. Addiction to any form of cocaine is a notifiable condition under the Misuse of Drugs (notification and supply to addicts) Regulations 1973.

Methods of use

Freebase and crack are smoked in specially made pipes or in small metal containers or from metal foil.

Effects of use

Extreme elation and euphoria, feelings of power, strength and well being.

Adverse effects

Feelings of tiredness and weakness, depression, feelings of being threatened. Heavy use can lead to paranoia and psychosis with the display of bizarre and often very violent behaviour, especially upon withdrawal.

Tolerance potential

Some tolerance develops with continued use.

Habituation potential

Both physical and psychological dependence develops very rapidly with continued use. Babies born to pregnant users may also be dependent.

Withdrawal effects

Feelings of aggression, agitation and panic, severe depression, risk of suicide.

Overdose potential

An overdose of freebase or crack can lead to coma and death.

Crack and Freebase Cocaine: In Depth Guide

Source

Crack cocaine is produced by freeing cocaine from its chemical base. The normal form of the drug cocaine is a compound of pure cocaine known as cocaine hydrochloride. Until the mid 1980s this was the only form of the drug commonly available on the streets. Suppliers of the drug in the US then began to seek for ways of producing it in a form that the human body would accept more readily, and would give the user a more intense 'hit', and enhance the effects that normal cocaine use provides. Pressure also came from users for a form of the drug that could be smoked more efficiently than ordinary cocaine. The normal habit of snorting cocaine had caused so many nasal problems for users that many were seeking a smoking form that would give them all of the effects of snorting without the attendant problems.

The first step in this process was the creation of a form of cocaine called freebase. The production of freebase involves dissolving cocaine hydrochloride with a powerful solvent such as ether, and then allowing it to evaporate off. This process is difficult and potentially dangerous. Fires and even explosions can be the common result of such processes. Freebase cocaine produced in this way is seen occasionally on the streets, but it is extremely rare and most freebase is made by the users themselves for their own use. Another process was then developed which involves dissolving the cocaine hydrochloride in an alkaline solution and then gently heating it. This causes the creation of crystals of freebase cocaine, known on the streets as crack. Chemically both freebase and crack are identical but the crack process is easier and safer and produces a drug that is in a form that can be used for smoking very easily.

Forms and appearance

Freebase cocaine is seen as a white powder. It is less crystalline in appearance than cocaine hydrochloride but has the same pure white colour. It can be as much as 95 per cent pure cocaine. It is not generally 'cut' or diluted with anything else. The remaining five per cent will normally be contaminants that have remained within the drug after processing.

Crack crystals and freebase cocaine

Crack cocaine is seen in the form of crystals of varying sizes. Many of these crystals will be very small, some as small as that of granulated sugar, but many will be as much as one centimetre across. Users of crack prefer the larger crystals, and producers will seek to produce as much of the drug in this form as they can. Purity levels can be very high, figures of between 80 and 100 per cent are usual. The colour of the crystals will vary a great deal. There is a common belief amongst users that crack is always a purer type of cocaine because of its crystal form. It is certainly harder to add adulterants deliberately to crack, but many of the contaminants that were present in the original cocaine hydrochloride will be carried over into the crystals during manufacture. These additional substances cause the colour variations that are seen. Some crack crystals will be transparent and have a yellow or pinkish hue. Others will be of a similar colour but cloudy and translucent, while many crystals have a white or yellow waxy appearance and are opaque.

Marketing

The promotion of freebase and crack cocaine has been a remarkable thing to observe. During the mid 1980s, stories began to emanate from the US about an amazing new form of cocaine, a form that gave the user an instant hit and had effects that far surpassed the ordinary form of the drug. Despite other stories that described the drug as being able to turn a user into an addict at the first use, there arose an immediate demand for supplies. Details of the production processes quickly began to circulate within the drug using community and many users began to produce their own at home. At the same time small amounts of American produced freebase and crack began to arrive in the UK. The freebase form of the drug failed to establish itself as a high demand drug but the market for crack cocaine rapidly began to grow. Producers in the UK refined their production processes and began to produce the drug in useful quantities and to the same standards as their American counterparts. Production has now increased to the point where around half of all the crack used in the UK is produced here from cocaine hydrochloride imported from elsewhere. There are enormous profits to be made from the production and sale of crack, and a great deal of criminal violence occurs where suppliers are involved in what are called 'turf wars' for control of areas in which they can establish a monopoly of supply.

Both freebase and crack are sold by the fraction of a gram. The market for these drugs is so new that no particular form of packaging has established itself as the norm. Freebase, when available, and the smaller crack crystals are commonly dealt in small plastic press seal bags or in the usual paper wrap. The larger crystals of crack cocaine are often sold separately with the price set according to weight. These crystals will normally be wrapped in a twist of clear plastic film or a single cigarette paper. The shape of this form of packaging has led to them being referred to as *bombs*.

Crack cocaine is also used by criminal elements as a means of controlling prostitutes, both male and female. The drug is first given either free or at a very low price to young males or females who the supplier sees as suitable for involvement in prostitution. Many of these will be very young, some in their very early teens, and will almost always be poor and unemployed, or have run away from home or institutions, and be living on the streets. The young person quickly acquires a dependence upon the drug, and being unable to afford the normal street price will be prepared to do whatever the supplier asks of them. The supplier acts as their pimp, introduces them to clients and take the majority of the earnings from them. A steady supply of crack is only assured if the young person continues to obey the pimp, and many fall into a lifestyle that most of us would have difficulty in imagining.

Crack cocaine has now established itself as an important drug of choice in the UK, and is readily available in most large centres of population. In some of the more socially deprived areas in some major towns and cities, it will be available from dealers operating on the streets. In other places it will be available from locations such as clubs, cafes, public houses and so on, from dealers who are known personally to the user. The drug will be available in other smaller towns and villages by special arrangement between the user and a local dealer in other drugs.

Cost

It is only in areas where crack is readily available that a market price has become established. In other areas the price will have to be agreed between the user and their particular supplier. Casual or first time users in such areas seem to be prepared to pay a much higher price in order to experiment with the drug.

In established areas both freebase and crack sell for around £100.00 per gram. The larger crystals are sold separately and will be weighed, using a small balance, and the price set accordingly. The very largest of the crystals are much sought after by many users. These crystals will often attract a premium price that will be considerably more than the equivalent weight of smaller crystals.

Legal position

Both freebase and crack cocaine are legally classified as being the same as cocaine, and as such are both class 'A', schedule two, controlled substances under the Misuse of Drugs Act 1971.

Offences involving freebase or crack cocaine attract the following penalties

Possession for personal use

The possession of any amount of freebase or crack cocaine for personal use is punishable on indictment by a maximum sentence of seven years imprisonment plus an unlimited fine.

Possession with intent to supply

Possession of freebase or crack cocaine with intent to supply by sale or gift to another person is punishable on indictment with a maximum sentence of life imprisonment, plus an unlimited fine and the seizure of all drug related assets.

Supplying

As for possession with intent to supply.

Importation and manufacture

As for possession with intent to supply.

Although freebase and crack cocaine are classified within schedule two of the Misuse of Drugs Act 1971, this part of the classification refers only to ordinary cocaine. These other two forms of the drug have no recognised medical use in the UK at the present time.

Any doctor treating a person who they have reason to believe is suffering from an addiction to the use of freebase or crack is obliged to inform the drugs branch of the Home Office within seven working days.

Methods of use

Both freebase and crack cocaine were designed to be smoked, and it is exceptionally rare for it to be used in any other way. These forms of cocaine are able to withstand the high temperatures achieved during smoking in a much better way than the ordinary form. However, if the temperature in the smoking bowl is allowed to reach too high a level, even these forms of cocaine begin to break down and a loss of effectiveness will result. Because of this the user will try to smoke their drug in a way that keeps the temperature down to as low a point as possible. It is not necessary to burn the drug in order to smoke it, it is merely necessary for the temperature to reach a point at which the drug will vaporize. It is this vapour that is inhaled. The smoker will try to keep the temperature as close to this vaporization point as possible to maintain maximum effectiveness.

Many smokers make use of smaller versions of the bottle pipes used by cannabis smokers. These pipes employ the same principle of having a smoking bowl connected to a water filled container through which the vapour is drawn before reaching the smoker. Most of the crack water pipes that are seen in use in the UK have been home made but there is a thriving trade in commercially manufactured water pipes of all descriptions.

However, it is not necessary to use anything as sophisticated as a water pipe to smoke crack cocaine successfully. Many will simply use a glass or metal tube with a bore wide enough to accommodate the average sized

Crack pipes

crack crystal. The user fits the crystal just inside one end of the tube and puts the other end in their mouth. The outer end of the tube is then heated with a match or cigarette lighter until the crystal vaporizes and the fumes are inhaled. Others will heat their freebase or crack cocaine on a piece of metal foil or in a metal bottle top, or indeed anything similar, and collect the fumes for inhalation with a tube, a match box sleeve or simply a cupped hand.

Effects of use

The effects of smoking freebase or crack cocaine are almost instant. The drug is readily absorbed through the lungs and passes via the bloodstream to the brain. The users will feel the *hit* provided by the drug within a matter of seconds of inhaling the vapour. The effects of the drug are extremely short lived. Depending upon the amount smoked at any one time, and the previous experience of the user, the duration of the effects can be as short at 15 minutes and certainly no longer than one hour.

As the *hit* reaches the brain the user will feel intense sensations of euphoria, great elation, almost superhuman strength, boundless energy and well being. It is hard to exaggerate the reported power and intensity of these sensations. Many users of these forms of cocaine claim that the drug provides the most powerful feelings of any street drug.

Adverse effects

As with most drugs the higher the freebase or crack user becomes, then the lower they will sink when the drug has run its course. The intensity of the euphoric feelings provided by freebase and crack cocaine are followed by equally powerful feelings of fatigue and weakness. These will be accompanied by depression, and in many cases, feelings of paranoia and of being under threat from those around them.

It only takes a small amount of the drug to produce its effect, and so each individual dose is inexpensive when viewed in comparison with some other drugs. The severity of the down side of the use of this drug, together with the shortness of the duration of the pleasant feelings, and the low price of an individual dose, can encourage users to continue its use. A frame of mind of 'just one more time' rapidly develops. The low cost of each dose of freebase or crack is, of course, a false impression. With many users taking repeated doses of the drug over a fairly short period, the monetary cost begins to mount rapidly. It is not uncommon for users to consume many hundreds of pounds worth of the drug over the course of one heavy session, lasting for only a couple of days.

Heavy or prolonged use of the drug leads, in a great number of users, to profound psychological problems. Many will develop a deep seated paranoia and be suspicious of and antagonistic towards other people. These feelings of antagonism will be particularly focused on those whom they consider to be trying to stop them using the drug that has become the centre of their lives. This may show itself in violence, often of a very extreme form, towards drug agency workers, police, doctors and indeed officials of all sorts. Many drug agencies give their workers special instructions on how to work with heavy users of freebase and crack cocaine. Even a relatively short period of continued use can lead to the development of complex psychosis in which very elaborate delusions may be created by the user which make it even more difficult to help them.

These psychological conditions can be very difficult, if not impossible, to control or cure, and may require prolonged periods of inpatient treatment at a psychiatric hospital.

One problematic area causing increasing concern is the use of the drug by pregnant women. Many of these will suffer spontaneous abortions, or their babies will die in the womb due to displacement of the placenta. They may also be still born. The chief cause of these problems is the way in which all forms of cocaine restrict the flow of blood along veins and arteries. This significantly reduces the volume of blood flowing through the umbilical cord into the foetus. This reduction together with the consequent decrease in oxygen supply often leads to the baby being born either physically or neurologically damaged, or both. Some of this damage can be extreme. No figures are available for the number of such births in the UK, but it has been estimated that some two per cent of all births in the US are from crack cocaine using mothers.

Tolerance potential

Some degree of tolerance to freebase or crack will develop with continued or regular use, although it is unlikely to be as marked as that seen with other street drugs. These forms of cocaine seem able to maintain the power of their effect without the need to increase dosage levels for much longer than is usual with other drugs.

Habituation potential

Many users of freebase and crack cocaine will develop a powerful physical dependence upon the drug. They will experience very severe craving for it when either trying to cease its use or when their supplies are not available to them. This often causes them to become very unstable and to lose control. Many of the instances of violence carried out by freebase and crack users have taken place under these conditions. Along with the development of a physical dependence will form a deep seated psychological dependence on the drug. The user will feel unable to face the world without it. The unpleasantness of the physical feelings that withdrawal can bring will only serve to reinforce the psychological feelings that life is too difficult or stressful to cope without the drug. Many users report that they are afraid, even terrified, to try to stop using.

Because of the degree of unpleasantness associated with coming down from the drug, many users are now experimenting with a practice called *mixing the gravies*. This practice involves mixing heroin powder in with the freebase or crack and smoking the two together. The heroin is absorbed more slowly by the lungs and the *hit* that it provides is masked by that of the crack. The effects of heroin are much longer lasting, however, and as the effect of the crack begins to fade, are then able to take over and ease the user through the come down phase. Users who have been 'bingeing' on freebase or crack cocaine by taking it repeatedly, will often add heroin to their last dose to achieve this. The addition of heroin exposes the user to the development of a physical dependence upon that drug, and whilst easing the user through the comedown from freebase or crack cocaine can eventually lead to greater problems.

Withdrawal effects

The speed at which dependence can develop means that any user who has experimented with this drug on more than an occasional basis is liable to suffer some form of withdrawal when its use is stopped. They may experience extreme agitation and feelings of disorientation, combined with a state of panic. They may become very depressed and this, together with the psychological problems that use of the drug often causes, can lead to the user becoming suicidal. This risk is very real and no one who has used this drug over any period of time should attempt to withdraw without seeking professional help.

Overdose potential

Heavy doses of freebase or crack cocaine can lead to both respiratory or cardiac failure, collapse, coma and death.

Street names

- Crack cocaine crystals – **rocks, wash, flake, cloud nine, eight ball, gravel, nuggets, roxanne**
- Freebase cocaine – **base, freebase, baseball**

Slang associated with use

- **Free basing, basing** – smoking freebase or crack
- **Washing** – producing crack cocaine from cocaine hydrochloride powder
- **Crack head** – crack user
- **Crack baby** – the infant of a crack using mother
- **Crack pipe, crack bottle** – pipe used for smoking
- **Bomb** – a single wrapped crystal
- **Mixing the gravies** – mixing heroin powder with freebase or crack and smoking the two together

Crack and Freebase Cocaine

Reasons for use   Problems

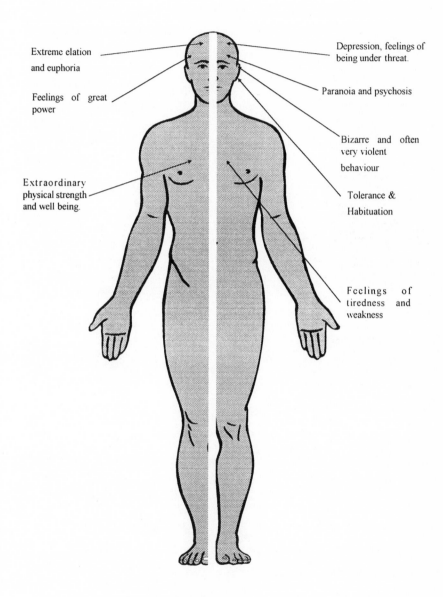

Extreme elation
and euphoria

Feelings of great
power

Extraordinary
physical strength
and well being.

Depression, feelings of
being under threat.

Paranoia and psychosis

Bizarre and often
very violent
behaviour

Tolerance &
Habituation

Feelings of
tiredness and
weakness

CHAPTER 5

Hallucinogens

LSD
Lysergic Acid Diethylamide

LSD: Quick Reference Guide

Source

Derived by a chemical process from ergot, a naturally occurring fungus of certain cereal grains.

Forms and appearance

Pure LSD occurs in the form of colourless crystals but as such is not seen as a street drug. LSD for street use is impregnated into small squares of blotting type paper, each with a picture printed upon them, and known as *trips* or *tabs* or in small squares of clear yellow gelatine, known as *windows*. It also appears in the form of pinhead sized pills of various colours.

Marketing

All the forms of LSD are sold by the dose.

Cost

A single dose of the drug will cost between £1.50 and £5.00.

Legal position

LSD is a class 'A', schedule one, controlled substance under the Misuse of Drugs Act 1971.

Effects of use

Hallucinations, visual, auditory and tactile. These can feel very real and may vary from extremely pleasant to extremely unpleasant.

Adverse effects

There is a real risk of the user becoming involved in an accident whilst hallucinating. Many users experience a reoccurrence of the hallucination many weeks or months after ceasing to use the drug, these being known as *flashbacks*. Use may bring to the surface a latent psychiatric disorder.

Tolerance potential

Tolerance to LSD develops quickly with repeated use over a period of a few days, but will disappear if the user abstains for a week or more.

Habituation potential

LSD is not thought to cause the development of any physical dependence in users. A regular user may, however, develop a psychological dependence on the drug, although this is not common.

Withdrawal effects

LSD produces little in the way of physical effects when a user ceases. A regular user may have to cope with feelings of anxiety, but these will be of a low level.

Overdose potential

It is not thought possible to overdose on LSD.

LSD: In Depth Guide

Source

LSD is produced by the chemical processing of a substance contained in ergot, which is a naturally occurring fungus that affects many cereal crops, the chief source of the fungus being rye, which is grown in the US.

LSD was first isolated in 1938 by Albert Hoffman, a Swiss chemist who was investigating the properties of the many compounds that can be derived from ergot. He was seeking compounds that would be of use for medical purposes. Having isolated and then synthesized the drug, he carried out some experiments with it on a range of animals. Because LSD has almost no physical effect on living organisms he noted no useful reactions and the drug was largely forgotten. In 1943 he returned to the study of the drug, and during the course of an experiment accidentally ingested a small quantity of it, probably by licking his fingers after handling it. During the course of the next few hours he experienced the world's first recorded hallucinogenic LSD *trip*. Being a scientist he recorded his impressions of the experience in his diary, which mentions that the shapes of objects and people around him changed and that he saw fantastic images of extraordinary clarity and with intense and changing coloration. The whole hallucinatory period lasted about two hours.

This experience was totally unexpected and so Hoffman set out to replicate it under more controlled conditions. He had no idea what the most effective dose would be, so he decided to take 0.25 milligrams, this being what he thought would be a very mild dose of the drug. Unknown to him, he was in fact taking a dose equivalent to five times the normal strength of the street forms that we see today. He then recorded, as carefully as he could, his impressions as the effects began to take hold. His notes refer to his beginning to feel a little dizzy after about 40 minutes and then beginning to suffer some distortion to his vision. He records that he felt as though he had left his body and was able to observe himself from outside. He also describes how the sounds in the laboratory were translated in his brain to images, and he was able to see the sound of people talking and of a tap running. Throughout the hallucination he remained aware that all that was happening to him was only the result of the drug, but still felt a great fear that he was going out of his mind. After several hours of this he fell asleep and woke up later feeling perfectly well.

Over the next few years supplies of LSD were made available to doctors in the US and in Europe for experimental use in the treatment of certain psychiatric disorders. Many psychiatrists felt that it would provide a useful tool in helping patients to vocalize their inner feelings and psychoses. Experiments were also carried out by the American Government into the possibilities of using it as a 'truth drug'. Some doctors working with terminally ill patients also used the drug as a way of helping these patients to approach their deaths with calmness.

All of these experiments were abandoned within a fairly short time due to the ineffectiveness of the drug as a therapeutic tool, and also because many of the patients who were given it had begun to experience what we now know as *flashbacks*.

It is worth noting that during 1995, fifty of the UK patients who were given LSD as part of these experiments were granted permission to sue the participating health authorities for damages due to the problems that the use of the drug caused them.

Forms and appearance

LSD 'trips' or 'tabs'

Pure LSD is in the form of small colourless crystals but it is never seen on the streets in this form. The vast majority of pure LSD is today manufactured on the west coast of America. The LSD required to service the demand in Europe is exported from the US in pure form for preparation into the familiar street forms, most of this work being carried out in Holland and Belgium. This was not always the position, for during the early 1970s extensive production of LSD took place in the UK. The police mounted a very extensive operation to close down this production which resulted in 'Operation Julie', which involved many hundreds of officers over several counties and resulted in the prosecution of 122 people for offences relating to the production and distribution of the drug. At its height it is thought that the production of LSD in the UK was supplying 95 per cent of the British market and 65 per cent of the American LSD market. Following the success of the police operation the market for LSD collapsed. It became very difficult to obtain and the price escalated wildly, causing many users to change to other drugs or cease use altogether.

The dose of LSD that is needed to produce the effect desired by the user is extremely low, an average dose being in the region of 40 to 60 micrograms (a microgram being a millionth of a gram). In order to understand just how small this dose is, it is worth considering that a full stop put on a piece of paper with a ball point pen contains around 120 micrograms of ink, therefore to dose the drug accurately for use is very difficult.

When it first appeared on the streets in the 1960s it was in the form of a dilute, clear, colourless and odourless liquid that was placed with an eye dropper onto a sugar cube and eaten. This is a very inconvenient method of use and it soon disappeared. Today most LSD is seen impregnated onto sheets of absorbent paper, similar to poor quality blotting paper. The sheets are then divided into five millimetre squares. This is the most common size, although larger sizes are also seen. These squares are called *trips* or *tabs* or occasionally *blotters*, and are each decorated with a small picture or symbol. Most commonly there will be a complete picture or symbol printed on each square but it is not unusual to see a single larger image covering multiple squares. There are many hundreds of different designs and new ones appear all the time. The exact reason for these pictures is unclear. To some users they indicate quality. If the manufacturer of the drug has produced good quality images on the squares, then they believe that it follows that the drug will also be of high quality. Others will have favourite pictures and have a belief that they have found the form that suits them best. The constant arrival of new designs also serves as a sort of 'sell by date'. Most users know that LSD deteriorates with time if not stored properly, and feel that if the picture is new to them then the drug is also fresh. With some users, particularly the very young, there is also a fascination to try as many of the different designs as possible, in the same way that they might have collected pictures of footballers or pop stars.

Many of the designs have survived from the earliest appearance of this form of the drug, for example, 'the strawberry' and the little figure that is known as 'sad ant' have survived from the 1960s. Many of the older designs have a quasi-religious significance, such as 'buddha', 'the keys to the heavenly kingdom', the Hindu 'om' symbol. Important figures from world affairs, such as Saddam Hussein or Mikhail Gorbachev, are also featured. More recently LSD tabs have been produced with images that appear to have been designed to attract a very young clientele. Images of 'Batman', 'Superman', 'Sonic the Hedgehog' and the 'Super Mario Brothers' have become very popular. The dosage of LSD contained on these paper squares normally varies between 40 and 60 micrograms, but because of failures in the production system, some squares contain none at all whilst others have been found that contain several hundred micrograms of the drug.

Sheets of translucent yellow gelatine impregnated with LSD are occasionally seen. The sheets are usually printed with a grid of cutting lines to enable them to be easily divided in five millimetre squares. These gelatine sheets are known as 'windows'.

Small tablets of inert material that have been impregnated with the drug are also available. These tablets are known as microdots, or simply dots, and are very small, most examples being no more than two or three millimetres in diameter. They are available in a wide variety of colours, the colour being simply the result of vegetable dyes added to the tablet mix.

Methods of use

LSD is normally taken orally by placing the paper square or small pill in the mouth or in a drink. The gelatine squares are normally placed under the eyelid so that the blood vessels of the eye absorb the drug, this practice being known as 'looking through the window'.

Special note – drug laced tattoos and transfers

At regular intervals over the past fifteen years or so vast numbers of unsigned and unaccredited documents have turned up all over the UK under the title of 'Drug laced tattoos and transfers', or the like. They are all very similar in wording and usually come to notice as a result of being circulated to parents and children by well meaning schools, community groups and so on.

The documents, recent examples of which claim to be a 'Metropolitan Police Warning', draw attention to the sale to children of tattoos or transfers that contain LSD. The document goes on to describe the drug laced tattoos as being called 'Blue Star' or 'Red Pyramid'. It also describes others as having pictures upon them. The reader is asked in three different places in the document to pass on the information to other parents and children and to 'feel free to reproduce this article and distribute it within your community'.

We have made extensive enquiries to trace the source of this document without success. The National Drugs Intelligence Unit (NDIU) at New Scotland Yard have made their own enquiries and have also drawn a blank.

The NDIU make the point strongly that extensive enquiries within this country and abroad have failed to turn up any examples of such drug laced tattoos or transfers or a child affected by one. Common sense would dictate that if they existed we would have seen an example by now.

The history of the document appears to be as follows. It first came to notice in Canada almost twenty years ago and early examples that we saw some years ago had an American feel to the wording, although this has disappeared in later versions. It next came to prominence by being circulated amongst families of the British Army on the Rhine in Germany. It then seemed to get into the international electronic mail system. Many companies run 'notice boards' within their electronic mail systems that can be used by employees to advertise articles for sale or local events and other matters of interest. For several years now this has been the apparent channel through which the document circulates. An individual will believe that it is important and accurate and then place it upon the electronic notice board. It is then picked up and printed out by some other employee, often the employee of another company with access to the same notice board, and brought to the notice of a school or community group for further copying and distribution. It has become an international electronic chain letter, the circulation of which to parents and children often results in panic and a flood of enquiries to the Police and the various drug agencies.

Much of what is said in the document is a mixture of half truths about LSD and its methods of use and complete nonsense. Anyone coming across such a warning leaflet or poster would be well advised to destroy it.

Cost

The street price of LSD is now at its lowest ever level. Prices for the paper *trips* vary from £1.50 to £5.00 with the gelatine *windows* and *microdots* attracting a slightly higher price because of their rarity. This represents an enormous drop in price since the drug was last in vogue during the 1960s. In those days a single paper square often cost as much as £5.00 which in today's values would be in excess of £25.00. This reduction in price is a reflection of the large quantities currently available on the streets, and places the drug well within the reach of even the youngest potential customer.

Legal position

LSD is a class 'A', schedule one, controlled substance under the Misuse of Drugs Act 1971. Offences involving it attract the following penalties.

Possession for personal use

The possession of any amount of LSD for personal use is punishable on indictment by a maximum sentence of seven years imprisonment plus an unlimited fine.

Possession with intent to supply

Possession of LSD with intent to supply the drug by sale or gift to another person is punishable on indictment with a maximum sentence of life imprisonment plus an unlimited fine and the seizure of all drug related assets.

Supplying

As for possession with intent to supply.

Importation

As for possession with intent to supply.

The position of LSD within schedule one indicates that is has no current medical use.

Effects of use

The level of dosage has shown a considerable reduction over the years. When LSD first became a popular street drug in the 1960s, it was usual for the paper squares to contain between 120 and 150 micrograms of the drug. This meant that the effects of the drug were very intense and precluded the user from being involved in any other activity. Today's user wishes to take the drug whilst taking part in other social activities, such as raves and parties. As a result, the general dosage level has declined considerably, most containing levels of between 40 and 60 micrograms.

The physical effects of taking LSD are very slight. The user will normally experience a dilation of the pupils of the eyes, the raising of their blood sugar levels, together with a small increase in blood pressure and pulse rate.

It is the psychological effects that the user is seeking. LSD has a powerful effect on the brain which becomes apparent about 30 to 40 minutes after taking the drug. The user will go through a period in which their perception of the world around them will begin to become distorted. The colours of objects will change, light and sound levels will rise and fall, and some tactile sensations will occur. This distortion will steadily increase over the course of a further 30 minutes or so until the user reaches the stage at which the full effects are experienced. At this stage a full state of halluci-nation or *tripping* will become established, in which the user will be assailed by a whole range of very realistic visions and sensations. Many users see strange creatures or extreme alterations to the form of people and objects around them, and may experience these same changes happening to their own bodies. The colour, shape and nature of everyday objects may change so dramatically, that the *tripper* feels they have entered a completely new world. Many users, but not all, are able to remain aware of their true identities throughout the hallucination and will know that what they are seeing and feeling is only a false, drug induced, reality.

The nature of the *trip* may be very pleasant indeed, it may be fairly neutral, unpleasant or even totally terrifying. It could be a person's worst nightmare brought to life. The degree of alteration to perception that a user experiences will depend upon several factors, the dose of the drug taken, their previous experience of it, and certain personal factors which are, as yet, little understood. The nature of the hallucination will depend largely on the mood of the person when they use it. This mood is known to users as the *mind set* or simply the *set*, and a person who takes the drug whilst in a good frame of mind and in congenial and relaxed circumstances and environment is more likely to experience a *good trip*. A person taking the drug whilst unhappy, under stress, depressed or in circumstances or environments that are stressful is more likely to have a much more unpleasant experience.

The duration of the hallucinatory effects of LSD is difficult to predict, and can vary between six and twenty-four hours. The duration does not seem to be affected by any particular factors and can be quite random.

As the effects begin to fade the user will normally experience a period of tiredness and disorientation that will last for several hours. A reasonable period of sleep will usually return the user to normal; however, many will take a considerable time to clear any unpleasant images from their minds.

Adverse effects

The physical effects of LSD use carry very little risk for the user. The state of hallucination can be extremely intense and so real that the user may put themselves at risk of becoming involved in a dangerous accident. During a *bad trip* it is not uncommon for users to try to escape from the frightening apparitions around them by running away, and many have suffered serious injury or death by running across roads or climbing out of windows. Some users do lose touch with reality during particularly powerful *trips* and will attempt impossible feats that place them in danger. Many deaths have occurred because the user thought that they could fly and launched themselves off a high balcony or out of a window. Others seem to think that they can breathe under water and try to do so with fatal consequences, whilst others have attempted to stop oncoming traffic physically by standing in its path.

There is no known antidote to LSD and anyone dealing with a user who is under the influence of the drug can do little else but keep them from harming themselves, and to keep reassuring them that what they are experiencing is not real and only the result of the drug.

Another major problem with LSD use is the likelihood of the user experiencing a rerun of the hallucinatory state long after use. These reruns or *flashbacks* can occur weeks, months or even years after the person has stopped using the drug. They are generally of a shorter duration than the original 'trip', but can be just as intense and are often unpleasant. They may occur at a most inappropriate moment, whilst the person is driving a car or operating machinery, or even whilst performing some very delicate task that requires great concentration. It is worth contemplating the possible results of a surgeon, who had used LSD in their youth, suffering a flashback whilst operating on a patient. Some recent research suggests that if cannabis is used over the same period that LSD is being used, then the likelihood of flashbacks is increased dramatically.

In the long term most LSD users will suffer little in the way of permanent harm but the action of LSD on the brain is little understood, and in some cases it has been known to bring latent mental disorders to the surface. In a small number of cases it may even contribute to the onset of a psychiatric illness.

Tolerance potential

Tolerance to LSD develops quickly if the drug is used repeatedly over a short period. This tolerance rises to the point where the user will get very little effect from their normal dose, and merely increasing the dose will seldom achieve the required degree of effect. This tolerance rapidly fades if the user abstains from the drug for a week or so. This pattern of use is well understood by regular users and they will build in periods of 'rest' or abstinence into their LSD use. If they wish to use the drug at a particular time or venue or with particular people then they will ensure that they have cleared their tolerance so as to achieve the highest level of effect.

Habituation potential

LSD does not produce any physical dependency in users. Most users will not experience any psychological dependence either, but in a few cases may feel unable to enjoy their lives without the added spice of LSD use.

Withdrawal effects

There are no physical withdrawal effects from the drug, even after prolonged use, and most users will suffer no psychological effects either. Some will need to reorganize their lives in order to avoid situations in which they had become accustomed to taking the drug, in order to avoid the temptation to reuse.

Overdose potential

It is not thought possible to fatally overdose on LSD and even quite heavy doses do not produce dangerous physical reactions.

Street names

- LSD – **acid**
- LSD impregnated paper squares – **trips, tabs, blotters**
  (There are hundreds of different printed designs, each having its own name, for example – Bart Simpson, smiley faces, Batman, Superman, Flintstones)

- LSD impregnated gelatine squares – **windows**
- Small LSD tablets – **microdots, dots, micros**

Slang associated with use

- **Tripping, dropping acid** – using LSD
- **Looking through the window** – placing a gelatine square under the eyelid
- **Trip** – hallucination
- **Good trip** – a pleasant hallucination
- **Bad trip** – an unpleasant or frightening hallucination
- **Mind set, set** – the mood of the user at the time of use
- **Acid head, psychonaut** – LSD user
- **Flashback** – a rerun of a previous trip without further use of LSD
- **Trips** or **tabs** – squares of blotting type paper, impregnated with LSD
- **Windows** – small squares of clear yellow gelatine, impregnated with LSD

LSD

Reasons for Use   Problems

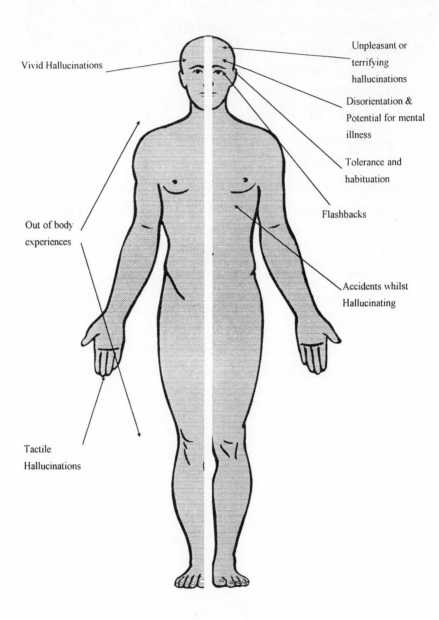

Vivid Hallucinations

Unpleasant or
terrifying
hallucinations

Disorientation &
Potential for mental
illness

Tolerance and
habituation

Flashbacks

Out of body
experiences

Accidents whilst
Hallucinating

Tactile
Hallucinations

Ecstasy
Methylenedioxymethamphetamine
MDMA

Ecstasy: Quick Reference Guide

Source

A totally synthetic product, similar to amphetamine but with hallucinogenic properties.

Forms and appearance

Commonly found in tablets and capsules in a wide range of colours, size and shape. Very occasionally seen as powders of different colours.

Marketing

The tablets and capsules are sold singly. The powder, when available is sold by the fraction of a gram. Major outlets for sales are the rave and dance club scene, although it is also commonly available from street dealers.

Cost

Tablets and capsules of ecstasy cost between £10.00 and £20.00 if bought singly, but as with most other drugs discounts are available for bulk purchases. Bought in quantity, the price can fall as low as £5.00 per tablet or capsule. There is no established price for the powder form due to its rarity.

Legal position

Ecstasy is a class 'A', schedule one', controlled substance under the Misuse of Drugs Act 1971.

Methods of use

Ecstasy is taken orally, but recently cases have also occurred where users are injecting crushed and dissolved tablets.

Effects of use

Feelings of euphoria, sociability, empathy to others, increased sexual arousal, energy, and changes in perception of surroundings.

Adverse effects

Ecstasy use may cause mood swings and irritability, nausea and vomiting, overheating (hyperthermia), high blood pressure, dehydration, convulsions and sudden death.

Tolerance potential

Tolerance develops with repeated use.

Habituation potential

There is little evidence of any physical habituation to ecstasy, but many users develop a low level psychological dependence. Other drugs used as adulterants in the manufacture may themselves cause habituation or addiction.

Withdrawal effects

Ecstasy causes no physical problems when use ceases but some users will suffer anxiety, mood swings, irritability and depression.

Overdose potential

Overdose can lead to coma and death.

Ecstasy: In Depth Guide

Source

Ecstasy is a completely synthetic hallucinogenic form of amphetamine. It was first synthesized in Germany in 1910 and patented by a German chemist as an appetite suppressant in 1914. The drug failed to find financial backing and was never marketed commercially. Military authorities in several countries showed an interest, and a number of experiments were carried out in order to assess its value as a stimulant and mood enhancer for soldiers engaged in physically strenuous and dangerous activities. It was considered as a possible chemical alternative to the traditional tot of rum. These experiments came to little, but for a short time the drug came into use in mental hospitals as a treatment for certain psychiatric disorders. The level of adverse side effects proved to be high and it again fell into disuse. It was then forgotten for many years until it next came to light in the US. During the early 1970s ecstasy was again experimented with as an aid to psychotherapy, and to put people into a relaxed frame of mind during counselling sessions. The level of side effects was still too high, and this led to the American health authorities banning it for medical use.

During this same period it began to appear on the streets of the US as a drug that seemed to offer the combined effects of amphetamine and of LSD. It was at this stage that it acquired the name 'ecstasy', a name that seemed to capture the effects that users were seeking. This name has now become universally accepted with all other street names used merely to describe different forms of the drug. It reached the UK during the late 1980s, and rapidly established itself as the drug of choice for people involved in the 'acid house music' craze. As this craze evolved into the 'pay party' and 'rave' scene, the drug moved with it, and along with LSD is now connected very firmly with young people who frequent the commercial dance scene. So close is this association that ecstasy is known as a 'dance drug'.

Forms and appearance

Ecstasy in its pure form is seen as a white powder. However, it is impossible to give a definite description of the drug in tablet or capsule form. Nowhere in the world is it manufactured commercially, and the form that it takes on the streets is determined by whoever manufactures it. The colour will

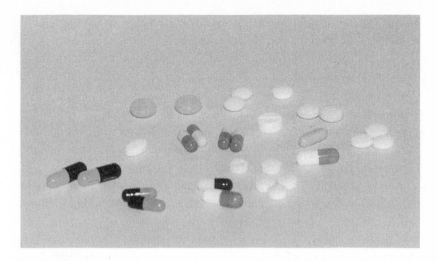

Ecstasy tablets and capsules

depend on whether any colouring agents have been added. Vegetable dyes are often added to produce a wide range of colours. The size and shape of the tablet forms will depend on the machines used to produce them, and any imprints on the tablet body will result from different formers used.

At least thirty different forms of ecstasy tablet are available on the streets and in dance clubs and raves. Some forms are much more popular than others, and include 'disco burgers' or 'disco biscuits' which are large, rather granular, tablets and, as the name suggests, light brown in colour. A small white form, often containing minute specks of other colours is known as 'adam' or 'eve'. Many forms exist that have images imprinted on their surface. Two in particular are very popular. One has a rather crude image of a bird imprinted into it, and is known as a 'dove' or 'love dove,' and in some circles as a 'rocking robin'. Another has a rabbit head imprinted on it and is known simply as 'rabbit'.

There are also a great number of capsule forms of ecstasy. It is fairly easy to obtain empty medicinal capsules as they can be purchased quite legally or obtained by theft from medical manufacturers. It is even possible in some places to purchase empty gelatine capsules from alternative medicine suppliers in order to make up your own herbal medicines. Many cases have occurred where ecstasy has been placed in the capsules of genuine medical preparations from which the original contents have been emptied.

All this means that the drug can be found in capsules of all sorts of sizes and colours. There are a number of popular forms including, a red and black capsule called 'Dennis the menace', named after the tee shirt of those colours worn by the comic book character. Another is red and yellow and called 'rhubarb and custard' for obvious reasons, while a red and white and a blue and white form are called 'united' and 'city' respectively after famous football teams.

All of this variation in form and colour has lead to a large trade in what are known on the streets as *snidey drugs*, substances that are falsely sold as particular drugs. A vast range of products are sold to young people as ecstasy with most of these snidey drugs being genuine tablets and capsules that were intended for other uses. Various proprietary pain relieving tablets are sold which have often been coloured by dipping them in vegetable dye, or even by spraying with a car touch-up paint. The brown disco burger is almost perfectly replicated by a proprietory brand of dog worming tablet, and many hundreds of these are sold in the dance clubs by dealers who make their escape before the fairly predictable results of taking such a preparation are experienced by their customers. The 'Dennis the menace' capsule is identical to a particular form of powerful antibiotic. There are thousands of young people who are allergic in some way to antibiotics, with reactions that vary from the simply uncomfortable to the extremely dangerous, and many have found themselves unknowingly being sold a powerful antibiotic when they thought they were buying ecstasy. Taking the antibiotic could therefore lead to disastrous results. Other drugs that have been passed off as ecstasy include hormone replacement therapy, contraceptive pills and kinds of tranquillizer. In many cases the drug filling in the capsules will be far from pure. Despite the relatively simple process involved in producing ecstasy, it is not uncommon to see amphetamine, LSD or a combination of both added to bulk out the filling.

A laboratory test would be required before a definitive identification of any tablet or capsule as ecstasy could be made.

Marketing

The major client group for ecstasy are the young people who frequent the dance and rave clubs that have sprung up all over the country in recent years. Many of these establishments do make a genuine effort to exclude the drug from their premises, but many cases have occurred where some club staff have been taking a percentage of the profits made by the dealers whom they allow to operate freely within the club. Even in clubs where care is taken to exclude the dealers, customers will simply buy their ecstasy from a dealer operating on the street outside and take it before they enter.

It is also available freely in a great number of public houses, cafes and in other places frequented by young people.

Cost

Tablets and capsules of ecstasy are usually sold for between £10.00 and £20.00. The price variation will depend a great deal upon the type of customer who the dealer is supplying. If the clientele of a particular venue are well off, the price may well be high. However if they are less well off it will be lower. The production costs of ecstasy are very low, and high profits can be made even when selling at the lower prices.

There is no established market for ecstasy in powder form and therefore no established price.

Legal position

Ecstasy is a class 'A', schedule one, controlled substance under the Misuse of Drugs Act 1971. Offences involving it attract the following penalties.

Possession for personal use

The possession of any amount of ecstasy for personal use is punishable on indictment by a maximum sentence of seven years imprisonment plus an unlimited fine.

Possession with intent to supply

Possession of ecstasy with intent to supply the drug by sale or gift to another person is punishable on indictment with a maximum sentence of life imprisonment plus an unlimited fine and the seizure of all drug related assets.

Supplying

As for possession with intent to supply.

Importation

As for possession with intent to supply.

The position of ecstasy within schedule one indicates that is has no medical use.

Methods of use

Ecstasy is most commonly taken orally, the tablet or capsules simply being swallowed. This gives it a real advantage over most other drugs as no paraphernalia is needed. This saves time and effort and means that there is no incriminating evidence for anyone to discover in the possession of the user. There is a reluctance on the part of many people to use drugs in smoking or injecting form, whilst a drug that can simply be swallowed in the form of a tablet or capsule raises no such reluctance.

There have been some examples of users experimenting with the drug by injecting it or snorting it up the nose, but these methods are still rare and show little sign of becoming popular with the vast majority of ecstasy users.

Effects of use

For most users, ecstasy provides a feeling of euphoria, of being at peace with the world, together with an increase in confidence and of empathy towards other people. At its best its effects can include a feeling of great warmth and even love to those around the user. Being an amphetamine derivative, it also provides the user with feelings of energy and freedom from hunger, allowing them to dance for long periods without the need to stop for rest or food. It is the combination of these effects, which may last for between two and six hours, which makes the drug appear so attractive for use within the party and dance club scene, and which has led to it becoming so closely associated with it.

Ecstasy is mildly hallucinogenic at the dosage normally used. These hallucinations will be of a much lower level than LSD, and will mostly comprise subtle changes in perception of the user's surroundings rather than the powerful visual and auditory effects associated with LSD. At much higher doses the hallucinogenic effects can rise to a much greater level and begin to rival those of LSD.

Adverse effects

Several recent tragic cases where ecstasy has led to sudden death have brought the drug into prominence with the general public. The fact that some of these cases have involved very young people, on the threshold of their lives, have made them even more poignant. Ecstasy is one of the few street drugs that has the power to cause death in such a sudden and often very distressing way. Many other drugs can lead to eventual death or even sudden death when used in overdose, but the use of ecstasy can be very much a case of playing 'Russian roulette' with your life. The causes of death can vary, but none of them appear to be particularly dose related. It is just as possible to suffer sudden death at what would be considered a normal street dose of the drug as it would be if the dose is much higher. Nor is this danger related to the user's previous experience of the drug. The fact that a person has used ecstasy on several previous occasions without mishap is no protection. The sudden adverse reaction can happen to an experienced user, as it can to a first time user.

Most of the sudden deaths associated with ecstasy seem to have been caused by two major effects of the drug. The first and the rarest is the formation of small clots within the blood system. These clots can migrate around the body until they lodge within the narrowest of blood vessels. Many of these very small blood vessels are to be found in the brain, and a clot lodging there can have disastrous results, and may lead to collapse and death in a very short time. The reaction that seems to cause the highest number of deaths is the drug's ability to raise the body's temperature alarmingly, and also to limit its ability to dissipate the heat. The exact mechanism of this is little understood, but it would appear that the drug has an effect on the hypothalamus, the organ that controls temperature. Along with this rise in temperature, the user is often involved in a prolonged session of energetic dancing in a crowded and very hot club. These two factors can make the temperature rise to such an extent that the user is at risk of suffering hyperthermia, a condition where the body temperature rises to a point where the user is at risk from potential convulsions and collapse. These can and often do lead to respiratory and cardiac failure and death. The heat will also cause profuse sweating and the user may become dehydrated in the extreme. Some dance or rave clubs recognize that their clients are likely to use ecstasy and provide cool rooms away from the dance area, called *chill out rooms*, where clients can rest, rehydrate with cold, non alcoholic drinks and cool down. On the other hand there are many clubs which provide no such chill out rooms and restrict the clients' access to water by closing off the taps in the toilets and so on. The reason for this behaviour is the desire to maximize profits from a vulnerable clientele. There are many unscrupulous club owners who will ruthlessly exploit the young user by charging re-entry fees to those who are forced to go outside to cool down, and then by selling the non alcoholic drinks needed to prevent dehydration at exorbitant prices. It is not uncommon to see tap water sold at several pounds per pint.

These dramatic and potentially fatal side effects of ecstasy are not the only problems that the drug can bring to its users. Many users complain of nausea, muscle pain and severe headaches. As the effects of the drug fade, users may experience a feeling of being drained of both energy and emotion.

Prolonged or heavy use of ecstasy can lead to profound changes in the user's personality. They may become depressed and irritable, suspicious of those around them, obsessed with the attitude of others towards them, and even, in extreme cases, show violence towards them.

There is some evidence that the effects of prolonged ecstasy use can lead to permanent changes within the workings of the brain. It is thought possible that the receptors within the brain that receive a chemical called serotonin, which we produce naturally when experiencing pleasure, can be changed in such a way that they become incapable of receiving this naturally produced substance. This change is thought to be of a permanent nature, and suggests that prolonged use of the drug can lead to a condition where the user is incapable of feeling naturally happy, and must rely on the drug to provide any happiness at all.

Recent research has confirmed that long term regular use can lead to permanent damage to kidneys, liver, heart and brain function.

Tolerance potential

A tolerance to ecstasy develops with repeated use. Users who take the drug on a regular basis soon find that it fails to provide the degree of effect that they are used to experiencing. This inevitably leads to them increasing the dose that they use. As the drug is normally available in tablet or capsule form it is only possible to increase the dose by increasing the number of such tablets or capsules that are taken. Thus a user who increases from one to two tablets is doubling their dose in a single step. Such a large increase can have unpredictable consequences.

Habituation potential

There is little evidence of any physical habituation to ecstasy, although this may occur with some people who have used the drug heavily over an extended period.

Many users develop a low level psychological dependence on the drug with prolonged use, some of whom begin to feel that it is not possible to have a really good time and that life begins to seem a little flat without it.

Withdrawal effects

Most ecstasy users will experience no physical problems as a result of ceasing their use of the drug. Many regular and heavy users will go through a period of anxiety and depression which will be eased if they are given support and care.

Overdose potential

Excessive doses of ecstasy can easily lead to collapse, coma, permanent brain damage and death.

Street names

- Tablet forms – **'E', disco burger, disco biscuit, love dove, rocking robin, rabbit, crystal splitter**
- Capsule forms – **city, dennis the menace, rhubarb and custard, united**

Slang associated with use

- **Getting cabbaged** – becoming completely intoxicated by use of the drug and energetic dancing
- **Chilling out** – allowing the body time to cool down and recover from overheating etc.
- **Chill room** – an area in a rave or club set aside to allow users to chill out

Ecstacy

Reasons for use

Problems

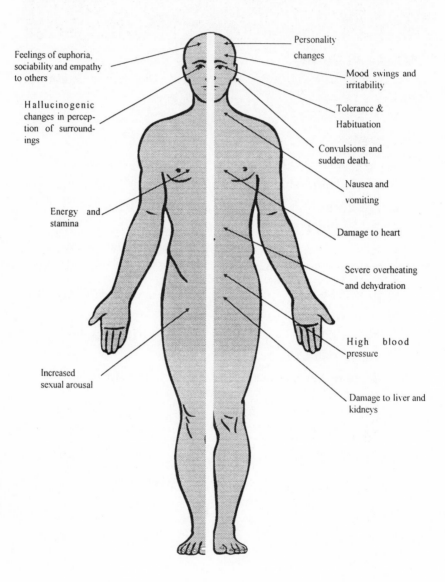

Feelings of euphoria, sociability and empathy to others

Hallucinogenic changes in perception of surroundings

Energy and stamina

Increased sexual arousal

Personality changes

Mood swings and irritability

Tolerance & Habituation

Convulsions and sudden death.

Nausea and vomiting

Damage to heart

Severe overheating and dehydration

High blood pressure

Damage to liver and kidneys

Hallucinogenic or Magic Mushrooms

Hallucinogenic or Magic Mushrooms: Quick Reference Guide

Source

Natural, found growing in woodland, heath and domestic gardens. Most varieties appear during September and October, the season extending into November if the weather remains mild and frost free.

Forms and appearance

There are several varieties of hallucinogenic mushroom, all very different in appearance. Identification of them can be very difficult and mistakes are common. Details of the main varieties are given in the **In depth guide**.

Marketing

Many users of hallucinogenic mushrooms pick their own when in season. Out of season they are available in a dried or very occasionally frozen form. The dried form are normally sold in bags containing between 50 and 60 of the smaller varieties. Their availability varies from one area to another and will be affected by the prevailing weather conditions during the previous growing season.

Cost

A bag of 50 or 60 dried hallucinogenic mushrooms, enough for one dose of the drug, will sell for around £5.00.

Legal position

The possession and eating of fresh hallucinogenic mushrooms of the genus psilocybe is not an offence. Any act that prepares the mushrooms for consumption, such as crushing, slicing, cooking or drying, renders the person liable to offences relating to psilocin and psilocybin, the active ingredients of most hallucinogenic mushrooms.

Both of these drugs are class 'A', schedule one, controlled substances within the Misuse of Drugs Act 1971.

Methods of use

Hallucinogenic mushrooms are normally eaten. If obtained fresh they may be eaten raw or after cooking. Dried varieties are usually infused in boiling water to make a drink.

Effects of use

Feelings of euphoria, high spirits and well being, bouts of laughter and giggling, visual and auditory hallucinations.

Adverse effects

Some users will suffer bouts of dizziness and nausea. There is the possibility of long-term mental problems. The major danger lies in consuming a poisonous variety of mushroom by mistake.

Tolerance potential

Tolerance develops rapidly with continued use.

Habituation potential

There is little evidence of any marked physical or psychological dependence developing.

Withdrawal effects

It is very rare for users of hallucinogenic mushrooms to experience any problems withdrawing from use of the drug.

Overdose potential

The potential for overdose is reduced due to the very large quantities of mushrooms that the user would need to consume.

Hallucinogenic or Magic Mushrooms: In Depth Guide

Source

Naturally occurring fungi of the genus psilocybe and amanita provide the varieties that are commonly called magic mushrooms. The two most commonly abused are psilocybe semilanceata, known as the 'liberty cap', and amanita muscaria, known as the 'fly agaric'.

The liberty cap is found in enormous numbers growing on open grasslands, such as pastures, domestic gardens, parks and road side verges. It prefers well watered soil with a high nutrient content. It produces the mushroom that we see above ground, during September and October. This fruiting season will extend into November if the weather remains mild and frost free.

The fly agaric is found growing in woodland, often around the roots of trees such as pine, spruce, birch, hazel and beech. It is capable of growing successfully on very poor and infertile soils. The main fruiting season is September although it can be found much earlier and later if the weather is wet and mild.

The use of various types of mushroom for hallucinogenic purposes has been known for many thousands of years. Extensive use of the mushroom has occurred in countries all around the globe, but there is little evidence of such historical use in the UK. In many other northern European countries complete cultures grew up around the fungi, which were often endowed with magical and religious properties. In northern Russia the fly agaric was found in large numbers growing around the roots of the birch trees that abounded in the forests. Their presence was thought to be a gift from the gods that were believed to inhabit these trees. The collection of the fungi was a right reserved for the priests, and their use often restricted to the wealthy classes. The human body transforms the active ingredient of the fungus into another substance which is excreted in the urine. This substance is itself hallucinogenic and many stories exist of the poor people of a village, who were not able to acquire the mushroom itself, waiting near to the houses of the rich and offering wooden bowls for them to urinate into, in order to drink it and enjoy the same experiences. It was common practice for reindeer herdsmen to save their own urine, after consuming fly agarics that they collected in their travels, and then feed it to their lead reindeer. So accustomed did these animals become to the sensations that the urine gave them, that it was only necessary for the herdsman to appear on the snow fields in the morning and urinate on the ground for the lead animals to rush towards them in order to eat the urine soaked snow and in doing so bring the whole herd together.

Forms and appearance

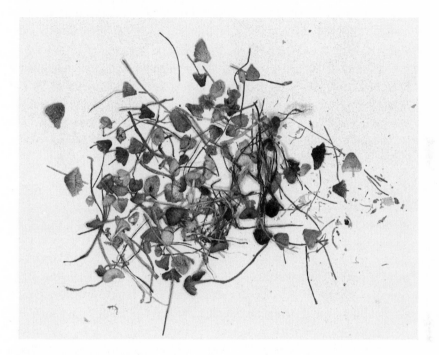

Dried 'magic' mushrooms

The liberty cap is the most commonly used magic mushroom in the UK. It is a very small fungus, its cap a pale creamy yellow or light brown in colour, and shaped like a female breast complete with a small nipple in the centre. The cap will measure between five and fifteen millimetres across. The stalk of the mushroom is very thin and fragile and measures between two and five centimetres in length. When seen out of the fruiting season it is almost always in a dried form. When dried the mushroom turns a dark brown to black colour and loses much of its shape. It shrivels up and in this form is almost indistinguishable from any other small dried mushroom.

On very rare occasions tablets made from dried and crushed liberty caps are seen. These have usually been imported from continental Europe and are about eight millimetres across and a light brown in colour.

The fly agaric is much less commonly used. It is a much larger fungus, the cap of which can grow to 30 centimetres in diameter and be supported on a thick stalk between 9 and 40 centimetres in height. The cap has a very distinctive appearance, for when young its surface is a bright red, almost scarlet colour, which fades to reddish yellow as the cap expands to maturity, and is covered in irregular white spots which protrude from its surface. The coloured part of the cap is sticky with an exuded substance that is poisonous to insects. Beneath the cap is a large frill of creamy white gills. It is the fly agaric that is often illustrated in cartoons and which many of us have in plaster form decorating our gardens. When prepared for use outside of the fruiting season it is usually cut up into pieces measuring approximately three centimetres across before drying. After being dried the red colour is lost and the fungi is seen as rather hard brown irregular lumps and is indistinguishable from many other varieties of large fungi.

Marketing

Many users of magic mushrooms pick their own during the fruiting season. Some will pick more than they need immediately, and dry the surplus for later use. Other collectors will harvest in very large quantities and then dry them for sale. The small liberty caps are commonly sold in plastic bags containing between 50 and 60 mushrooms. This quantity of liberty caps is enough for one dose for the average user.

The fly agaric is much more rarely available and there is no established market for it. Users who wish to experiment with this fungus will obtain an amount that they think is sufficient and then try out different doses until they achieve the result they want.

The supply of all magic mushrooms is irregular. Following a prolonged warm and damp autumn there may be a glut of them and ample supplies of the dried forms may be available for months afterwards. If the fruiting season has been affected by cold and dry weather they may not be available at all.

Cost

A bag of 50 to 60 dried liberty cap mushrooms will cost the user around £5.00. There is no established market for fly agaric and no set price.

Legal position

There are no legal controls applicable to use of the fly agaric mushroom. The possession of fresh mushrooms of the genus psilocybe is not illegal, but the active ingredients of such mushrooms, psilocin and psilocybin, are class 'A', schedule one, controlled substances under the Misuse of Drugs act 1971. If the mushrooms have been prepared for consumption in any way, by slicing, crushing, drying, cooking or infusing with water, then the following penalties apply.

Possession for personal use

The possession of any amount of the prepared mushrooms for personal use is punishable on indictment by a maximum sentence of seven years imprisonment plus an unlimited fine.

Possession with intent to supply

Possession of prepared mushrooms with intent to supply them by sale or gift to another person is punishable on indictment with a maximum sentence of life imprisonment plus an unlimited fine and the seizure of all drug related assets.

Supplying

As for possession with intent to supply.

Importation

As for possession with intent to supply.

It is worth noting that the picking of magic mushrooms on land without the land owner's permission could result in a charge under the Theft Act. All wild fungi growing in the UK are protected by conservation legislation and offences under this legislation may also be committed by the picker.

Methods of use

Magic mushrooms are commonly taken orally. The fresh or dried forms can be eaten raw or cooked in some way. We have known both fresh or dried mushrooms added to quiches, omelettes, stews, pancakes or even eaten on toast. They may also be infused in boiling water to make a sort of soupy tea which is then drunk. The tablet forms of the drug are also taken orally.

Occasionally the dried form of the mushroom is mixed with tobacco or cannabis and smoked in hand rolled cigarettes or in pipes. A small number of users have even tried liquidizing mushrooms in a domestic food processor, straining the resultant liquid and then injecting it.

Effects of use

The effects of magic mushrooms vary a great deal. The exact amount of active ingredient in each mushroom is impossible to determine and so the dosage is difficult to get right. The normal dose for a first time user is between 50 and 60 of the small liberty cap mushrooms and between 100 and 150 square centimetres of the much larger fly agaric.

The effects will begin some 20 minutes or so after consumption, and may last between six and eight hours. Younger users seem to feel the onset of effects more quickly than older users. The mood or *mind set* of the user prior to use will play a great part in determining what effects are achieved. Most users will experience feelings of euphoria and happiness. Many begin to giggle, often uncontrollably, and become excitable and animated, and may be unable to keep still. Users also experience a mild level of visual and auditory hallucination. The *trips* achieved with magic mushrooms are usually of a lower level than those achieved with LSD but of a similar nature. They may range from mild distortion of the shape and colour of objects and people, to the appearance of strange shapes, objects and even creatures. The user may also experience some tactile hallucinations during which they may feel that insects are crawling all over them or that they are dissolving or changing shape. These hallucinations will be of much shorter duration than those created by LSD, and the *flashbacks* common with LSD are very rare.

Adverse effects

Magic mushrooms sometimes cause bouts of nausea and dizziness, particularly in first time users. This can often lead to the user becoming very concerned that they have eaten a poisonous variety by mistake and will therefore alter their state of mind just as they are entering the hallucinatory phase. This will usually guarantee that they will have an unpleasant or even frightening experience.

As with all mind altering substances, there is always the danger of bringing to the surface any latent mental illness within the user. Many cases have occurred where regular users of magic mushrooms have become depressed or suffer delusions, and have required inpatient treatment in a psychiatric hospital.

The main danger with the use of magic mushrooms lies in using the wrong variety. This can not be stressed too strongly. It is difficult enough to be sure of what you are getting when the mushrooms are fresh, let alone when a user is buying them in dried form. It would require careful study by a fungi expert to correctly identify the little brown wisps that are all that is left of the liberty cap after drying. It is not uncommon for bags of so called magic mushrooms offered for sale to contain many other varieties than those that the user expects. These will have been added either by mistake on the part of the collector or cynically by the dealer to bulk out shortages of the correct fungus. There are many varieties of mushroom that are superficially similar to the hallucinogenic types, but which contain very powerful poisons. This is particularly true of the fly agaric, a fungus that has highly poisonous relatives within its genus. Some of the poisons contained within fungi will cause mild discomfort, sickness and diarrhoea while others can cause respiratory arrest, collapse, coma and death.

Tolerance potential

Tolerance develops very rapidly with continued use of magic mushrooms. The dosage required to achieve the desired effects rises quickly to such a point that it becomes very difficult to achieve anything at all. Users are aware of this and will rest for a week of so following a bout of mushroom use. This restores their tolerance level to normal and they can make effective use of the drug again. Users of mushrooms develop a cross tolerance to LSD, and switching to that drug will achieve nothing.

Habituation potential

Because of the rapid development of a high tolerance to mushrooms, to the point where no effects are achieved, it is rare for anyone to keep on taking the drug over any extended period of time. There seems to be little danger of the user developing any marked physical or psychological dependence upon the drug.

Withdrawal effects

Once a user ceases using this drug, they will experience very little in the way of withdrawal effects. Some may find their lives a little flat, and will have to devise other ways of getting enjoyment and pleasure, but with a little help and support should succeed in this.

Overdose potential

The potential for overdose of genuine magic mushrooms is low due to the very large quantities of the fungi that the user would need to obtain and consume. The overdose potential from other varieties of more dangerous fungi is very high. Some of the poisonous varieties require minute amounts to be consumed in order to cause very real problems.

Street names

- **Shrooms, mushies** – hallucinogenic mushrooms.
- **Fly agaric, liberty cap** – varieties of mushroom.

Slang associated with use

None known

Hallucinogenic Mushrooms

Reasons for use

Problems

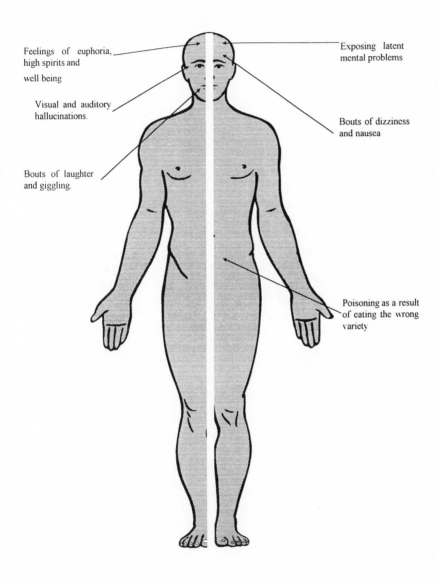

Feelings of euphoria,
high spirits and
well being

Visual and auditory
hallucinations.

Bouts of laughter
and giggling.

Exposing latent
mental problems

Bouts of dizziness
and nausea

Poisoning as a result
of eating the wrong
variety

Opiates

Heroin
Diamorphine

Heroin: Quick Reference Guide

Source

Produced by chemical processes from raw opium collected from the opium poppy.

Forms and appearance

In its pure pharmaceutical form, heroin is a pure white, fine grain powder. In its street forms it is coarser and varies in colour from a pinkish cream to dark brown.

Marketing

Heroin is sold by the fraction of a gram, commonly contained in a paper wrap or press seal plastic bag.

Cost

Prices vary according to availability and quality from £50.00 to £90.00 per gram.

Legal position

Heroin is a class 'A', schedule two, controlled substance under the Misuse of Drugs Act 1971.

Addiction to heroin is a notifiable condition under the Misuse of Drugs (notification and supply to addicts) Regulations 1973.

Methods of use

Heroin is most commonly smoked or injected. It can also be sniffed into the nose or taken orally.

Effects of use

Feelings of euphoria and inner peace, freedom from fear, worry, pain, hunger and cold.

Adverse effects

Depressed breathing, severe constipation, nausea and vomiting are common, also loss of body condition and a lowering of general health, with some effect on the immune system. Injecting can cause vein collapse and ulceration, and the risk of serious illness through the use of infected needles.

Tolerance potential

Tolerance to heroin rapidly develops with continued use.

Habituation potential

Continued heroin use can lead to severe physical and psychological dependence.

Overdose potential

Overdose of heroin can lead to coma and death.

Heroin: In Depth Guide

Source

Heroin is produced by chemical processing of raw opium. Opium is a natural product obtained from certain varieties of poppy, in particular the oriental opium poppy, Papaver Somniferum. This is a very much larger plant than our familiar hedgerow poppy, and produces very large flowers which may be red, white or purple in colour. The plant does not grow well in the UK, as it does not flourish in this climate, preferring higher temperatures and light levels. In any particularly warm summer, attempts are made to cultivate it but these produce such small amounts of opium that they play no part in the heroin trade.

The plant is cultivated in vast quantities in two distinct areas of the world. One area is known as the golden triangle, centred in South East Asia and includes such countries as China, Afghanistan, Thailand, Pakistan, northern India and Indonesia. The second main area is sometimes called the golden crescent, and is centred on the eastern Mediterranean and includes Iran, Lebanon, Turkey, Cyprus and Greece. The plant is also cultivated in south eastern Russia, central south America and in South Africa, but these are very much smaller players on the international heroin scene.

As the plant matures and the flower is pollinated, a large seed pod begins to swell beneath the fading flower. This pod is green in colour as it develops, and will swell to the size of a small orange. It is segmented internally with each segment containing many hundreds of minute seeds. The seeds are suspended in milky white, sticky, fluid. As the seed pod nears maturity the opium farmer will walk along the lines of his poppies and, often using a special knife with three sharp spurs on it, will incise a number of cuts in the pod running from top to bottom, with each cut penetrating one of the segments containing the seeds. The pod will then begin to bleed its milky sap through the cuts onto the surface of the pod. The heat of the sun will cause the sap to dry to a sticky dark brown material. This is pure raw opium. The plant is revisited at regular intervals and the opium is scraped from the pod into a pouch. The pod is then incised with a number of fresh cuts to different segments and begins to bleed again. This process is repeated until the pod is exhausted of its sap.

The special properties of opium have been recognized for a very long time. Archaeological evidence exists in South East Asia of the use of opium, both in medicine and as a drug for social use, going back at least six thousand years. Its powerful pain killing properties were well known, and opium was exported to all the countries of the ancient world.

When being used as a pain killing agent in ancient times, it was generally smoked or dissolved in water or alcohol for drinking. These same methods were also employed by others who were seeking the many other effects of the substance. Opium is a very powerful drug and induces feelings of peace, euphoria and dreaminess, it drives away emotional and physical pain, hunger, and makes the user feel very much at peace with the world. Slowly the practice of using opium for these effects began to spread out from Asia, and from Roman times onwards was an increasingly common phenomenon.

During the first half of the nineteenth century raw opium was examined and its active ingredients were identified and isolated. Opium contains two very powerful and useful drugs, morphine and codeine, both of which still have their uses in modern medicine.

By the end of the nineteenth century, further work with morphine had produced a more powerful version called diamorphine, or more commonly heroin.

Both morphine and codeine are misused in the UK, but little street trade takes place. Heroin has displaced both of these to become the leading opiate street drug.

Forms and appearance

Heroin produced for pharmaceutical use is normally a fine powder, pure white in colour. It is also seen in tablet form and in ampoules of clear injectable liquid. These pharmaceutical forms are occasionally seen on the streets when they have been obtained by theft from doctors or from chemist shops. This is very rare, such are the security precautions that are employed to protect the legally held drug. The normal heroin that we see sold as a street drug is in the form of a coarse powder, varying in colour from a creamy, almost pinky white, through various shades of brown to a dark coffee colour. The degree of reddish brown colour depends on the process used to produce the drug. Generally speaking, the lighter the shade of brown the better the quality of the heroin. Street samples of the drug are usually around 20 per cent pure. The remainder will be made up from impurities resulting from the processing, or deliberately added 'cutting' or diluting agents used to increase the bulk of the drug and therefore increase

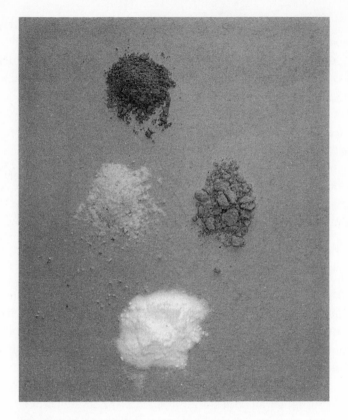

Heroin powder forms

profits. These cutting agents can be, if the user is very lucky, fairly innocuous substances such as caffeine, glucose or sugar. If the user is not so lucky, they may be curry powder, soup powder or gravy powder, and if they are really unlucky it could well be something such as powdered brick dust.

Occasionally heroin is seen on the streets in the form of small granules, most of which has been produced in South East Asia, and is intended specifically for smoking.

Marketing

Heroin is commonly dealt in fractions of a gram. This amount will vary according to the local market. It can be as little as a fifteenth of a gram, but is more usually either a quarter or an eighth of a gram. It is also common for heroin to be sold by value, such as in bags costing £5.00 and £10.00

each. The amount of drug will vary according to prevailing prices and quality.

Usually packaged in paper wraps like other powder drugs, heroin has been seen in small press seal plastic bags, wrapped in plastic film, and contained in cooking foil.

It is available in all major centres of population in the UK, and its use has now spread across all social groupings. In smaller centres it will be available without difficulty by arrangement with a local street dealer.

Cost

There is a great deal of variation in the price that heroin attracts on the street. It normally varies between £50.00 and £90.00 per gram. The variations are the result of the financial situation of the users, the activities of the local police, the amount of the drug that is available, and its quality.

Legal position

Heroin is a class 'A', schedule two, controlled substance under the Misuse of Drugs Act 1971.

Offences involving heroin attract the following penalties.

Possession for personal use

The possession of any amount of heroin for personal use is punishable on indictment by a maximum sentence of seven years imprisonment plus an unlimited fine.

Possession with intent to supply

Possession of heroin with intent to supply the drug by sale or gift to another person is punishable on indictment with a maximum sentence of life imprisonment plus an unlimited fine and the seizure of all drug related assets.

Supplying

As for possession with intent to supply.

Importation

As for possession with intent to supply.

The position of heroin within schedule two recognizes that there are some medical uses for the drug but these are strictly controlled.

Any doctor treating a person who they have reason to believe is suffering from an addiction to the use of heroin is obliged to inform the drugs branch of the Home Office within seven working days.

Methods of use

A great deal of heroin use in the UK is by injection. The drug will have been acquired by the user most likely as a powder or very occasionally as a tablet and will have to be prepared into an injectable liquid. If the heroin is in tablet form they will need to be crushed, usually between two spoons, to as fine a powder as possible. If in powder form, the user will need to ensure that it is as fine as possible and free from any obvious contaminants. The required amount of drug is then placed in the bowl of a spoon, a desert spoon is usual and known as a *cooking* spoon. The powder must now be dissolved, and this is best achieved if the liquid added to it is a little acidic. It is common for users to add water to the heroin powder together with a little lemon juice (citric acid) or vinegar (acetic acid) to give the water the right degree of acidity, in order to dissolve the heroin completely. Lemon juice remains a popular acid for use by injectors because of its easy availability and convenient packaging in small plastic bottles. However lemon juice can contain a fungus that comes from the skin of the fruit. This causes no problems when the juice is drunk or used on food, but can attack the optic nerve if injected, causing users to run risks with their sight. Because of this users are advised to use dissolved vitamin 'C' powder (ascorbic acid) to add to their heroin. Indeed many drug agencies issue vitamin 'C' powder to their injecting clients.

The heroin and the added liquid are then heated gently from underneath with a match, cigarette lighter or candle to speed up the dissolving, and may be stirred with a match. All of the equipment used in this process should be sterilized to reduce the risk of infection, but hygiene is not a matter that many users take very seriously.

Once the powder has been dissolved, a small twist of cotton wool or more commonly a cigarette filter is dropped into the liquid. The injector then impales the cotton wool or cigarette filter with the end of the needle, and draws up the liquid through it into the syringe. The filter will help to remove any undissolved particles, and prevent them being drawn up where they may block the needle or, if they pass through the needle, and are then injected, may go on to block small blood vessels within the user's body and cause very serious problems.

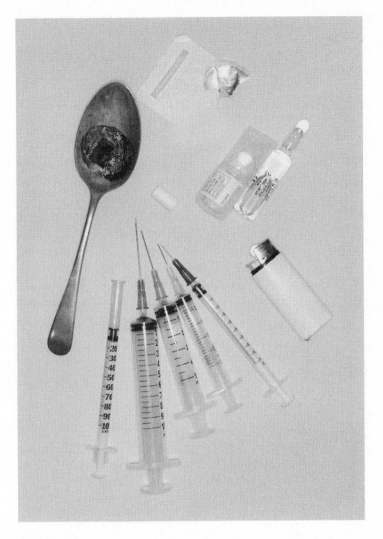

Injecting equipment

The syringe is now ready, and the user must choose a site to inject into. Most first time injectors will seek the assistance of an experienced friend to guide them. Many people are given their first few injections by these 'friends', until they feel confident to do it themselves. Some first time users will inject their heroin into muscle tissue under the skin rather than into veins. This practice is known as *skin popping* and is a simpler and safer process than intravenous injection. It has the disadvantage for the user that the effect from the heroin is felt more slowly and without the intense *hit* that most heroin users are seeking.

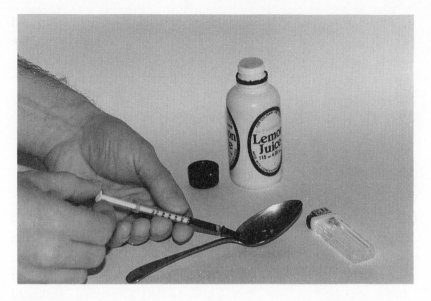

Heroin being drawn into a syringe

If the user is going to inject into a vein, then they have a wide choice of suitable locations all over the body. It is very important to make a careful choice and inject into a vein and not an artery. An artery carries blood at high pressure from the heart to more distant parts of the body and attempting to inject into one can cause very rapid and sometimes uncontrollable bleeding that could have serious if not fatal results.

The veins of the hands and arms are often chosen. Some female users will choose the veins of the upper leg or the ankle, as it is easier to conceal the marks left by injections at these sites than in the arms, which are left uncovered in women more frequently than in men. Some users have veins that lie close to the surface of the skin and are easy to see and to reach with a needle. Other users have to encourage their veins to stand out by slapping the skin, or by the use of a belt or a leather thong as a tourniquet. Most users start by injecting into the smaller veins that lie close to the surface of the skin, but it is not possible to continually inject into the same site. The area can become inflamed and very painful, may develop ulcerous sores and the vein may even collapse. Users will then have to seek out the deeper lying veins of the thighs, the neck or the stomach. When seeking these deeper and therefore less visible veins, it is much easier to make the mistake of striking an artery, or even a nerve, with the needle.

Having selected the vein, the user normally inserts the needle and then draws back a little blood into the syringe to check that a good connection has been established. This practice is called *flushing* or *back tracking*, and means that any infections present in the user's blood will contaminate the needle and syringe. The user will then depress the plunger of the needle to inject the heroin into the vein where it will be carried to the brain within a few seconds to create the *hit* that is being sought.

Because of problems caused by blunt and dirty needles, and the very real risks that users run if they share needles and syringes with others, most Health Authorities have set up needle distribution schemes where injecting users can obtain what are called *clean works*.

Another popular method of using heroin is by smoking. This can be done by adding the powder to tobacco or cannabis, and smoking it in a hand rolled cigarette or in a pipe, but this is not common. Most smokers of the drug use a method called *skagging* or *chasing the dragon*. The heroin is placed on a piece of cooking foil and heated from underneath with a match, cigarette lighter or candle until it turns into beads of liquid that then begin to spit and emit thin tendrils of smoke. This smoke is collected and inhaled with the use of a tube, sometimes made from a rolled piece of foil or paper, or from glass or metal. Sometimes the sleeve of a match box will be used. The origins of the expression *chasing the dragon* are unclear. Some suggest that it is the drug's connection with China and Chinese dragons, whilst others claim that the smoke looks like the tail of a dragon as it floats in the air, and it is further suggested that the deposit left on the foil looks like the shiny scales that the dragon is supposed to possess.

The *hit* achieved by smoking is very quick to occur and is second only to injecting in its speed of onset.

It is possible to use heroin orally by *dabbing* it on a wet finger into the mouth, but this is very rare. A little more common, although still rare, is to use the drug by sniffing, or *snorting* into the nose and using the membranes of the nose to absorb it into the bloodstream. This is a fairly slow way of achieving the *hit*, but does avoid the real problems that injecting can bring.

Effects of use

Most users of heroin, especially if the drug is injected, will experience a distinct 'hit' when the drug reaches their brain. They will feel overpowering euphoria and a deep inner peace that then leads to a dreamy and in some cases a trance-like state. In this state all feelings of stress, anxiety and fear will disappear, and the user will feel at total peace with the world. Heroin is a powerful analgesic and will remove all traces of pain, cold and hunger. It is this dream-like state, which can last for between two and six hours, that makes the use of heroin so attractive to its users.

Adverse effects

Heroin is a very powerful drug, whose exact strength when purchased on the streets is impossible to determine. This means that the dose that a user will administer can vary considerably. Current average street strengths of around 20 per cent are common, but they can vary from less than 10 per cent to over 60 per cent. This presents obvious problems to the user and increases the risk of overdosing. Many first time users experience feelings of nausea and may suffer bouts of vomiting. A high dose of heroin may depress the breathing rate and consciousness level of the user, and if vomiting takes place in this state, there is the very real risk of it being inhaled, leading to sudden death.

Heroin use can quickly become the central activity in a person's life and they may fail to take any care of themselves. They may not eat properly or keep themselves clean, and their general bodily condition can decline rapidly. There is some evidence to suggest that the efficiency of their natural immune system will be reduced, leaving the user more prone to developing infections and other illnesses.

Tolerance potential

Tolerance develops very quickly with continued use. The body soon learns to cope with heroin, and the same dose of the drug produces weaker and weaker effects as time passes. The general state of health of the user is likely at the same time to be in decline, and the user may even be feeling unwell. A point is soon reached where the drug is being used merely to mask or drive away these unpleasant feelings, and return the user to a more normal state. In order to achieve a measure of the original uplifting effects of the drug, the user has to increase the dose they are using or its frequency of use. The process of developing tolerance continues until even this increased amount of the drug will do nothing more than drive away the bad feelings.

Habituation potential

Most heroin users very rapidly develop a real physical and psychological dependence upon the drug. The body chemistry of the user changes until it becomes vital to keep on taking the drug just to feel normal. No heroin addict starts their use of the drug with the intention of becoming habituated to it. Most users feel that they can keep control of their use, and stay in control. This is very rarely true, and the 'power of the powder' soon defeats them until they become totally dependent upon it. The heroin user's physical habituation can be immensely powerful and the cravings for the drug so strong, that their whole life become a journey from obtaining the means to pay for the drug, buying supplies, using, and experiencing its effects, until the craving drives them to repeat the whole process again and again.

The average heroin habit in the UK is estimated to cost the user some £45.00 per day, that is £315.00 each week, or £16,380.00 each year. Dependent users will employ any method to raise this level of money. Most will turn to crime of one sort or another, either the theft of property by burglary, theft from motor cars, or street robbery. Some become drug dealers themselves, buying heroin in the largest quantities that they can afford, and then reselling it at sufficient profit to sustain their own habit. Many others, both male and female, turn to prostitution as a way of raising sufficient cash. Prostitution exposes the user to all sorts of health risk. In desperation for cash for their drug, some may even agree to unprotected sex with clients, and run the risk of becoming infected with HIV, which they can then spread to other users through the sharing of needles, syringes, cooking spoons and other injecting paraphernalia.

As well as a physical dependence, most users also develop a powerful psychological dependence upon the drug. They begin to rely on the feelings that the drug can give them to defend them from the pressures of the real world. They may not want to have to think for themselves or to make decisions, other than those around their drug use, and may simply hide within their own drug induced reality.

Withdrawal effects

Sudden withdrawal from repeated use of heroin without medical assistance often leads the user to experience all of the symptoms of a severe bout of flu, such as aching muscles, severe cramps and stiff joints. They will also sweat profusely and their body and skin temperature will fluctuate wildly. All this may be accompanied by a runny nose, sore eyes, diarrhoea, stomach cramps, a sore throat and a headache. Withdrawal from heroin in this way is called *going cold turkey*, because of the similarity in appearance between the cold and clammy skin of a dead turkey and the appearance of the skin of the user.

On top of these physical problems the user will feel a real psychological craving to continue use of the drug. They know that just one more use of the drug will remove all of their physical problems and reintroduce them to the dream-like state that they have found so comfortable.

So powerful are these urges to return to use of the drug, that relapses in those attempting to give up are very much the norm. No regular user of heroin should attempt to give up the drug without professional assistance. The user can be helped through their physical symptoms with medical drugs, and also offered support and counselling for the psychological cravings. It is worth saying that with all of the best help and support available, it is a very difficult process to withdraw totally from heroin once use has become regular or heavy. It is a very difficult road back to full health.

Overdose potential

Heroin use carries real risks of overdose. Street samples of the drug are of uncertain strength and it is easy to use too much. Some users get into such a state that they are not capable of thinking clearly and will make grave mistakes in the amount that they use. Overdose with the drug can quickly lead to severe respiratory depression and coma. Unless medical help is obtained quickly, the breathing rate will continue to fall until it ceases altogether and death is inevitable.

Street names

- Heroin – 'H', horse, skag, smack, stuff, shit, harry, brown, gravy

Slang associated with use

- **Cooking** – preparing the heroin for injection
- **Cooking spoon** – spoon used to prepare heroin for injection
- **Shooting up, fixing** – injecting
- **Back tracking, flushing** – drawing blood back into the syringe before and during injecting
- **Works, gun, spike, pistol, barrel** – needle and syringe
- **Track marks** – scars caused by injecting
- **Skagging, chasing the dragon, chasing** – smoking heroin
- **Dabbing** – using heroin orally via a wet finger into the mouth
- **Snorting** – using heroin by sniffing
- **Hit** – user's experience when the drug reaches their brain
- **Going cold turkey** – sudden withdrawal from repeated use of heroin

Heroin

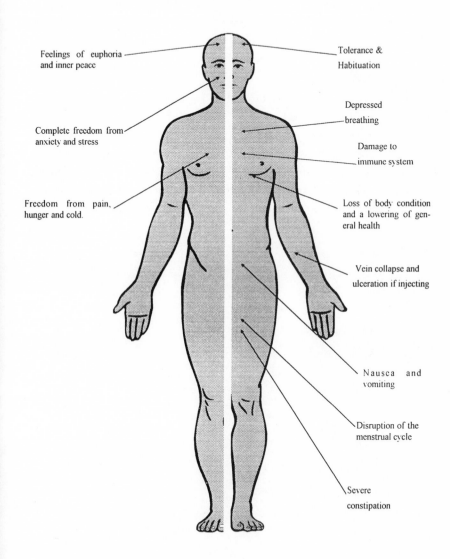

Reasons for use

Feelings of euphoria and inner peace

Complete freedom from anxiety and stress

Freedom from pain, hunger and cold.

Problems

Tolerance & Habituation

Depressed breathing

Damage to immune system

Loss of body condition and a lowering of general health

Vein collapse and ulceration if injecting

Nausea and vomiting

Disruption of the menstrual cycle

Severe constipation

Methadone
Methadone Hydrochloride

Methadone: Quick Reference Guide

Source
A totally synthetic product.

Forms and appearance
In its pure state methadone is a white powder. It is more commonly seen in the form of small white tablets, clear injectable ampoules, and as a brown, orange or green linctus and mixture.

Marketing
Methadone is prescribed occasionally as a pain killer and a treatment for chronic and painful coughs. It is frequently prescribed in the treatment of heroin addiction, where it is used to control withdrawal symptoms. It is also seen as a street drug and appears in all its forms except that of its pure state. There is no established packaging for methadone. Almost all of it will have originated from prescriptions and will be sold in its pharmaceutical packaging or other containers.

Cost
There is no established price for street methadone due to the irregularity of supplies.

Legal position
Methadone is a class 'A', schedule two, controlled substance within the Misuse of Drugs Act 1971.

Methods of use
Methadone can be used orally or by injection.

Effects of use
Feelings of relaxation, bodily warmth, freedom from pain and worry, suppression of the withdrawal effects of heroin addiction.

Adverse effects

Some users experience bouts of sweating, disruption of the menstrual cycle, constipation, nausea, itching and tiredness.

Tolerance potential

Tolerance to methadone will develop slowly with continued use. A previously acquired tolerance to heroin can be transferred to methadone.

Habituation potential

A powerful physical and psychological dependence develops with continued use.

Withdrawal effects

Symptoms of fever and influenza, diarrhoea, restlessness, anxiety and aggression.

Overdose potential

Overdose can cause respiratory depression, collapse, coma and death.

Methadone: In Depth Guide

Source

Methadone is a totally synthetic product that is similar in chemical composition to naturally occurring opiates such as morphine and heroin. It was first developed during World War II by German scientists searching for a powerful painkiller that would replace the natural opiates from whose source they were largely cut off.

Forms and appearance

Methadone mixture

Methadone hydrochloride in its pure form is a white powder and in this form is almost never seen as it has no medical use. The forms that are seen on the streets are those which are produced by various pharmaceutical companies for therapeutic use.

It is produced under two trade names:

Physeptone. Under this name the drug is produced in the form of small white tablets or as a colourless injectable liquid contained in glass ampoules.

Methadone. This name is used for the drug when produced in the form of a liquid mixture or linctus. These will vary in colour from brown or orange to a bright green, according to which colouring agents have been added.

Marketing

Methadone is sometimes prescribed to provide relief for patients suffering from extreme pain. It is also prescribed in an attempt to control very painful and chronic coughing. Both of these conditions are usually associated with a terminal illness, such as lung cancer. For pain relief the drug is commonly prescribed in its tablet or injectable form, while the linctus is usually prescribed for the alleviation of chronic coughing.

The drug is also available as a mixture which is some two and half times as strong as the linctus form. Here the picture can become very confusing, because many methadone users and even some professionals refer to the mixture also as linctus. Methadone mixture is commonly prescribed by doctors for people who are addicted, both physically and psychologically, to heroin or other opiates. The other forms of methadone are sometimes also prescribed for this purpose. The drug is prescribed to alleviate the symptoms that arise as a result of withdrawing from heroin use, often with the intention of slowly reducing the dose of methadone prescribed in order to wean the user away from opiate use altogether. Some users are prescribed their methadone by their own general practitioners, but the majority are issued with their prescriptions by specialist doctors who are attached to drug treatment services. Practices vary, but most drug services prescribe methadone in its mixture form to be taken orally.

In order to control the amount of methadone that the user takes, many services issue prescriptions only on a daily basis for enough of the drug for that day. Other services will issue prescriptions for a one week supply, and will in certain circumstances issue for longer periods. This sometimes applies to users from the travelling fraternity, who often live a wandering life style that prevents regular contact with any particular drug service. It is also possible for the user to obtain Home Office permission to take over 500 milligrams or more than 15 days supply of methadone out of the country with them whilst on business or holiday, and some services will provide prescriptions to cover this.

Some drug services dispense their own methadone, but more commonly it is obtained from local pharmacies. Where services operate a policy of keeping very tight control on the issue of methadone to prevent it reaching the streets, they usually only prescribe the drug in mixture form. They then request that the pharmacist only issue the drug in an open receptacle, so that the user has to drink it then and there in their presence. The pharmacist will then require them to speak, to ensure that they have swallowed the methadone and cannot spit it back into a bottle for sale on the streets.

Despite the best efforts of doctors, pharmacists and the drug services, a great deal of methadone in its various forms does reach the illegal street trade. The drug can be attractive to heroin users who are unable to afford the generally higher prices asked for heroin, or who are unable to obtain supplies of their preferred drug during times of shortage.

There is no established trade in illegally produced methadone. All of the methadone available on the streets will have originated from legally prescribed methadone or by theft from dispensaries who hold supplies of the drug.

When sold on the streets it will usually be in its original pharmaceutical packaging as this will reassure the buyer that they are getting the genuine article.

Cost

Methadone mixture bought on the streets may be priced as low as £1.00 for each ten milligrammes. Prices may vary according to availability.

Legal position

Methadone is a class 'A', schedule two, controlled substance within the Misuse of Drugs Act 1971.

The possession of methadone is only lawful if the person in possession of it has obtained it by means of a doctor's prescription. This methadone is lawful for their use only.

Offences involving methadone attract the following penalties

Possession for personal use

The illegal possession of any amount of methadone for personal use is punishable on indictment by a maximum sentence of seven years imprisonment plus an unlimited fine.

Possession with intent to supply

Possession of methadone with intent to supply the drug illegally by sale or gift to another person is punishable on indictment with a maximum sentence of life imprisonment plus an unlimited fine and the seizure of all drug related assets.

Supplying

As for possession with intent to supply.

Importation

As for possession with intent to supply.

Any doctor prescribing methadone as a treatment for opiate addiction is obliged to supply details of the patient to the drugs branch of the Home Office within seven working days.

Methods of use

The tablets, linctus and mixture forms of methadone are designed to be taken by mouth, the ampoules by injection. When misused the tablet form is also crushed and dissolved in water, usually with a mild acid added, and then injected (see *In depth guide* to heroin, page 142 for further information on injecting methods). The mixture and linctus are sometimes injected, although this is rare due to the volume of liquid that would have to be injected and the thick syrupy nature of the liquid, which can lead to severe pain.

Effects of use

The effects of methadone use can vary a great deal from one person to another, and the drug is not suitable for all. In most users the effects are similar to those of heroin. The drug does not produce the intense *hit* that heroin use achieves. The effects are slower to build up, but generally last much longer, perhaps as long as twenty-four hours or more. The user will experience relief from any physical pain, together with feelings of relaxation and freedom from worry, anxiety and stress. There will be a levelling off of the user's emotions, so that no extremes are felt. The majority of users experience a comfortable feeling of bodily warmth and well being. Because of its similarity to heroin in its effects, methadone is purchased on the streets as a substitute when heroin itself is not available or beyond the financial means of the user.

Most people who use methadone are doing so to assist them in 'coming off' heroin. The drug will largely prevent the worst of the physical effects of withdrawing from heroin, and provide some support in dealing with the psychological and emotional effects. Once stabilized on methadone, efforts are normally made to reduce the dosage in order to wean the user slowly and carefully away from opiate use altogether.

Adverse effects

The potentially adverse effects of methadone use can vary greatly from user to user. Some people experience nothing adverse at all, while a small number of others find the drug completely unacceptable to them. Most users of methadone will experience some excess sweating and itchiness of the skin. They may become flushed, with a noticeable reddening of the face and neck. Some users find that the drug can cause drowsiness in varying degrees. At its least this may result in the user simply feeling tired, and at its most pronounced it may cause the user to fall asleep 'at the drop of a hat'.

As with all opiates and their substitutes, methadone can cause nausea, vomiting, severe constipation and retention of urine. These last two conditions can lead to stomach and back pain.

Some female users report that the drug causes disruption and loss of regularity to their menstrual cycle, whilst both male and female users often experience a loss of sexual drive.

Tolerance potential

Tolerance to methadone will develop with continued use, although its development will generally be fairly slow, much slower than that to heroin. This is complicated, however, by the chemical similarity between heroin and methadone. In tolerance terms the body does not make a great distinction between them. If a user has developed a marked tolerance to heroin before starting to use methadone, then that tolerance will apply to methadone also. If the heroin user has only developed a tolerance to certain effects of heroin, but has not built a marked tolerance to some of the other effects, then that pattern of tolerance will transfer to the methadone.

Tolerance to methadone is lost very quickly if the user has a week or so free from all opiate drugs. This presents a great danger for the user should they lapse and return to methadone or heroin use. With their tolerance now lowered almost to zero, they may inadvertently take what appears to them to be a normal dose when in fact they are placing themselves in grave danger of overdosing.

Habituation potential

Regular use of methadone produces in almost all users a powerful physical and psychological dependence. Much debate goes on amongst opiate users as to whether the dependence produced by methadone is stronger or weaker than that produced by heroin. This varies from user to user and for different people either may be true.

Withdrawal effects

The withdrawal effects of ceasing to use methadone can be every bit as severe as those of heroin. Indeed in some users they can be more severe, and in most they will certainly take longer to pass. No regular methadone user should attempt to make a sudden and unsupervised withdrawal from its use. If they do, they will experience many of the symptoms of a severe fever or influenza. Their body temperature will be high but they will feel very cold. They may have a sore throat, runny nose, and suffer bouts of sneezing. Many will become tremulous, very restless, anxious, and display aggression to those around them. The constipation that use of the drug has caused them will turn to severe and debilitating diarrhoea. Their appetite may be lost and they may suffer long periods of insomnia. All of these will lower their general bodily condition and leave them feeling extremely unwell. This period of withdrawal can last for several weeks or even months, gradually getting less severe as time passes.

None of these symptoms is dangerous in the long term but they are very unpleasant to live through.

No one should try and make a sudden withdrawal from long term methadone use without professional help.

Overdose potential

Methadone is a powerful and potentially dangerous drug. Many cases of overdose have occurred in the children of users who have left the attractive orange or green liquid forms unattended at home. Overdoses amongst established users of the drug are rare due to the control exercised over their methadone use by the prescribing services. Problems occur when inexperienced users try the drug and take too much, or previous users return to the drug after a period of abstinence and fail to adjust their dose downwards to take account of their body's loss of tolerance. Overdose of methadone will result in the user's breathing becoming severely depressed and their heart rate lowered. Both may decline to the point where consciousness is lost and death may follow shortly afterwards.

Street names

- Methadone – **doll, dolly, red rock, tootsie roll**
- Ampoules of methadone – **phy-amps, phy**

Slang associated with use

- **Script, paper, reader** – prescription for methadone
- **Scripted, on a script** – in receipt of a prescription for methadone from a doctor

Methadone

Reasons for use   Problems

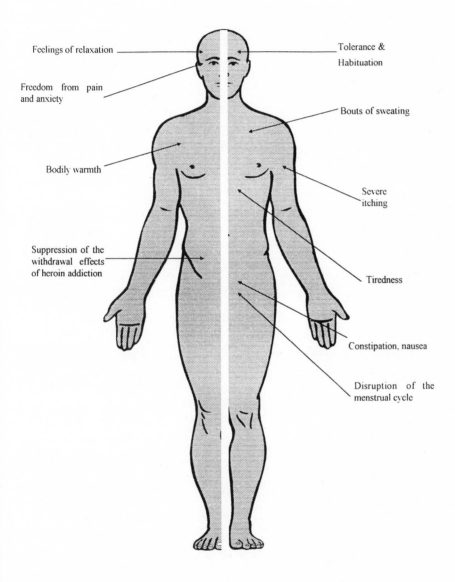

Feelings of relaxation ——————————— Tolerance &
                                                Habituation

Freedom from pain
and anxiety

                                                Bouts of sweating

Bodily warmth

                                                Severe
                                                itching

Suppression of the
withdrawal effects
of heroin addiction

                                                Tiredness

                                                Constipation, nausea

                                                Disruption of the
                                                menstrual cycle

CHAPTER 7

Volatile Substance Abuse
'Sniffing'

Solvents

Solvents: Quick Reference Guide

Source

A wide range of domestic and commercial products.

Forms and appearance

The range of products that can be abused is immense, and they are present in every home in the land. They fall into three main groups as follows:

Liquid petroleum gases (LPGs) contained in aerosols, camping gas cylinders and lighter gas refills.

Liquid solvents such as fire extinguisher fluid, document correction fluid and its thinner, certain types of paint and its remover, nail polish and its remover, anti-freeze and petrol.

Solvent based glues, impact adhesives that are used in the application of laminate surfaces, vinyl floor tiles, wood and plastic.

Marketing

Solvents in one form or another are for sale in the majority of shops and garages.

Cost

Priced according to product, but it is possible to purchase enough solvent to achieve a very high level of intoxication for about £1.00.

Legal position

The possession and use of solvents is not controlled. The sale or supply of solvents to young people under the age of 18 can be an offence in certain circumstances.

Methods of use

LPGs are usually sprayed directly into the mouth of the user and deeply inhaled. Liquid solvents and solvent glues are commonly plastic bag, a rag or handkerchief, from the collars and cuffs or from a drinks can or other such container.

Effects of use

Intense intoxication, excitability, auditory and visual hallucinations.

Adverse effects

Very real danger of sudden death caused by over stimulation of the heart, or asphyxiation caused by swelling of throat tissues or inhalation of vomit. Users often expose themselves to the danger of accidents whilst intoxicated or hallucinating. Loss of short-term memory and cognitive skills may also be experienced, together with problems with speech and balance. Personality changes may also occur.

Tolerance potential

Tolerance can develop with continued use

Habituation potential

There is little evidence of any physical dependency developing, but a powerful psychological dependence can develop with repeated use.

Overdose potential

Overdose can lead to collapse, coma and death.

Withdrawal effects

No physical problems, but user may experience bouts of anxiety and mood swings when use ceases.

Solvents: In Depth Guide

Source

The deliberate inhalation of solvents for intoxication purposes is known as Volatile Substance Abuse or VSA. It is a practice that has a long history that may go back several thousands of years. Stories abound of priests and priestesses who inhaled the fumes escaping from cracks in certain volcanic mountains around the Mediterranean, and then predicted the future from the visions that they saw. It may well be that the fumes they were inhaling were simply hydrocarbon gasses similar to many of today's solvent products.

The discovery of ether and chloroform in the last century led to the science of anaesthetics, but also provided two very powerful solvents that could be inhaled easily. Ether parties were popular with medical staff of all ranks who got together and used ether to get extremely intoxicated. Cases of similar behaviour amongst medical students still occur occasionally today.

The next phase in the story took place in the US in the years immediately after World War II. Many thousands of military vehicles were unwanted once hostilities came to an end, and were shipped back to America for disposal. While the military authorities were deciding what to do with these vehicles, they were stored in vast compounds with very little security. Local children took to exploring the vehicles and discovered that many of them were fitted with fire extinguishers containing a solvent fluid. These young people soon discovered that they could achieve a powerful level of intoxication by inhaling this fluid, and several deaths occurred before security was tightened and the extinguishers removed.

The practice was first noted in the UK in the late 1950s. It was reported in two places at the same time at opposite ends of the country. Both Glasgow and Portsmouth reported problems with young people inhaling the fumes of impact adhesives from milk bottles. The glue was placed in the bottle and the nose of the users placed into the opening while deeply inhaling. It is this practice that gave birth to the expression *glue sniffing*. From these beginnings the practice spread throughout the country, leaving no community untouched. At the same time the range of products being used and the methods of use changed and evolved, with each locality seeming to have its own favourite substance.

An enormous range of ordinary products are currently used for inhalation. These can be household products or those used everyday in offices and workshops. It has been estimated that there are around 30 solvent products in the average house, all of which can and often are used for purpose of intoxication.

Forms and appearance

A range of household solvents

The solvent products that are commonly used for intoxication in the UK can be divided into three main groups, which are listed in their order of popularity with young people, and the danger that they represent for their users.

(1) Liquid Petroleum Gases such as butane, propane, and less
    commonly pentane, are the most popular range of solvents that are
    used for intoxication. These gases are used as the propellant in
    most aerosols, since the manufacturers stopped using various
    chlorinated fluorocarbons as propellants, because of concern over
    possible damage to the earth's ozone layer. LPG is also found in

cylinders that provide the power source for camping stoves, portable lamps and blowtorches. It is also available in aerosol type canisters for refilling gas cigarette lighters, cooking stove lighters and some portable heated hair rollers. It is this last aerosol form of LPG that is the most popular with young people who use solvents for intoxication, and it is also the most dangerous.

(2) Powerful solvents such as benzene, amyl acetate, hexane, acetone and carbon tetrachloride are available in liquid form in a wide range of everyday products. This range would include nail polish and its remover, document correction fluid and its thinner, dry cleaning fluid, suede cleaner and adhesive plaster remover. This range is vast and the above list is merely given to illustrate some of the more popular types. Another liquid solvent that has caused a lot of problems in recent times is halon. This solvent is contained in the green bodied fire extinguishers that are to be found in most commercial premises, many vehicles and homes. It is a superb fire retarding fluid that can be used with safety in contact with electricity, but also a popular and dangerous substance for inhalation. Recent changes in legislation will place some controls on this type of fire extinguisher and may make it more difficult for young people to gain access to it.

Liquid solvents also includes petrol which can be found not only in the family motor car but in lawn mowers, boat engines and so on.

(3) The final group of products which are used for intoxication are the solvent based glues. These are the impact adhesives, which contain substances such as toluene and hexane, and are commonly used to fix laminate surfaces to desks, kitchen tops and tables. They are also used to glue tiles to floors and ceilings, as well as a wide range of other do-it-yourself tasks. This group also includes the modelling glues used in the construction of plastic model aeroplanes, boats and so on.

Marketing

All of the solvent products that have been listed above can be purchased from shops all over the UK. It is unusual for a shop not to sell at least one product that can be used in this way. Most young people are given their first experience of inhaling a solvent by being offered a share in a product being used by another young person. These may be friends from school, older brothers and sisters or their friends. It is a practice that is dominated by males. Females do engage in VSA, but they are outnumbered by males to a ratio of perhaps ten to one.

Any young person can become involved in VSA, but in general terms they can be divided into three basic groups as follows.

Experimenters and thrill seekers

Young people who will try anything, any new craze or fashion, are often talked into trying by their friends. They will experiment a few times and will almost always then cease using.

Those seeking to change their self-image

Young people who perceive something lacking in their personalities or the image they have of themselves. They will use solvents to change and enhance certain aspects of their personality. However solvents can never achieve the change that they seek, and they often move onto other, stronger and more dangerous, substances.

Escape seekers

This is the saddest group of all. They simply want to escape from a life that they find frightening, boring, stressful or empty, into a solvent-induced world where their problems don't exist. Unfortunately, however long they remain in that false reality, they will eventually have to return to normality, and their problems will still exist.

Cost

The prices of solvent based products vary tremendously, but most are well within the reach of young people's finances. One of the most popular products used for intoxication are the canisters of LPG that are used for refilling cigarette lighters and so on. A standard sized canister will cost around £1.00, and will be sufficient to achieve a very high level of intoxication for several hours.

Legal position

The possession and use of solvents for intoxication is not controlled under any legislation. The sale or supply of solvents is regulated by the Intoxicating Substance Supply Act 1985. This act makes it an offence for anyone to sell or supply a solvent based product to a person apparently under the age of eighteen, or a person who is suspected of acting on behalf of a person under the age of eighteen, if the supplier has reason to believe that the product is going to be used for the purposes of intoxication.

This piece of legislation, usually applied to retailers, is often misunderstood. It is not illegal to sell solvent-based products to those under eighteen. Many young people have a legitimate need for these often very useful products. The Act simply requires the retailer to exercise care as to the use that they think the buyer is going to put the product to. This Act also covers the situation where a person shares some solvent with another young person. No purchase needs to take place, simply supply, and a young person giving some solvents to a friend could be guilty of an offence under this Act.

Offences under this legislation carry a maximum penalty of six months imprisonment and a £2000.00 fine.

Methods of use

LPGs are normally used by being sprayed directly into the user's mouth. The favourite form of LPG is the canister refills of lighter fuel. These are designed with an upright spigot valve at the top that is inserted into a ball valve at the base of the gas reservoir being refilled. The spigot valve is depressed by pushing it into the ball valve, and the liquid gas is transferred into the reservoir. The VSA user grips the spigot valve between their teeth, and pushes the body of the canister inwards. This releases a stream of liquid gas directly onto the back of the throat. The user inhales air sharply at the same time, and thus draws the gas into the lungs. If other types of LPG cylinders are being used, the user will release the gas through whatever form of valve is fitted to it, and again draw the gas deeply into the lungs.

Domestic aerosols have been the subject of VSA for many years. Up until the late 1980s, the propellants used were mostly one of a number of CFCs, a range of powerful solvent gases that gave users the effects that they were seeking. With the advent of international concern over the depletion of the earth's ozone layer, the CFCs have been removed from aerosols and replaced with LPG. This has made the aerosol more ozone friendly but more deadly for the VSA user. If the product itself is also solvent based, then this will only increase the effects that are achieved. Providing that the product is not too repulsive or unpleasant, then the user will spray the aerosol directly into the mouth, sucking in air as they do so. Most VSA users will spray products such as deodorant, air freshener and furniture polish, directly into the mouth.

If the product is unacceptable to the user, then they will devise methods of taking in the LPG without taking in the product. Shaving foam aerosols

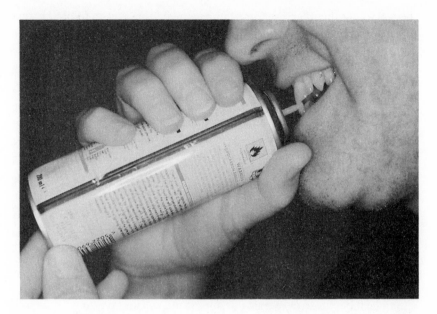

Lighter gas being sprayed

are often inhaled. The user will cover the mouth with a handkerchief or even a surgical mask, and then spray the foam onto the fabric at very close range. The foam is trapped by the fabric while the gas passes through into the user's mouth. Products such as aerosols paint canisters are used by being sprayed onto the surface of a bowl of warm water, while the user holds their face close to the water under a towel that is positioned to cover their head and the bowl. This is similar to the method used to inhale various medications. The paint is trapped on the surface of the water and the gas freed for the user to inhale. The warm water also evaporates any solvent used in the formulation of the paint and makes that available to the user. VSA users are very adept at finding ways in which they can inhale the gas propellant from almost any aerosol.

There are many liquid solvents that are commonly used for VSA. These can be sniffed directly from the container that they were supplied in, but this limits the amount of solvent vapour that is available to the user and is rare. Most users will pour a quantity of a solvent, such as document correction fluid or dry cleaning fluid, into a plastic bag prior to inhalation. Some users will use small plastic bags such as crisps packets, whilst others will favour the larger plastic carrier bags issued by most supermarkets. After the fluid has been poured in, the bag is opened out to get as much air into it as possible and then the top will be gathered together and held over the mouth and nose. The body of the bag is pumped with the hand to drive the vapour laden air into the user's mouth. The bag is then opened out again and the process repeated until the solvent has evaporated away. Some users will place their solvent into a very large bag and put it completely over their heads. This is known as space helmeting, and carries obvious dangers of asphyxiation should the user lose consciousness. If users are unable to obtain a plastic bag they will sometimes pour the solvent into a cardboard box or similar container and use that in the same way.

Liquid solvents can be poured onto a handkerchief or a piece of rag which is then held over the mouth and the vapours inhaled. These liquids are sometimes sprinkled onto collars or cuffs so that users can sniff directly from the fabric without it being evident exactly what they are doing. This is sometimes done in class at school, although the obvious smell of solvents usually gives them away. These types of liquid solvent can also be poured into an empty drinks can. The user holds the can in their hands until their body heat begins to evaporate the solvent. All the user has to do is to hold the ring pull opening to their mouth and deeply inhale the vapours being given off. This method also has the advantage of it not being obvious what the user is doing. To the casual observer they appear to be drinking.

Solvent based glues can be sniffed directly from their containers, but are commonly used from plastic bags in the same way as the liquid solvents. In confined spaces such as a garden shed or a dustbin bay, some users will spread the glue thickly onto any handy surface and then breathe the fume laden air.

Effects of use

The deep inhalation of solvent fumes will bring about a state of intense intoxication within a very short time. If the user is fairly new to the practice, they will become extremely intoxicated within a matter of seconds, certainly less than half a minute. This state of intoxication will be obvious to any sober observer. The user will become flushed of face, their speech will be slurred and they will have difficulty in standing or keeping their balance. They will become very excitable and may laugh uncontrollably, or may become morose and burst into tears. In their intoxication, the user may fall over repeatedly and may even become unconscious.

If the user carries on inhaling, they may experience the onset of auditory and visual hallucinations. Some users report that they hear voices. A 14-year-old boy known to us reported that he spoke with the birds in the trees and they spoke to him. Others report that the shapes and colours of objects around them change dramatically and they sometimes see creatures and objects that aren't really there. One 16-year-old male user reported that he was frequently chased along the road by a six foot gold tooth. If he stopped and looked round the tooth stopped as well and 'just looked at him'. He was so frightened that he often ran blindly for several miles, and often had no clear idea where he was when the effects wore off. The duration of the effects from VSA can be very short lived. If the user inhales only until they are intoxicated, and then stops, the effects normally wear off within 30 minutes or so. If they keep inhaling to the point at which hallucinations occur and then stop, then it may take two to three hours before they recover.

Adverse effects

It is very difficult to quote accurate figures for the number of young people who die as a result of the deliberate inhalation of solvent fumes. Figures published by St George's Hospital Medical School, London, indicate that approximately two young people die each week in the UK from a variety of causes associated with the practice. These figures represent a minimum, as there is no mechanism for recording deaths centrally, and the hospital has to rely on its own enquiries. Some authorities in the field of VSA suggest that the true figure may be nearly double that. Whatever the true figures are, it is clear that by becoming involved in this practice young people place their lives at real risk. Another disturbing fact emerges from St George's Hospital's enquiries. It seems that at least 25 per cent of these deaths are of users with no previous history of solvent use. It needs stating very clearly that there is no room to experiment with solvents. They may, and often do, kill first time. Most sudden solvent deaths are the result of one of two causes.

The inhalation of LPG can cause the body to over-produce the hormone adrenaline. This is sometimes known as our 'fight or flight' hormone, as it is produced naturally by the body when we are startled, frightened or excited. The reflex action that triggers its production is very ancient and may date from primitive times, when our survival depended much more on being able to fight or to run away from danger. The hormone closes down the small blood vessels close to the surface of the skin, in order to prevent excessive bleeding should we be injured. It also stimulates the heart to beat faster and to therefore pump oxygen carrying blood around the body at a faster speed, to provide our muscles with the fuel needed to exert ourselves strenuously. LPG can cause this production to become excessive, and the result of this excess production of adrenaline can over-stimulate the heart and cause major disturbance to its rhythm. The normal rhythm may become irregular, and there is a real danger that it may arrest. Such an arrest will lead very quickly to death unless help is immediately at hand. Even if full arrest does not occur, such heart problems can lead to the user vomiting with the danger that in their intoxicated state, they may inhale the vomit and choke to death.

The second major cause of death is associated with the method of use of LPG and aerosols. When any pressurized gas or liquid is decompressed, its temperature drops dramatically. LPG and aerosol users often spray the contents directly against the back of their throats. This causes the tissues of the throat, and more importantly the larynx, to swell. This swelling can be of such a degree that the passage of air through the throat becomes severely restricted, if not cut off all together. This can lead quickly to asphyxiation, with death following closely behind if expert help is not obtained very quickly.

The intoxication from solvent use can be very intense, and that together with the powerful hallucinations often lead solvent users into situations of grave danger. They become reckless about their own safety and many deaths and serious injuries have occurred where users have wandered out into the road, or onto railway lines, or fallen into deep water. Most solvents are highly flammable and many horrific fires have resulted from their careless use in what are often very confined spaces.

Prolonged and repeated use of solvents can lead to very profound changes in the user's personality. They may exhibit very wide mood swings, often being in a state of ecstatic happiness one minute, and seeming to change to an aggressive and sometimes violent character shortly afterwards. It is often as a result of such mood swings that parents begin to suspect their child's involvement with solvents.

Some heavy users may also begin to experience a loss of short-term memory, and have difficulty concentrating on any task that they are engaged in. This often begins to show itself at school as a marked reduction in the quality of their work, and should lead teachers to investigate the possibility of VSA.

Extensive use of solvents over a long period can lead to problems with the user's speech and balance. Although they may have not used for some time and be therefore 'sober', they may exhibit slurred speech and difficulty in finding the right words to use, and show signs of staggering and unsteadiness on their feet. In some users these problems do not clear up when use ceases and may become permanent.

It is worth noting that there are a number of notifiable industrial diseases that effect workers within the solvents industry who may be exposed to low levels of solvent fumes over an extended period.

Tolerance potential

Tolerance to solvents builds up fairly quickly with repeated use. The user finds that they need longer exposure to the substance to achieve the same effects. Some users also learn how to control their intake of fumes so as to maintain themselves at the level of intoxication that they desire.

Habituation potential

There is little evidence of the development of physical habituation from continued solvent use, but many long-term users do develop a powerful psychological habituation to the practice. They come to rely on it to cope with everyday life, or to add the degree of excitement that they require into lives that they consider dull or empty. Some chronic users also feel that they need solvents as a form of escapism, and are frightened to face the world without them.

Many chronic users of solvents go on to become heavy alcohol or drug users in later life.

Withdrawal effects

No physical problems occur when withdrawing from solvent use. The user may feel anxious and unsure, and will require the help and support of those around them.

Overdose potential

The risk of sudden death is not particularly related to the amount of solvents inhaled. Death can and does occur at very low levels.

Street names

- **Glue** – impact adhesives
- **Gas** – LPG
- **Can** – A canister of LPG
- **Cog** – A Can of Gas

Slang associated with use

- **Glue sniffing, sniffing, sucking** – inhaling solvents for intoxication
- **Cogger, gasboy** – LPG user
- **Bagging** – inhaling solvents from a bag
- **Space helmeting** – placing a large bag completely over the head

Solvents

Reasons for use

Problems

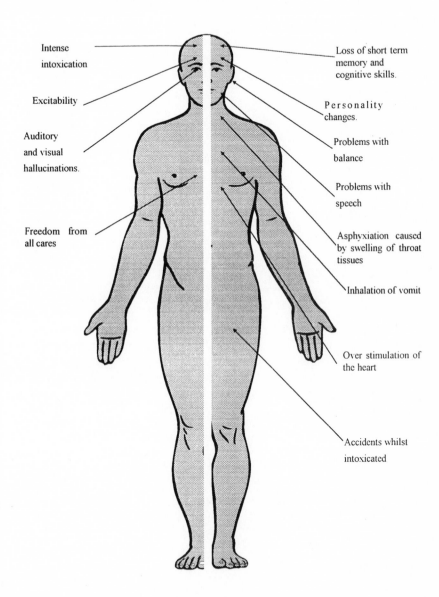

Intense intoxication

Excitability

Auditory and visual hallucinations.

Freedom from all cares

Loss of short term memory and cognitive skills.

Personality changes.

Problems with balance

Problems with speech

Asphyxiation caused by swelling of throat tissues

Inhalation of vomit

Over stimulation of the heart

Accidents whilst intoxicated

Nitrites
Amyl Nitrite – Butyl Nitrite – Isobutyl Nitrite (poppers)

Nitrites (Poppers): Quick Reference Guide

Source

A range of synthetic volatile chemicals.

Forms and appearance

Sold in small glass bottles under trade names of Rush, Liquid Gold, Locker Room, Ram etc.

Marketing

Sold openly in sex shops and other similar establishments, from street markets and through mail order.

Cost

Between £3.00 and £8.00 for a small bottle.

Legal position

There are no legal controls on the sale of these products, although the Intoxicating Substance Supply Act could be applied in certain circumstances.

Methods of use

Nitrites are used by inhaling their fumes.

Effects of use

Feelings of excitement and exhilaration may be experienced, along with sexual arousal and increased sensitivity of the sexual organs. It is also claimed that it enlarges the penis in some users and relaxes smooth walled muscles allowing easier anal intercourse.

Adverse effects

Inhaling nitrites can cause nausea and vomiting, together with head-aches and dizziness. It is poisonous if swallowed, and can cause damage to vision if it comes into contact with the eyes. Skin problems are also seen in some users.

Tolerance potential

Tolerance develops quickly with repeated use.

Habituation potential

No marked physical or psychological dependence develops with use.

Withdrawal effects

No marked effects.

Overdose potential

Little risk of serious overdose.

Nitrites (Poppers): In Depth Guide

Source

A range of synthetically produced nitrites, that are designed to be inhaled, has been freely available in the UK for many years. Until the advent, in recent years, of a range of specific drugs for heart disorders, nitrites were sold in chemist shops as a treatment for heart problems such as angina. A small quantity of the liquid was contained in small glass capsules called vitrellae which the sufferer carried with them at all times in a special case. When chest pains were felt, the sufferer placed the glass capsule inside a handkerchief and crushed it with the pressure of the fingers. The 'popping' of the capsule in this way gave rise to the common name now used universally for this type of substance. The fumes released were inhaled from the handkerchief and had the effect of dilating the blood vessels supplying blood to the heart muscle. This increased the blood flow and eased the pain. Little medical use is now made of these products.

Forms and appearance

Liquid gold 'poppers'

Poppers are sold in small glass bottles under various brand names. The bottles are usually between five and seven centimetres high, made of brown glass, and have very bright, often fluorescent, labels. The brand names used are intended to indicate the sort of uses that they might be put to. These include Ram, Stud, Locker Room, Liquid Gold, Liquid Incense, TNT and many others.

Marketing

Poppers can be seen on open sale in sex shops, some market stalls and in establishments that specialize in soft pornographic magazines. They are also sold in certain dance and night clubs. Certain magazines often carry advertisements for supplies of poppers that can be bought by mail order.

Cost

A small bottle of poppers will cost between £3.00 and £8.00. This will be enough for several doses for one person or for a number of people to use.

Legal position

The sale and supply of poppers is completely legal. The only restriction that could apply would be the provisions of the Intoxicating Substance Supply Act 1985. This act makes it an offence for anyone to sell or supply a solvent-based product to a person apparently under the age of eighteen, if the supplier has reason to believe that the product is going to be used for the purposes of intoxication. It can be argued that the range of nitrites, that are sold under the title of poppers, are solvents within the meaning of the act, and that the effects of nitrites can be called intoxication.

This piece of legislation is usually applied to retailers and is often misunderstood. It is not illegal to sell nitrite-based products to those under eighteen. The Act simply requires the retailer to be satisfied that it is not going to be used to induce intoxication. As this is the primary purpose of the product when sold in such places today, it is difficult to see what argument retailers could use in defence of a sale to those under eighteen. This Act also covers the situation where a person shares nitrite with a young person. No purchase needs to take place, simply supply, and a young person giving some nitrite to a friend could be guilty of an offence under the Act.

Methods of use

Instructions for the use of these products are usually given on the sides of the bottle. These instructions tell the user simply to remove the cap and leave the bottle in a room 'so that the aroma can develop'. The suggestion is that this aroma will bring about the sexual arousal that the brand name suggests. The instructions go on to tell the user never to inhale the product directly. This is a complete sham, as the majority of users of poppers have no interest in creating a background odour. They purchase it with the intention of doing nothing else but inhaling it directly.

Most users will either inhale directly from the bottle or from a handkerchief, tissue or piece of fabric. Very small quantities of the liquid are needed to achieve the effects, and it evaporates very quickly leaving a chemical solvent smell if used in a room.

Effects of use

The original use of poppers as a vaso-dilator for angina gives a clue as to the effects that today's users are seeking. The fumes dilate all of the blood vessels in the body, and lead to an increase in the flow of blood to the brain. The user will therefore feel a *head rush* as the brain receives the increased oxygen supply. This will be followed by short-lived feelings of excitement and some exhilaration. The heart beat will increase and there may be pleasant feelings of dizziness and disorientation. The blood supply to the sexual organs will also be increased which may lead to sexual arousal and erection in males. Some users claim that the increased blood flow causes an increase in penis size and enhances their ability to maintain the erection for longer periods.

Some users claim that poppers relax the smooth wall muscles of the anus and therefore facilitates anal intercourse.

Adverse effects

The dilation of the blood vessels within the user's body leads to a dramatic drop in blood pressure. The heart beat rises in an attempt to maintain adequate blood pressure, but severe dizziness and blackouts are common. There may also be nausea and vomiting. These factors together increase the risk of a user inhaling their own vomit and choking to death. There have been reports of strokes and heart attacks following extensive use of poppers in people who may have had some underlying defect to their cardio-vascular system. Some users report that their use of poppers leaves them with severe headaches and sore eyes.

Poppers can cause a variety of skin problems, including dermatitis, if it is allowed to come into contact with the skin. Users who place the chemical on hankerchiefs or rags to inhale it obviously run the risk of the chemical coming into contact with their hands and face.

Poppers can cause damage to the eyes if allowed to come into contact with them. There have been a number of cases where the liquid has been splashed into a user's eyes and a loss of sight in one or both eyes has resulted.

It is not unknown for inexperienced users to attempt to drink the liquid instead of inhaling its fumes. All of the different nitrites that are sold as poppers are poisonous, and present a very real danger to health and even life if swallowed, and medical help will need to be obtained very quickly if a tragedy is to be avoided.

Tolerance potential

Regular users of poppers soon develop a tolerance. The effects achieved become less and less, until its continued use becomes a waste of time. This tolerance soon fades once use is stopped, and within a week or so will have returned to normal levels. Most regular users manage their use so that tolerance does not develop to any great degree and they are always able to achieve the effects they desire.

Habituation potential

There appears to be no physical habituation to these chemical, and very few users ever develop any psychological dependence. For the vast majority of users it is simply one substance amongst many others that they will experiment with and then leave alone. Even for those who use it regularly, it becomes simply an important but not essential part of their lifestyle.

Withdrawal effects

There are no known withdrawal effects associated with cessation of the use of poppers.

Overdose potential

It is not generally thought possible to overdose on poppers. The very real problems that it can cause do not appear to be particularly dose related.

Street names

- The range of inhaled nitrites – **poppers, nitro, nitrite**

Slang associated with use

- **Popping** – inhaling nitrites

Nitrites

Reasons for use   Problems

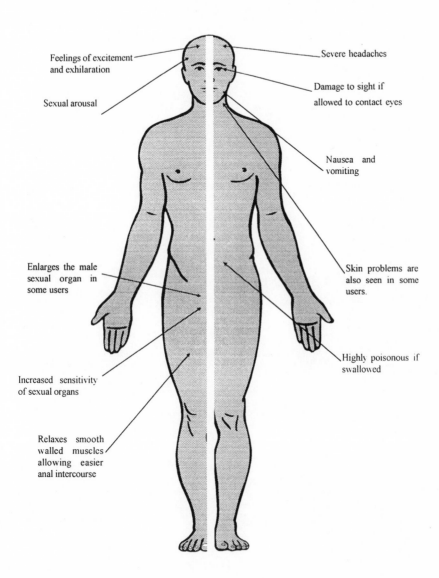

Feelings of excitement
and exhilaration

Sexual arousal

Enlarges the male
sexual organ in
some users

Increased sensitivity
of sexual organs

Relaxes smooth
walled muscles
allowing easier
anal intercourse

Severe headaches

Damage to sight if
allowed to contact eyes

Nausea and
vomiting

Skin problems are
also seen in some
users.

Highly poisonous if
swallowed

Tranquilizers

Tranquilizers: Quick Reference Guide

Source

A wide range of synthetically produced drugs manufactured by the pharmaceutical industry to treat patients with problems of anxiety, depression and insomnia.

Forms and appearance

Most tranquilizers are either based on benzodiazepine or, more rarely, barbiturate. They are seen in tablet or capsule form in a wide variety of shapes, sizes and colours.

Marketing

Tranquilizers remain the most commonly prescribed mind altering drug in the UK. The drugs reach the street market from people who have been prescribed them by a doctor then selling them on, and as a result of thefts from pharmacies and manufacturers premises.

Cost

Their is no firmly established price for tranquilizers, except in areas where use is common. In other areas, where supplies are irregular, the vendor will set the price to suit the prevailing market. Prices can vary from as little as three for a pound to £2.00 per tablet or capsule.

Legal position

Benzodiazepine based tranquilizers are classified as class 'C' controlled substances within the Misuse of Drugs Act 1971. Possession for personal use is not illegal, but supplying them to a person other than as a result of a doctor's prescription is.

Barbiturate based tranquilizers are classified as class 'B' controlled substances under the same act.

Methods of use

Tranquilizer tablets and capsules are taken orally or prepared for injection. There is evidence of a considerable rise in the use of these drugs by injection.

Effects of use

When used as prescribed, the user will experience some relief from their symptoms of anxiety, depression and insomnia. When used in higher doses the user will experience feelings of euphoria, dreaminess, elimination of worry, fear, hunger and cold.

Adverse effects

When used in high dose the user may experience violent mood swings, aggression, bizarre sexual behaviour, deep depression, lethargy, tiredness, physical weakness and disorientation.

Tolerance potential

Tolerance develops very quickly with continued use.

Habituation potential

A powerful physical and psychological dependence to tranquilizers can quickly develop with continued use.

Withdrawal effects

Withdrawing from regular tranquilizer use can lead to confusion, nausea, violent headaches, bizarre behaviour and depression. Sudden withdrawal from heavy use can lead to convulsions and even sudden death.

Overdose potential

Overdose of both types of tranquilizer can lead to convulsions, depression of the breathing reflex, coma and death. This is far more common with barbiturate based products. The potential for overdose for both types is increased if their use is combined with alcohol consumption.

Tranquilizers: In Depth Guide

Source

Tranquilizers are based on synthetically produced substances and are manufactured by the million in a variety of forms by the pharmaceutical industry. They are designed for use in the treatment of patients who suffer from a wide range of problems, mostly of a psychological nature. These problems would include anxiety, stress, panic attacks and general restlessness, depression and insomnia. They are also used in the treatment of certain mental illnesses and epilepsy.

Most commercially produced tranquilizers fall into two groups.

The oldest group, now little used, are the tranquilizers based on barbiturate. This substance was first isolated at the end of the nineteenth century and rapidly became popular in the treatment of a wide range of nervous disorders and to induce sleep. It became a prescription only drug early in this century and was prescribed in vast quantities by doctors who saw it as an effective and safe way of treating people for the disorders already outlined. During the 1950s and 1960s it became clear that its use was not without problems. Many thousands of users were prescribed barbiturates over a long period and became totally dependent upon them. Overdoses were common, both accidental and deliberate. Barbiturates can be very dangerous if their use is mixed with that of alcohol, and in the 1970s barbiturate overdose accounted for almost fifty per cent of all suicides recorded in the UK.

Chemists all over the world searched for a safer tranquilizer that could offer the benefits of barbiturate but without the serious problems that its use was causing. During the 1950s a group of Swiss chemists isolated the active ingredient of the plant Rauwolfia Serpentina, a bush that occurs in Asia and Africa and which has been used as a herbal medicine for hundreds of years. Shortly after that first breakthrough they managed to produce a synthetic form of the same substance, and an enormous industry was built up around the production of a whole range of benzodiazepine-based tranquilizers.

Benzodiazepine tranquilizers offer all of the advantages of the earlier barbiturate based products without some of the more dangerous side effects. As a result, their use has grown very rapidly, and they now represent the biggest group of all the mind altering substances prescribed by doctors.

They are not without their own problems, for tolerance to them builds up quickly and it is necessary to take larger doses as time goes on to achieve the beneficial effects. Continued use can lead to profound dependence and withdrawal can be very difficult. All of these problems can occur for users who are taking tranquilizers on doctor's advice and adhering to the recommended dosage. The problems that occur for the street user make these pale into insignificance, and are fully covered later in this chapter.

Forms and appearance

Tranquilizers are produced by the pharmaceutical industry in both tablet and capsule form in a bewildering array of different shapes, sizes and colours. It is impossible to list all of the brand and generic names that describe the range of tranquilizers currently available, but it is worth mentioning a few that have become popular with street users.

Diazepam, known commonly under its trade name of valium, is a benzodiazepine-based tranquilizer and is manufactured as small tablets that are either white, pale yellow or blue in colour. The white type are the lowest strength and the blue the highest. There are also veterinary forms of diazepam available that are seen on the streets occasionally in the form of small white tablets. Diazepam is sometimes seen in the form of a syrup or an injectable liquid.

Tuinal is a barbiturate product that is manufactured in the form of blue and red capsules or, more rarely, as an injectable liquid.

Temazepam, sometimes known under the trade name Normison, is a benzodiazepine-based hypnotic that is prescribed by doctors to overcome insomnia. It is has been produced in the past few years in the form of jelly-filled capsules in a variety of colours, the two commonest being a bright yellow and dark green. They come in a variety of sizes: the larger the capsule, the higher the strength. Because of the problems that have occurred with the misuse of the jelly-filled capsules, detailed in full later in this chapter, manufacture in this form is being phased out and replaced with tablet forms.

Marketing

Many millions of tranquilizers of all sorts are prescribed by doctors every year in the UK. The vast majority of these are used in a perfectly proper and responsible fashion by the recipients and do not find their way into the street trade. A small percentage of prescriptions are written for patients who are only too willing to sell on their tranquilizers to others. Some users will visit a number of different doctors in order to obtain multiple prescriptions to feed their habit, and for selling on. In order to increase the amount of tranquilizers that they have available for sale, some will attempt to increase the amount of the drug that has been prescribed by altering the prescriptions. This is becoming much more difficult to do now that the majority of general practitioners are using computer generated prescriptions. The money raised by patients selling their tranquilizers is often used to buy other street drugs. This source accounts for the majority of street tranquilizers, the rest arriving on the street scene from a variety of sources. Prescription pads are stolen from doctors surgeries and from their cars and bags, and then written out in imitation of that doctor's handwriting to obtain supplies for sale. Supplies of tranquilizers are also obtained by burglary of pharmacies and hospitals and even of manufacturers premises. Some employees of pharmaceutical companies have been known to steal tranquilizers for sale on the streets.

Tranquilizers will be available in most urban centres of population. Some areas have an established use of tranquilizers amongst the street drug using population. This has been particularly true of temazepam in the urban centres of Scotland in recent years. It is still true to say that tranquilizer use is patchy, and there are areas where its use is still rare, but this is rapidly changing. It is our view that it will not be much longer before the regular use and availability of tranquilizers will have spread all over the UK.

Cost

Prices can vary widely. In areas where there is established use it will have settled to a recognized level. In areas where the use is a relatively new practice and supplies are more irregular, it will be set by the supplier, reflecting the amount available and the financial means of the buyers. A typical price range for tranquilizers would be between fifty pence and £2.00 per tablet with higher prices applying to any supplies of the drug in injectable form. As with other street drugs there are discounts available for bulk purchases.

Legal position

The legal position of tranquilizers is somewhat confused.

Products based on barbiturates are class 'B', schedule three, controlled substances within the Misuse of Drugs Act 1971. As its inclusion in schedule three would indicate, possession is only permissible when they have been obtained as a result of a doctor's prescription, otherwise the following penalties apply.

Possession for personal use

The possession of any amount of barbiturate for personal use is punishable on indictment by a maximum sentence of five years imprisonment plus an unlimited fine.

Possession with intent to supply

Possession of barbiturate with intent to supply the drug by sale or gift to another person is punishable on indictment with a maximum sentence of fourteen years plus an unlimited fine and the seizure of all drug related assets.

Supplying

As for possession with intent to supply.

Importation

As for possession with intent to supply.

The position of benzodiazepine products is less clear. Some of them are only controlled by the Medicines Act 1968 which allows unauthorized possession but forbids the supply of them by unlicensed persons. Other forms are controlled substances under class 'C', schedule four, of the Misuse of Drugs Act 1971. As schedule four substances, it is not an offence to possess them, even without a prescription, providing that the tranquilizer is still in its original form. If it has been altered in any way, for example by crushing tablets to prepare them for injection, then class 'C' penalties apply.

Possession for personal use

Possessing a benzodiazepine that has been altered in any way so that it is not in its original medicinal form is punishable on indictment by a maximum penalty of two years imprisonment and an unlimited fine.

Possession with intent to supply

Possessing benzodiazepine in any form with intent to supply them by gift or sale to another person is punishable on indictment by a maximum penalty of five years imprisonment plus an unlimited fine and the seizure of all drug related assets.

Supplying

As with possession with intent to supply.

Importation

Importing benzodiazepine is not an offence provided that they are in their original medicinal form.

Methods of use

Both the tablet and capsule forms are taken by mouth, but an increasing amount are being prepared for injection. The tablets are simply crushed between two spoons into as fine a powder as the user can achieve. It is then dissolved in water. It is less common with tranquilizer use to add acidic substances, such as lemon juice, than it is when preparing drugs such as heroin. Most tranquilizer preparations will dissolve easily in plain water. The resultant mix is drawn up into a hypodermic needle and syringe through a filter of some sort to remove any undissolved particles. A portion of a cigarette filter is commonly used for this purpose or a twist of cotton wool. The drug is then injected into a suitable vein. Even if the user is an experienced injector, and takes a great deal of care, it is common for small undissolved particles of the drug to get through into the syringe and then to be injected. These particles can lodge within the veins or tissues around them, and cause ulceration, infection and even gangrene. We once had dealings with the suicide of a valium injector, whose veins of choice were in the back of his hands. He developed an infection at one injection site that developed into gangrene, resulting in it being necessary for him to have the hand amputated above the wrist. He carried on injecting into the stump until he took his own life a year or so later.

In recent years there has been a dramatic increase in the injecting of the sleeping pill temazepam. This drug is commonly seen in the form of a range of brightly coloured oval capsules that contain the drug in the form of a jelly. These are known on the streets as 'eggs', 'jellies' or 'jelly beans' because of their appearance. It was thought at first that this would make it much more difficult to use it for injection, but the ingenuity of determined users was up to the task, and the problem was soon solved. Users found that if the capsules were heated, for example in a microwave oven for a very short time, the jelly would liquidize and could be drawn out of the gelatine case of the capsule with a needle and syringe. The required number of capsules were emptied to provide the user with their chosen dose and the liquid injected into a vein. The liquid was injected whilst still warm and in concentrated form. If the liquid was diluted with water there was a tendency for the jelly to reform and make injection more difficult. The same applies if it is allowed to cool too much. It is not uncommon for the jelly to reform once inside the veins of the user and cause, in some cases, a total blockage. Because of the problems that have occurred in recent times with temazepam in jelly form being used for injection, it has been decided to phase out the capsules. Temazepam will then only be available in tablet form; this will not prevent the product being injected, but will simply remove one of the problems for injectors.

Effects of use

Tranquilizers can bring great relief when prescribed by doctors to those suffering from conditions which respond to these drugs. It is not this use that we are concerned with here. It is the misuse of these drugs that has grown to problem proportions in recent years.

Many street users of these drugs take them in high doses to achieve feelings of euphoria and dreaminess. The user will drift off into a drug-induced state of mind where all anxiety, stress and fear disappear, and they will exist in a sort of twilight world of intoxicated peace, congeniality and sociability which can last for several hours. They will often combine the use of these drugs with alcohol which exaggerates the effects of the tranquilizers. For those whose living circumstances are extremely poor, they will use the drugs to help them escape all feelings of hunger and cold.

Other users take them to alleviate the withdrawal problems associated with other drug use. Opiate users often inject tranquilizers to obtain relief from the withdrawal symptoms of dependence when supplies of their usual drug are not available, due to a lack of supplies or because of the cost. Some opiate users will 'self medicate' with high levels of tranquilizers when attempting to deliberately withdraw from opiate use without medical help.

Because of the calming effects of tranquilizers, many users of stimulants such as amphetamine, cocaine or ecstasy will take them towards the end of a prolonged 'spree' of stimulant use, to ease the unpleasant effects that result when stimulant use ceases, such as insomnia.

The use of tranquilizers by injection will increase the speed of onset of their effects and their intensity.

Adverse effects

It is very common for street users of tranquilizers to take very high doses and many times the normal medicinal dose is not unusual. This can be further exacerbated by heavy alcohol use and the additional use of other drugs. The combined effects of such use can be extremely unpredictable and often very unpleasant.

The users may experience very extreme changes of mood, with feelings that swing between euphoria and peace, to extreme agitation, irritability and aggression. This can be coupled with paranoid feelings that every one around them is against them, and often results in acts of violence. Others will display bizarre behaviour, often acting in a totally inappropriate way in relation to the circumstances they find themselves in. These displays of bizarre behaviour are often sexual in nature. Exposing oneself in an indecent manner on the dance floor, or making sexual advances to someone in the presence of their partner, are common examples of this form of behaviour.

Long-term users will often become extremely depressed and withdraw from the world completely. They may experience extreme tiredness and loss of strength and have no energy to do anything. This would include keeping themselves clean and taking adequate food, and as a result their general bodily condition will often decline alarmingly.

Injecting the drugs also carries with it all of the risks associated with injecting any drug. Ulceration and infection of the injection site is common, with the added potential for the infection to become gangrenous, often requiring the amputation of limbs to prevent its spread. The sharing of injection equipment with other users carries the risk of passing infections from one person to another, and such users run very real risks of contracting HIV, hepatitis and septicaemia.

Tolerance potential

All tranquilizers have the potential to create a tolerance rapidly. The body quickly learns to adapt to the drugs and their effects begin to decrease. It is then necessary for the user to increase the amount of the drug that they are using or the frequency of use. Another way of overcoming the tolerance is to increase the amount of alcohol that is used at the same time, so that effects are strengthened. Little is gained by changing to another form of tranquilizer, as tolerance developed to one form is almost always carried over to the new form.

Habituation potential

Both barbiturate and benzodiazepine tranquilizers have the potential to create very deep dependence within their users. This dependence will often be both physical and psychological and can be very powerful. The higher the dose taken and the longer the period of use, the more risk there is of dependence developing. It can reach a point where the user becomes totally dependent upon the drug to cope with their lives and feels afraid to attempt to cease their use.

Withdrawal effects

The withdrawal effects of heavy or long term use of tranquilizers can be very unpleasant to experience or to observe. It has been said on many occasions that such withdrawal is more difficult and more unpleasant than withdrawal from heroin.

Sudden withdrawal is particularly dangerous and can result, in the case of barbiturates, in convulsions, fits and even sudden death. Withdrawal from tranquilizers can be achieved if it is managed and carried out over a period, but if sudden withdrawal is attempted the user may experience very unpleasant bouts of psychosis, depression, agitation, insomnia together with panic attacks, hallucinations and confusion. They may also experience heavy and unpleasant levels or perspiration, nausea and vomiting which may be accompanied by a high degree of weight loss.

Withdrawal from heavy or long term misuse of tranquilizers should never be attempted without seeking professional help.

Overdose potential

Both forms of tranquilizers can be very dangerous if taken in overdose. This danger is exacerbated by the fact that the difference between the high doses needed to achieve the desired effects of misuse are very close to the overdose levels of these drugs. It is very easy to overdose accidentally, particularly if the user's judgement is impaired by other drugs or alcohol at the time. Similarly, if the user has been tranquilizer free for a period of time, their tolerance level will have reduced, and returning to their usual dose can lead directly to overdose. The effects of overdose would include a depression of the breathing reflex leading to very slow and shallow breathing, a very weak pulse, cold and clammy skin and dilated pupils. This can quickly lead if untreated to coma and death.

Street names

- Tranquilizers – **tranx, barbs, barbies, blockers, blockbusters, downers, tueys, chewies, traffic lights, goof balls**
- Temazepam in jelly capsules – **jellies, jelly beans, M & Ms, yellow eggs, green eggs, rugby balls**

Slang associated with use

- **Freaking, pill popping** – use of tranquilizers
- **Losing the plot** – being heavily under the influence

Tranquilisers

Reasons for use

Problems

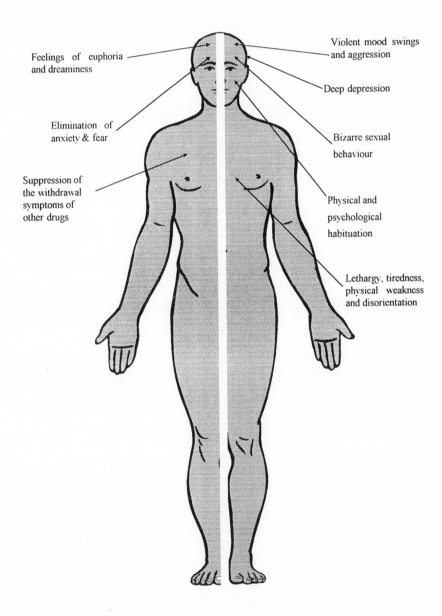

Feelings of euphoria and dreaminess

Elimination of anxiety & fear

Suppression of the withdrawal symptoms of other drugs

Violent mood swings and aggression

Deep depression

Bizarre sexual behaviour

Physical and psychological habituation

Lethargy, tiredness, physical weakness and disorientation

Anabolic Steroids

Anabolic Steroids: Quick Reference Guide

Source

A group of synthetic products formulated to imitate certain natural hormones produced within the human body.

Forms and appearance

Anabolic steroids are produced in capsule and tablet forms in a variety of colours, and in injectable liquid form.

Marketing

The solid and liquid forms are usually marketed in their original packaging. Many of them will have been manufactured outside the UK with little control being applied to quality and purity. A large proportion of the anabolic steroids used for non-medical purposes have been specifically produced for veterinary use.

There is little or no street trade in steroids. The street drug dealer is not the usual supplier of these substances, with most users buying them from someone within their circle of associates who share their interest in body building, body sculpturing or sport. By following up advertisements in certain body building magazines, it is sometimes possible to obtain steroids by mail order.

Cost

Due to the limited nature of the market for steroids, no established prices exist. Vendors of these drugs will set their price to suit the customers that they are in contact with.

There have been many instances where steroids have been supplied free of charge, by unscrupulous sports coaches, to young people engaged in competition.

Legal position

Anabolic steroids are not controlled by the Misuse of Drugs Act 1971. Their supply without prescription is controlled by the Medicine Act 1968.

Methods of use

Steroids can be taken orally in the form of tablets and capsules, but the commonest form of misuse is to inject the liquid forms intramuscularly.

Effects of use

Most users will experience an increase in muscle growth and body bulk, together with greater stamina and strength.

Adverse effects

There is a very large list of differing problems associated with excess use, and these include bone growth irregularities, high blood pressure and heart disease, liver and kidney dysfunction, liver and kidney cancers, hepatitis, shrinking of the testicles, uncontrollable erections, impotence, mood swings, aggression and irritability, damage to foetal development, development of breasts in males and irreversible enlargement of the female clitoris.

Tolerance potential

Tolerance develops with continued use.

Habituation potential

There is little evidence of a purely physical dependence developing with continued use, but many users experience a profound psychological dependence upon these drugs.

Withdrawal effects.

Some users will experience a catastrophic collapse of muscle strength and stamina together with extreme irritability and mood changes.

Overdose potential

Overdosing with steroids can lead to collapse, coma, convulsions and death.

Anabolic Steroids: In Depth Guide

Source

Anabolic steroids are produced by the pharmaceutical industry for use in the treatment of certain human health disorders and for veterinary purposes. They are designed to imitate certain naturally occurring hormones. Those that they imitate all have both anabolic and androgenic properties. The anabolic properties help in the formation of muscle tissue and body bulk which give the user extra strength and stamina. The androgenic properties control the development of the sexual organs in both sexes and the development of other masculine or feminine features.

The synthetically produced steroids that are misused are almost always those designed to imitate the anabolic properties of the natural hormones. Although this is the intention when the anabolic steroid products are manufactured, it is impossible to eliminate completely the androgenic properties, and all anabolic steroids will also have an effect on the sexual development of the user.

Forms and appearance

The steroids that are misused will have normally been produced commercially for medical and veterinary use and will be found in tablet and capsule form in a wide range of colours. Anabolic steroids are also manufactured in liquid form for injection. It is in this form that most misusers administer their steroids. The liquid forms will sometimes be in single dose vials or in multi-dose bottles, with a self-sealing rubber membrane at the top that allows the entry of a hypodermic needle.

Marketing

Anabolic steroids are not normally available through the normal channels of supply that apply to other street drugs. The trade in anabolic steroids is established within a fairly tight circle of like-minded people. Most misuse of steroids occurs by people engaged in body building or body sculpturing, either for competition or recreational purposes, or in athletic competition. Body builders are interested in developing their physique to a form that is seen by those involved in the sport as being ideal. Body sculptors are interested in achieving a body form that they see as being beautiful or attractive to others, or as expressing the image that they wish to create of themselves. It is the muscle building effect of anabolic steroid products that these people are seeking, and they will almost always be supplied with their drug of choice by someone connected with the gymnasium, sporting establishment or club that they are part of. There have been many instances of these drugs being supplied to often quite young people involved in sport by their coaches.

Most of these drugs will have been obtained legally from outside the UK. It is not illegal to import these drugs for your own use and there is little to stop the unscrupulous importer then selling on what they have obtained. A lot of the steroids now being used have been manufactured in the old Eastern Bloc countries, where standards of purity and quality control are often very poor. The instructions for dosage are often in a foreign language and methods of expressing the strength of any particular product may not be easy to interpret. A large proportion of these imported steroids were manufactured for use in veterinary medicine, and these products were never intended for human use. Dosage instructions therefore will not relate to human use.

By following up some advertisements in certain magazines that serve the body building and body sculpturing community, it is possible to obtain these drugs by mail order. The respectable magazines in this field would not carry such advertisements but others will often have advertisements that tell the reader to apply for a list of 'natural body building substances' that the company has available. On application they will be sent lists that include imported anabolic steroids.

Cost

Because of the nature of the steroid market, no regular price structure has become established. The vendor will set the price according to what they perceive the particular group of users that they are in contact with will bear. The price will also be affected by the relationship that exists between supplier and user. Many users will get together and share steroids that have been obtained by one of their group. Other users will have their drugs supplied at reduced cost or even without charge by coaches or other members of the same team. When ordered by mail order or obtained from legitimate sources, steroids cost between £3.00 and £5.00 per dose.

Legal position

Anabolic steroids are not controlled substances under the Misuse of Drugs
Act 1971. The government has recently considered including them in this
act, but has decided that for the time being they will remain outside of its
control. Most anabolic steroid products are available only on a doctor's or
veterinary surgeon's prescription and are thus controlled by the Medicine
Act 1968. To import, purchase or possess them for personal use is not an
offence. It is an offence, however, under the Medicine Act for an unlicensed
person to supply them to another person either by sale or as a gift. This
offence carries a maximum penalty of six months imprisonment and a
£2000 fine.

Most professional or amateur sports and body building coaches have
to be licensed by the governing body of their particular sport. All of these
organizations have very firm anti-drug policies, and any coach supplying
or allowing the use of steroids by people under their supervision will risk
instant revocation of their licence.

Methods of use

The tablet and capsule forms of the drug are usually taken orally, but
sometimes are prepared for injection. The use of steroids in this form is
very much overshadowed by the use of the liquid injectable forms. The
drug is much more effective when injected into the muscle tissue of the
user, and this method is the one most favoured by far by regular users.
Many users will obtain their steroids in large multi-dose packages. The
liquid steroid is marketed in bottles which contain a large number of doses.
The bottle will have a rubber membrane at the top which allows the
repeated insertion of a hypodermic needle to draw up each dose.

The use of such multi-dose packs reduces the cost of the drug but
introduces a potentially deadly risk. Many of these bottles are shared by
groups of users who will each take their dose from it. It is not unknown
for such groups to share the same injecting equipment. There is a common
belief amongst such groups that they are not at risk from diseases such as
AIDS, hepatitis or septicaemia, because they are all fit and live healthy life
styles. There is the often expressed belief that body builders and sports
people are always 'straight', and therefore not likely to have been exposed
to these problems, particularly AIDS, through unsafe sexual practices.
These beliefs can expose user groups to the very real risks of contracting
and then spreading very dangerous and potentially fatal diseases by sharing
infected injecting equipment.

Effects of use

The use of anabolic steroids is usually combined with a strict regime of diet and strenuous exercise in order to build the type of muscle tissue that the user is seeking. The drug will encourage the body to convert the high protein diet into muscle which is further toned and strengthened by the exercise.

Many steroid users achieve a very marked increase in body bulk and will develop very powerful and clearly defined muscles all over their bodies. This will lead to a considerable increase in strength and stamina which, with the right regime of exercise, can result in a useful increase in sporting performance.

Adverse effects

There is little clear knowledge about the effects of long-term and regular use of anabolic steroids. Many of the products used were never intended for use with humans, and little research has been carried out concerning such use. From the knowledge that we do posses at this time, it is clear that misusers of steroids run very grave risks with their bodies' natural development and long term health. The following health problems have been associated with steroid misuse.

Because of the androgenic properties of steroids, many adolescents who use them will experience changes in their sexual drive. Young males may see enlargement of their penises and suffer problems with frequent and uncontrollable erections. These erections can last a very long time and become extremely painful. Adult male users will often experience the shrinking of their penises and testicles, with consequent difficulty in achieving an erection at all. They may also develop breasts of a distinctly female nature with nipples that become very pronounced and often painfully inflamed.

Female adolescents will often suffer disturbance to their menstrual cycle with pre-pubescent girls often failing to develop a proper menstrual cycle at all. In others the female clitoris may become painfully enlarged and inflamed. Some female users will experience an excessive growth of dark facial and body hair, while others will develop patterns of irreversible baldness normally only seen in men. Pregnant users also run the risk that the drug will interfere with the proper development of the foetus within their womb, with the result that miscarriages may occur or the child will be born dead or with physical or mental abnormalities.

Other users, both adolescent and adult, may experience severe personality changes. These may take the form of an increase in irritability, aggression and the potential for violent behaviour, known as the *roid rage*. This may be coupled with the increase in sexual drive and lead some users into inappropriate sexual behaviour, and even into committing very violent sexual crimes.

When use of steroids has been heavy or prolonged, the user may develop clear signs of mental illness. Bizarre behaviour, extreme paranoia and delusions may become apparent, and lead on to the user requiring inpatient treatment in a psychiatric hospital.

Dysfunction of the liver and kidneys can occur, and in some cases complete failure of these organs can result, leading to serious illness and even death. Cancers of these organs have been reported in some long-term users.

There may be visible signs of use in some heavy steroid users. Their skin and the pupils of their eyes will take on a yellow colour, with the skin showing frequent outbreaks of acne or rashes of red spots. Their breath will also take on a very powerful and unpleasant odour.

The development of groups of abnormally large and powerful muscles in certain parts of the body may put an unnatural pressure on other muscle groups, and lead to strains and other injuries that take an unusually long time to recover.

When used by young people who have not as yet achieved full growth, the drug may cause a premature closure of the bone ends in the legs, which will prevent them growing to full length. This condition will lead to a loss of height potential and is irreversible.

Tolerance potential

As with most drugs, the body learns to adapt itself to steroids, and the user will find that they achieve less and less from them as time passes. This will mean that they will have to increase the individual dose taken or the frequency of use. At the same time the user's body bulk will be increasing, and so more of the drug is needed for that reason also. This will lead into a pattern of constantly increasing use which will expose users more and more to the adverse effects that the drugs can cause.

Habituation potential

There is little evidence of the development of any physical dependence to steroids. Many users become psychologically dependent on the drug due to their need to maintain the body shape and performance that they see as being so important. They have used the drug to achieve a body that gives them the status and self-image that they desire, and are consequently afraid to stop using it in case it should lead to a loss of muscular definition, strength and performance, with a loss of that status and self-image.

This dependence can be very powerful and the user may become locked into a pattern of use that they feel unable to break out of, even when they become aware of the adverse effects of steroids.

Withdrawal effects

Sudden and unsupervised withdrawal from heavy or long term use of anabolic steroids can be very dangerous. The user may suffer complete muscular collapse leading to an almost total loss of strength and stamina. This has resulted in hospitalization in many cases, and in some, confinement to a wheelchair for long periods before their bodies can be rehabilitated.

Other users will suffer considerable psychological problems during withdrawal and they will experience violent mood swings together with periods of severe depression and anxiety.

No regular or heavy user of steroids should attempt to withdraw from their use without seeking professional help.

Overdose potential

Heavy doses of steroids can lead to dangerous increases in body temperature and blood pressure. This will increase the possibility of heart failure and stroke occurring. Overdose can also lead to convulsions, collapse, coma and the possibility of sudden death.

Street names

None known

Slang associated with use

- **roid rage** – aggression and violence associated with long term steroid use
- **stacking** – the combination of using fast and slow acting steroids to achieve particular effects over a specific time scale

Anabolic Steroids

Reasons for use   Problems

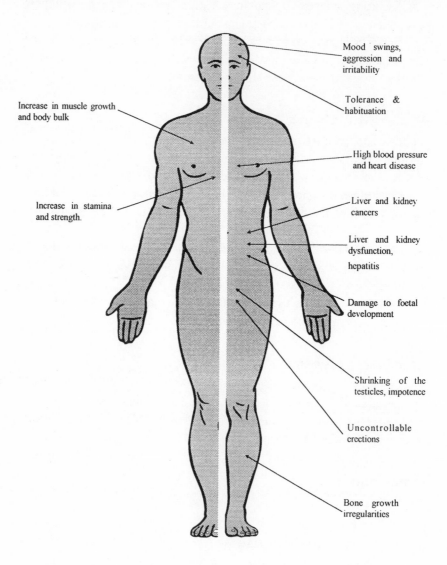

Increase in muscle growth
and body bulk

Increase in stamina
and strength.

Mood swings,
aggression and
irritability

Tolerance &
habituation

High blood pressure
and heart disease

Liver and kidney
cancers

Liver and kidney
dysfunction,
hepatitis

Damage to foetal
development

Shrinking of the
testicles, impotence

Uncontrollable
erections

Bone growth
irregularities

Over the Counter Medicines

CHAPTER 10

Over the Counter Medicines: Quick Reference Guide

Source

A wide range of proprietary medicines available with or without prescription from pharmacists and general stores.

Marketing

Medicinal preparations that are sold under a number of brand or generic names. They fall into three basic groups: opiates, antihistamines and sympathomimetic products.

Cost

Prices vary from product to product but in general terms the misuse of these preparations can cost less than the misuse of street drugs.

Legal position

Some of these preparations contain substances that are controlled by the Misuse of Drugs Act 1971 or by the Medicines Act 1968, whilst some are free from control.

Methods of use

The vast majority of misused over the counter medicines are taken orally, although some are occasionally injected.

Effects of use

The effects achieved will vary from product to product and according to the dose taken.

Adverse effects

These too will differ according to the product being used and the dose taken.

Tolerance potential

Tolerance will develop with continued use of many of these drugs.

Habituation potential

All of these products have the potential to create a physical or psychological dependence with repeated or long term use.

Withdrawal effects

Withdrawal from many of these products can produce unpleasant effects.

Overdose potential

Serious overdose of many of these products can be very dangerous and may even be fatal.

Over the Counter Medicines: In Depth Guide

Source

The term 'over the counter medicines' in drug misuse terms is used to cover a wide range of medicinal products that are available to treat a variety of medical conditions. Some of these preparations are available only by means of a doctor's prescription. Others are available without prescription, but can only be sold by registered pharmacists. Many others can be purchased without restrictions from general stores and similar outlets.

Marketing

The list of preparations that can be misused is very long and would include a large number of products sold under various brand and generic names. It would not be practical to try and produce a comprehensive list of branded products that can be misused in this way, as new products are constantly being added to those already available. Most of the products that are misused fall into three basic groups, and it would perhaps be useful to look in more detail at these groups.

Opiate products

There are a number of products that contain opiate substances. Most of these are naturally occurring opiates, such as morphine and codeine, that are obtained from the opium poppy, whilst others contain opiate-like products that have been produced synthetically.

These products are intended for use as painkillers, cough treatments or as medicines for stomach disorders and diarrhoea. All opiates have good analgesic properties and are often added to other substances in preparations intended to provide pain relief. Some of these will contain morphine and will generally be available only on prescription, whilst others will contain codeine and be available without prescription from pharmacies.

Opiate substances have a calming effect on the nerves that produce the coughing reflex, and many brand-named cough medicines contain either codeine or low levels of morphine. Gee's Linctus, one of the most popular generic cough medicines, is commonly misused. It contains a compound of codeine and is very efficient at alleviating many forms of cough. It is available without prescription but only from pharmacies, and then only if sold directly under the supervision of the pharmacist.

Many stomach and diarrhoea treatments contain morphine or codeine. The analgesic effect of these substances will alleviate the pain of stomach disorders whilst also slowing down the action of the bowel, and therefore easing the debilitating effects of constant diarrhoea.

Although now considered a little old fashioned in these days of branded medicines, Kaolin and Morphine, a generic stomach medicine, is still available from pharmacies without prescription. It can only be sold under the supervision of the pharmacist but is relatively inexpensive and contains a substantial level of tincture of morphine, a substance that is sometimes called 'opiate squill'. If allowed to settle, the purified kaolin falls to the bottom of the bottle, leaving above it a clear brown liquid that is high in morphine. It is this liquid that the misuser is seeking.

Antihistamine products

There are an enormous range of medicinal products that contain antihistamines of one sort or another. They are commonly used to alleviate the symptoms of hay fever and other allergies. They are also used in some cough preparations, in many travel sickness remedies and to aid sleep.

Most of these preparations are available without prescription but must be purchased from pharmacies.

Sympathomimetic products

The term sympathomimetic is used to describe a range of substances whose actions mimic a number of naturally produced substances within our bodies. They are included in a range of branded products used to alleviate the symptoms of colds and flu. They are used particularly in the so called 'cold cure' products that dry up runny noses and clear congested chests. Similar substances are also found in many laxative products. Some young people use laxatives constantly and in large doses in order to assist them in losing weight. This use is often associated with sufferers from anorexia nervosa. Many of these products contain substances that are chemically similar to amphetamine and have similar effects. Most are available without prescription but must be purchased from pharmacies.

Cost

The cost of these products vary greatly from one type to another. A 250ml bottle of Gee's Linctus or a similar sized bottle or Kaolin and Morphine will cost between £1.50 and £2.00, whilst some of the cold remedies will cost as much as £5.00 for ten tablets.

Legal position

Preparations that use opiate products are controlled by the Misuse of Drugs Act 1971. As opiates, they are Class 'A' substances that are in schedule five. Their place in this schedule allows them to be sold over the counter without prescription, but only by registered pharmacists. Having purchased them lawfully, it is an offence to supply them to another person other than for a medical purpose. If they are supplied to another person for misuse, then the full penalties of any class 'A' drug can be applied.

The antihistamine and sympathomimetic preparations are controlled by the Medicines Act 1968, which regulates their availability through pharmacies and other retail outlets. Supplying these products for misuse could make the supplier liable to a maximum fine of £2000.

Methods of use

All of these preparations have been designed to be taken orally and it is by this method that most misuse occurs. Some users who are seeking extreme effects or are experimenting will crush the tablet forms and prepare them for injecting or inject the liquid forms.

Effects of use

The effects that the preparations were intended to produce are very rarely those that the misuser is seeking. The sought after effects can usually only be produced by taking very much higher doses of the products than are recommended for medicinal purposes.

Opiate products

When taken in high doses, these products will produce the effects of heroin but in a much milder form. The user will not experience the *hit* or *rush* that heroin will produce, but will feel relaxed, calm and free from worries, and physical and emotional pain. Many users of heroin will turn to opiate medicinal products such as Gee's Linctus or Kaolin and Morphine to control the withdrawal effects of heroin when they are unable to obtain or afford their usual drug of choice. Some users, however, will never use heroin but will exclusively use opiate products as a matter of choice.

Antihistamine products

Most of these products will cause drowsiness if taken to excess. This effect is increased if alcohol is used at the same time. This drowsy state can be very relaxing and allows the user to feel free from the responsibility of facing their problems. Most antihistamine products also have an anti-emetic effect, controlling feelings of nausea and preventing vomiting. Heroin along with most opiates can produce nausea in some users, and they will sometimes use large doses of antihistamine to control these effects. Some users will crush antihistamine tablets, particularly those intended for travel sickness relief, and mix the resultant powder with their heroin and inject both substances at the same time, thus achieve the effects that they desire whilst avoiding the nauseous effects.

Sympathomimetic products

Because of the chemical similarity of some of these products to amphetamine, the most sought after effect of their misuse is to achieve stimulation. The user will take high doses of the product to achieve feelings of uplift and exhilaration, together with an increase in energy and stamina. Some people will use these products when supplies of their usual stimulants are not available to them, but some users will only use the over the counter products through choice, and never use their street equivalents.

Adverse effects

Most misusers of over the counter medicines use them in vastly higher doses than the manufacturers recommend in order to achieve the effects that they are seeking. This can mean that they will also experience adverse effects that a person using the product at its normal dosage will never run into.

Opiate products

Most misusers of opiate-based products will experience the normal adverse effects of street opiate use, such as depression of the breathing and heart rate, together with the risk of vomiting. They are likely also to suffer psychological problems and changes in their personality.

Heavy users of opiate-based medical preparations also run the risk of suffering from other problems such as serious kidney disease. This can become so severe that total kidney failure can occur. Such a failure would place the user's life under serious threat, and require a great deal of medical care to overcome. They may also suffer serious digestive problems with extreme constipation, ulceration of the stomach lining and internal bleed-ing. Long term use may also lead to anaemia and to problems with the immune system.

Many misusers of opiate-based pain killing products will also suffer serious health problems caused by the other ingredients in the product. A commonly combined substance is paracetamol which can cause serious and even fatal damage to the liver if used heavily over a prolonged period.

Antihistamine products

The excessive misuse of preparations containing antihistamines can lead to the user experiencing serious eye problems, including blurred and double vision. These can be very long lasting and difficult to treat. This may be accompanied by persistent headaches, nausea and vomiting. Long-term use can also lead to problems with the user's digestive system with alternating bouts of constipation and diarrhoea. This can be very debilitating and may lead to a serious reduction in general bodily health.

Sympathomimetic products

Excessive and prolonged use of these products exposes the user to the risks associated with the use of amphetamine-like drugs. There may be profound psychological changes in the user, and the appearance of latent mental problems. Many of these products can cause heavy and continuous diar-rhoea which can lead to the loss of vital vitamins and trace elements from the body, leading to a serious reduction in health. It can further lead to becoming prone to all sorts of disorders that the body would normally be able to resist. The stimulant effects acting on a severely weakened body can lead to cardiac arrest and sudden death.

Tolerance potential

All of these products will create the potential for tolerance to develop within the misuser. This will result in more and more of the product being required to achieve the effects sought. As the dose rises so does the risk of adverse effects being experienced, and serious damage to general health may occur.

Habituation potential

Those products that contain opiates as part of their formulation have the potential to cause a serious physical dependence in their misusers. This dependence can become so severe that the misuser's whole life becomes built around their use of the product. This is commonly seen if Gee's Linctus or Kaolin and Morphine is misused. It can reach the point where up to five bottles of the preparation are used each day. They may have a particular preference for one or the other, but will use whichever is available if necessary. As these products can only be purchased from pharmacies, they may spend a great deal of time travelling around from one pharmacy to another buying a bottle in each so as to avoid arousing suspicion. On one occasion a user's car was searched by the police and twenty-two empty bottles of Gee's Linctus were found scattered on the floor. From the labels affixed to the bottles it seemed that they had been sold over the course of a week or so, from eight different pharmacies in the area around the user's home. Another misuser of Gee's Linctus, who was in his mid thirties, whilst looking at his history of drug use with his drug counsellor, estimated that he had consumed 30,000 bottles of the product in his life time.

The other types of over the counter medicines all have the potential to create psychological dependence within their misusers. They will feel that life is too difficult or unpleasant to face without the chemical prop provided by their substance of choice.

All of these dependencies can be very difficult to treat and will require a great deal of skilled help and support if there is to be any chance of success.

Withdrawal effects

The opiate based products will all produce the withdrawal effects that are experienced by users of street heroin (see section on heroin withdrawal, p.147).

Most heavy and prolonged misusers of other over the counter medicines will experience problems of anxiety and panic when use of their chosen drug ceases. They may also experience abrupt and unpleasant bodily reactions which could include vomiting, constipation and diarrhoea, as their bodies try to adapt to going without the large amounts of drug that previously were being used. Anyone who has been regularly misusing products of this nature over any length of time is well advised to seek professional help before trying to withdraw abruptly.

Overdose potential

All of these preparations are being used in overdose, when misused in the ways that have been described. It is often only by taking them in overdose that the desired effects can be achieved. In extreme overdose situations, many of the products can produce very real risks. Heart, breathing and circulation problems can occur which could lead to collapse, coma and death.

Street names

None known

Slang associated with use

None known

Part II

The Signs and Symptoms of Substance Misuse
Things You will Need to Look Out For

The misuse of substances in this country is, due to its anti-social or illegal nature, mostly a covert activity, carried out in privacy, away from direct public gaze, or in venues where others too may be indulging in the same, and consequently the practice is tolerated, accepted, or even positively encouraged.

Indeed, some recent research into the drug misuse activities of 16- to 19-year-old students showed that the majority used their drugs at their friends' homes while parents were absent, or in parks and other such open spaces (Hettiaratchy and Baines 1993[1]).

Detection and recognition of such misuse is therefore made extremely difficult for the untrained and uninitiated observer. They may never witness the effects of direct drug misuse, and they may easily overlook the physical and behavioural symptoms of such activity, or pass them off as being due to some other cause. Perhaps only the symptoms of withdrawal may be seen, and these may be very similar to those brought about by other circumstances such as the stresses and pressures of being a young person today, and therefore easily discounted.

Even the paraphernalia and refuse of substance misuse can be easily overlooked, for much of it utilizes everyday materials and objects which in their own right would not give rise to suspicion.

It is therefore necessary, if you are to be able to recognize instances of substance misuse, to have an appreciation and understanding of certain behavioural signs and physical evidence that may be apparent. It is worth stating again that many of these behavioural symptoms may exactly mimic those of other causes, and consequently these alone should never be used as the basis for making assumptions or accusations that somebody is

---

1   Hettiaratchy, S.W. and Baines, S. (1993) *Survey of Young People 1993.*

misusing harmful or illegal substances. Further investigation is always advisable.

Marked and uncharacteristic mood swings, aggression or apathetic behaviour

Substance misusers usually administer their chosen drug or solvent in order to bring about, what is to them at least, a positive change in their mood or activity. Regular usage may quickly build up a tolerance to the substance, requiring ever increasing amounts of that substance in order to achieve the hoped for result each time. As the effects of each use fades, the user will begin to suffer the onset of withdrawal symptoms. Unless a further dose of the drug or an alternative is used, there are likely to be changes in the person's mood and behaviour that are visible to outside observers. Basically speaking, what goes up must come down; the 'high' gained from using a particular substance may result in a corresponding 'low' once its use ceases.

Because continued substance misuse may lead to a succession of highs and subsequent lows, the user may appear to be on an emotional roller coaster. They may be at one moment energetic, confident, happy, friendly or just at peace with the world, and then change to being drained, apathetic, emotionally withdrawn, morose, irritable, depressed, isolated, paranoid or even aggressive, over a short period of time.

Marked mood swings may indeed be a characteristic of some forms of substance misuse, but they may also be the usual signs of adolescence or a reaction to pressures in that person's life, and therefore can never be used as a guaranteed pointer to the use of drugs or other substances.

Truancy and lateness for school, college, work etc

Many users will not exhibit these symptoms in public, preferring to re-adjust as best they can to a state of near normality before allowing themselves to be seen in public. If they are unable to achieve this re-adjustment within the necessary time scale, they may report that they are sick, and therefore unable to attend school, college or work. Others may truant or arrive late, without any real explanation being given, in order to give themselves valuable time to return to a reasonable state of equilibrium.

Deterioration in personal hygiene and dress

Due to the debilitating effects of many substances and the lack of recovery time available to the user, attention to personal hygiene and grooming may suffer badly. Many users, who had previously kept up a good standard of personal appearance and cleanliness, become unkempt, dirty and unshaven. Many will fail to change their clothes or wash themselves and may well begin to smell.

Covering suspicious behaviour by lying, being vague etc

Working standards, reliability and time keeping may also be put at some risk due to the debilitating effects of the 'comedown' from some substances. Users will often adopt strategies of deception to cover their mistakes and their odd behaviour, and there may be evidence of deteriorating relationships with peers, work mates, siblings and other family members.

Unusual conflict with authority figures

Conflict may also erupt with parents, teachers, employers or other authority figures where none existed before.

Sudden and marked change of habits, loss of purpose in life, lacking motivation or goals

Favoured tasks, hobbies, activities and personal goals that were previously considered to be important to a user may quite suddenly lose their appeal, and be dropped from the daily routine altogether. This loss of purpose in life has proved in many instances to be an important indicator of drug and other substance misuse. Again it must be stressed that the pressures and strains of ordinary life, or even mental states such as depression or schizophrenia, may offer another explanation for this sort of behaviour. The exhibition of such behaviour is in any case worthy of further investigation so that the exact cause and possibly a remedy may be found.

Excessive borrowing of money

Once a regular drug habit has become established, funding it may become a real difficulty. This will be particularly true if a tolerance level has been reached that necessitates the use of ever increasing quantities of the substance being misused. Regular users, and particularly young users, may never seem to have any spare finances despite regular salaries, pocket money or other sources of money. Their continuing habit may force them into patterns of excessive begging or borrowing from family members, friends, colleagues and even complete strangers, without any real hope or intention of paying back the amounts borrowed.

Stealing from family, friends, school, shops, work etc

The stealing of money or goods to sell on may also become commonplace from home, shops, work or school. Users may become involved in stealing goods to order for other people, and they may reach the point where they are so desperate for money that nothing and nobody is sacred. Many users realize the inevitability of being found out or caught in the act, but the lure and promise of a drug can wipe these thoughts from their minds leaving them without any feelings or conscience.

Selling of own property with little or nothing to show for it

One of the more obvious pointers to possible substance abuse, especially amongst the young, who generally do not have much in the way of expensive saleable goods, is the selling of one's own property. Even items of great sentimental value or which have brought the owner much previous pleasure and pride may be disposed of. Items such as televisions, video recorders, bicycles, guitars, stereos and jewellery may be disposed of at a fraction of their true value without a flicker of remorse, as a result of their owner's desperate need to raise the necessary cash to buy more drugs. In some cases, goods of this nature may be directly exchanged for amounts of the user's chosen drug. This kind of behaviour can be taken to extremes at times, and we have known cases where users have disposed of their cars, houses and even businesses in order to realize the funds needed to finance a long-term drug habit.

More recently we have come across a 21-year-old unemployed heroin addict, who has confessed to selling irreplaceable family heirlooms with great sentimental value at prices that do not begin to approach their true market value, in order to fund his habit. Perhaps the saddest case that has come to our notice in recent times was that of a young mother addicted to amphetamine who, after selling most of her own property and committing a number of frauds, was ashamed to admit that she had been reduced to selling her seven-year-old daughter's toys in order to pay for her drugs.

Young people do sell their own property for genuine reasons, but in most of these cases they will use the money raised to buy something else. If the items are sold to buy drugs, there will be nothing to be seen in replacement for the goods sold. The money that was raised may quite literally have gone up in smoke.

Another area to be aware of by all those who are attempting to detect substance misuse, is that of the user becoming involved in the selling or supplying of drugs in order to generate profits that can be used to fund their own habit. This may only occur in a minor way to begin with, bringing in just enough to cover the user's own habit, but because it can be an easy and quick way to raise quite large sums of money, it can easily escalate into a much more serious business activity. Funding a drug habit by dealing generally involves buying drugs from more major suppliers in larger quantities than an individual would normally need for themselves, in order to obtain the discounts that are commonly available for buying in bulk. The excess drugs are then offered for sale to friends and acquaintances of the user at normal street prices, thus recouping the whole of the original outlay. Some user-dealers will attempt to increase their profit margins by adulterating or 'cutting' the drugs that they sell with other substances to increase their bulk and weight.

Furtive telephone calls and use of drug slang

Even small time dealers will need to advertise when they have drugs for sale and what drugs they have. They may make and receive a large number of furtive telephone calls to and from potential customers. It is likely that the use of drug related slang will be prevalent during these telephone calls, in order to try and conceal their real purpose to anyone overhearing them. As with many other forms, drug related slang is used in order to exclude those who do not understand it whilst bestowing credibility on those who can use it in the right context.

Frequent short visits from new or older friends, and many short excursions away from home

These telephone calls may be followed up by a succession of brief visits to the home of the dealer by a large number of familiar or not so familiar callers, many of whom may be outside the normal age range or social group of the dealer. There may also be frequent occasions when the dealer will have to go out to see someone for a short while, usually straight after a telephone call. It is not easy to recommend that anyone should deliberately eavesdrop on another person's private telephone calls, but in some instances it can be the only way to find out exactly what is going on.

As most substance misuse is carried out in private, the signs and symptoms that become apparent to the observer may only be those of withdrawal or 'come down'. It will therefore be necessary to understand certain characteristics that are peculiar to particular drugs.

Wearing dark glasses even in dull weather

Cannabis, for example, may cause a condition in some of its users that is known as 'red-eye', a condition in which the user's eyes become very bloodshot. This condition may be particularly noticeable in the morning following use of the drug, and this may prompt the user to wear dark glasses in order to hide their eyes from the view of others. They will wear the dark glasses at very inappropriate times, in dull weather and even indoors.

Short-term memory loss and deterioration in performance, loss of concentration and loss of co-ordination

Cannabis use may also lead to the loss of short-term memory, as well as a marked reduction in the user's powers of concentration. This together with generally apathetic behaviour on the part of the user may make tasks such as driving or operating machinery difficult, and in many cases very dangerous.

Poor appetite and weight loss or eating binges

Eating binges after cannabis use are also very common, and are affectionately known in drug slang as the *munchies*. Indeed, so effective is cannabis at stimulating the appetites of most of its users, that some people consider its use beneficial in the alleviation of some symptoms of wasting diseases, such as AIDS or multiple sclerosis, where the sufferer's appetite is severely reduced.

At the other end of the scale, many drugs, especially the stimulant type, can powerfully suppress the appetite. Both cocaine and amphetamine have this effect and, as they also speed up the user's metabolism giving them feelings of energy and stamina, usage on a regular basis or over an extended period of time will inevitably lead to a loss of body weight, making some users lean and thin.

Suffering a succession of colds and episodes of 'flu which may persist for an unusually long time

This disruption to the normal intake of nutrients may go on to cause damage to the body's immune system, leaving the user open to many ailments such as colds and 'flu. Having developed these ailments, the user may seem unable to shake them off, and the condition may go on for an unusually long time.

Depression, shyness and poor self-image

Certain people will actually use some substances as a way of self-medicating their problems away, without ever being aware that they may have a medically recognizable condition. Depression, anxiety and lack of confidence, and some other mild psychiatric disorders may be dealt with in this way, but also the reverse can be true. Disorders such as these may also arise as a direct result of the use of certain substances. This is especially true of amphetamines, which can cause paranoia, psychosis, or even bring to the fore latent mental illnesses such as schizophrenia, which may otherwise have remained dormant.

The remedy for adverse withdrawal symptoms, in the view of some users, is simplicity itself. Just administer another dose of the drug. But to carry on in this way could very soon lead to the building of a high level of tolerance, or even to the development of a full blown psychological or physical addiction. All this means, of course, more business for the dealer, but is very bad news for the user whose general health and well being will undoubtedly suffer.

Spending time away from home, usually overnight

Seeking out and using drugs may necessitate the user being away from home overnight or for even longer periods. To avoid detection the reasons given to explain this time away may be extremely vague, misleading and muddled, if any explanation is forthcoming at all.

Excessive sleeping, usually after time away from home

On returning home, the user may need to sleep for long periods, especially in order to offset the effects of stimulant drugs, and recover from strenuous activity.

Drunken behaviour and slurred speech

If depressant drugs have been used, this may affect the user's co-ordination and speech, making them appear out of control and sluggish.

In order to verify your suspicions of possible drug use, it will be necessary for you to back up your observations with some form of physical evidence, if any can be found.

Quick Reference Guide

- Marked and uncharacteristic mood swings, aggression and apathetic behaviour.
- Truancy and lateness for school, college, work etc.
- Deterioration in personal hygiene and dress.
- Covering suspicious behaviour by lying, being vague etc.
- Unusual conflict with authority figures.
- Sudden and marked change of habits, loss of purpose in life, lacking motivation or goals.
- Excessive borrowing of money.
- Stealing from family, friends, school, shops, work etc.
- Selling of own property with little or nothing to show for it.
- Furtive telephone calls and use of drug slang.
- Many short visits from new or older friends and many short excursions away from home.
- Wearing dark glasses even in dull weather.
- Short-term memory loss and deterioration in performance.
- Loss of concentration and loss of co-ordination.
- Poor appetite and weight loss, or eating binges.
- Suffering a succession of colds and episodes of 'flu which may persist for an unusually long time.
- Depression, shyness and poor self-image.
- Spending time away from home, usually overnight.
- Excessive sleeping, usually after time away from home.
- Drunken behaviour and slurred speech.

NOTE: Many of the above may simply be normal signs of adolescence or due to some other cause rather than drug use. It will be wise to make further investigations.

CHAPTER 12

Physical Evidence of Possible Drug or Substance Use

The paraphernalia and refuse of drug and substance misuse, such as needles, syringes, tablets and the like, will be quite evident to everybody, but things may not always be quite so easy. Many everyday objects can be utilized for taking drugs and can therefore easily be passed off as innocuous, insignificant and totally unrelated to drug or substance misuse.

Cigarette lighters, matches and candles (especially if a non smoker)

A large number of illegal drugs can be administered by being smoked, using a wide variety of methods and equipment. Obviously there has to be first of all a source of heat, and so matches, cigarette lighters and candles are items that have to be taken into account as possible evidence of drug use. That will be especially true if the person in possession of them is not known as a tobacco smoker.

Knives, metal foil, drink cans and bottle tops discoloured by heat; funnels, outer covers of match boxes and large straws

Many substances can be smoked merely by heating them gently and inhaling the resultant fumes that are given off. Cooking foil, metal bottle tops and drink cans can all be used for this purpose, and the fumes produced directed into the user's mouth or nose by use of a straw, paper or card tube. Other users favour the use of a funnel made by cutting off the top part off of a plastic bottle, or even the outer sleeve of a matchbox to collect and direct the fumes. The holding of a matchbox cover in the mouth to collect fumes is called in drug slang *playing the mouth organ*.

Heated knife blades can also be used to smoke certain substances. Heating the blade of a knife and pressing it directly onto the substance will make it smoulder and produce vapours that can then be inhaled. This can also be done by heating two knife blades and holding the substance between them both. These practices are known as *hot knifing* and are often utilized by cannabis users who wish to smoke their drug without the use of tobacco.

Clay, wooden, glass or ceramic long stemmed pipes (chillums)

Cannabis smokers will sometimes use specially made long stemmed pipes, made from wood, clay, ceramics or even glass. These pipes are known as chillums, and help to cool the cannabis smoke so as to prevent burning of the user's lips, tongue and throat, for cannabis burns at a far higher temperature than plain tobacco.

Home made hubble bubble pipes (bhongs), and similar devices

Other devices for cooling cannabis smoke are home made versions of the hubble bubble or hookah water pipe, known as 'bhongs'. These items are generally made from water tight containers such as glass or plastic bottles, or metal or plastic cans with tight fitting lids. They are half filled with water and have a tube inserted at an angle through the side of the container, far enough to have its lower end below the level of the water. At the outer end of the tube will be some form of heat proof metal bowl, sometimes merely fashioned from a milk bottle top, in which to burn the cannabis. Using the neck of the bottle or a vertical pipe fitted to the top of the water tight container, the user simply draws the smoke through the water by sucking. As the smoke bubbles through the water it is cooled, and some of the tar and other impurities are removed. This cooled and less irritating smoke can then be taken deeper into the lungs and held there for a longer period of time, resulting in more of the drug's active ingredient (THC) being able to pass into the bloodstream.

These devices are usually quick and easy to produce and may therefore be discarded after use just as easily, especially when the user is under the influence of the drug and not thinking clearly. Others, however, are much more painstakingly and lovingly created, and will be far more elaborate and durable affairs and intended for more permanent long-term use. It has been known for bhongs to be fashioned from buckets or other large containers for use by many smokers at once, and we have even seen a fully automatic electric bhong.

Another device for smoking cannabis has recently come to our notice. This is known as a *lung* and consists of a small plastic bottle with the base removed. To this open end is then attached a plastic bag, and a smoking bowl is fitted to the top of the bottle. Some cannabis is then placed in the bowl and lit. The bag will be pumped to draw the smoke down into it, and once full, the smoking bowl is removed. The user inhales the smoke through the top of the bottle by again pumping the bag.

No object should therefore be overlooked as a possible device for the smoking of drugs.

Large cigarette papers, short cardboard tubes (roaches)

Cannabis cigarettes, known today as *spliffs* or *joints*, are in the main constructed or 'built' with the use of extra large cigarette papers or multiple smaller ones. When smoked in this way it is still necessary to cool the cannabis smoke, and so a small cardboard tube, about the size of a commercial cigarette filter, is inserted in the end that is to be placed in the mouth. This tube, known as a *roach* or *roach end* in drug slang, keeps the burning material from spilling out of the *spliff* or *joint* and distances the lips and mouth from the burning material.

Packets of cigarette rolling paper with pieces torn from them

Many *roaches* are simply made from pieces of the cigarette paper packet, and therefore the finding of *roaches* or such torn packets are a good indication of cannabis use. Some ex-cannabis users will still use *roaches* when hand rolling ordinary tobacco cigarettes out of habit.

Razor blades, modelling knives or scalpel blades

Herbal or resinous cannabis can be inserted into a factory-produced cigarette by carefully slitting it with a modelling knife, scalpel or razor blade, adding the drug, and then resealing the cigarette with a cigarette paper. In these cases the filters are always removed before lighting as they filter out most of the active ingredient of the cannabis if left in place.

Cigarette filters and cotton wool

Cigarette filters, however, are of great benefit to injecting drug users who employ them to filter out undissolved solids from powdered drugs or crushed tablets in solution. If this is not done, these solids may clog the needle and syringe, or if injected they may block small blood vessels causing serious medical problems, and in some extreme cases loss of limbs.

Spoons discoloured by heat, often with bent stem

Drug injecting often involves a great deal of ritual. The usual method employed is to dissolve a quantity of powder drug or crushed tablets in a small amount of water in the bowl of a spoon, known in drug slang as a *cooking spoon*. The stem of the spoon may have been bent to allow it to stand or be held on a flat surface without spilling any of the contents.

Lemon juice, vinegar, ascorbic and citric acid

A few drops of a mild acid, commonly vinegar, ascorbic acid (vitamin C) or even lemon juice is then added to help break down the drug. The spoon is then heated from below to speed up the dissolving process. This is known as *cooking up*, and when the drug has completely dissolved a cigarette filter or a small piece of rolled cotton wool is then dropped into the solution. The needle attached to the syringe, or sometimes just the syringe, is then inserted into the filter and the liquid drug drawn up into the barrel of the syringe. The drug is then ready for injecting it into a vein, a process known as *shooting up*, or under the skin, known as *skin popping*. The undissolved solids hopefully remain in the filter.

Some users will save their old filters for occasions when they are unable to obtain or afford their drug. They will then use any residue left in the filters for their next 'hit' by reheating the filters in a small amount of water.

Tourniquets, syringes, needles, swabs and water ampoules

Tourniquets are utilized by many users in order to raise the profiles of their veins to facilitate injection. Many injectors will clean the injecting site on their skins with a spirit swab, and some will even obtain and use ampoules of sterile water produced especially for injection. Many pharmaceutical drugs are produced in ampoules ready for injection and the finding of any of these items would be indicative of an injecting user.

Folded five centimetre squares of paper (wraps or deals)

Drugs sold in powder form, such as heroin, cocaine and amphetamine are generally marketed in small quantities, usually fractions of a gram. They are commonly marketed in small pieces of folded paper, about five centimetres square, known as *wraps* or *deals*. The paper is folded in such a way that the powder held inside will not come out, despite rough handling, and due to their small size once folded, can be easily transported and concealed. Wraps may be as small as three centimetres by one and a half centimetres when folded. The finding of empty wraps would be a good indicator of drug use, whilst the finding of quantities of full folded wraps could indicate drug dealing. All powder drugs and crushed tablets can obviously be taken by mouth also. This is commonly done by *dabbing*, lifting the powder into the mouth on a wet finger. They may also be added to drinks. Sometimes they can also be taken by wrapping them in a piece of cigarette paper. The powder is placed in the centre of the paper which is then twisted together to hold the powder in a shape known as a *bomb*. The *bomb* is then swallowed.

Coloured powders, sets of scales

Those who deal street drugs in powder form may, in order to increase their profit margins, adulterate the drug with other substances to increase its bulk and weight. Indeed this may already have been done much further back in the dealer chain, long before it reaches the street dealer. Other powdered substances such as coffee, talcum powder, glucose or even rat poisons may be used depending upon the colour and consistency of the drug being adulterated. It has even been known for brick dust to be mixed with street heroin. The discovery of quantities of such powdered substances in abnormal circumstances may therefore be important.

Small, portable and accurate sets of scales, together with a set of small weights usually in fractions of a gram, are often used by drug dealers, and the possession of such items can often be used to successfully prosecute a person suspected of dealing in illegal substances.

Lighter fuel, lighter gas, hair sprays, spray deodorants, solvent glues, spray polishes, correcting fluids and dry cleaning fluids

With a resurgence in solvent abuse in recent years, mostly confined to the young, all volatile substances, lighter fuels and gases, plus aerosol cans of hair spray or deodorants may need to be viewed with some suspicion. This is especially true if found empty and in more than usual quantities, or if an attempt has been made to conceal them. One recent search of a playing field used by young people from a nearby school in our area yielded over 150 empty aerosol cans, indicative of this resurgence.

Plastic bags, crisp packets, drink cans and clothing that smell of solvents

Solvents can be used in a number of different ways. Some users will spray the substances directly into their mouths, or alternatively into plastic bags or crisp packets, which are then held over the nose and mouth. It is not unknown for much larger plastic bags containing solvents to be placed completely over the user's head, a method known as *space helmeting*.

Drinks cans too can be used for sniffing solvents. The solvent is poured into an empty drinks can and then held in the hand. The heat from the hand will cause the solvent to evaporate, so that it can be sniffed by the user through the ring pull opening.

It is possible to sniff directly from rags, clothing and paper towels, and it is therefore important to view with some seriousness any such items found that smell of solvents.

Use of strongly scented products

In order to mask the smells produced by smoking drugs or solvent abuse, some users will utilize other strong smelling aromatic items such as air fresheners, after-shaves and incense sticks in large quantities, and such behaviour will need to be checked out in order to establish the reason for such use.

To try and detail all of the varying forms of substance misuse paraphernalia would necessitate a much larger volume than we have here, and new ways of using substances are constantly being dreamt up.

All pills, tablets, capsules, powder and dried plant material, very small mushrooms, often dried, small stamp-like paper squares with coloured motifs printed on them (trips or tabs)

We can not emphasize enough that the discovery of any piece of equipment unfamiliar to you, along with any form of capsules, tablets, powders, crystals, plant material and solvents, must be regarded very seriously indeed and should be thoroughly investigated, perhaps with expert assistance from your local community drugs service, your doctor, pharmacist or the police. All of these will usually be most helpful and sympathetic in these matters, and can be approached anonymously.

Quick reference guides to the possible behavioural signs and symptoms are provided in the previous chapter (p.232) and a list of associated physical evidence are provided in this chapter (pp.240–1).

Quick Reference Guide

Physical evidence of possible drug use

- Cigarette lighters, matches and candles (especially if a non smoker).

- Knives, metal foil, drinks cans and bottle tops discoloured by heat.

- Funnels, outer covers of match boxes and large straws.

- Clay, wooden, glass or ceramic long stemmed pipes (*chillums*).

- Home made hubble bubble pipes (*bhongs*).

- Large cigarette rolling papers, short cardboard tubes (*roaches*).

- Cigarette rolling paper packets with pieces torn from them.

- Razor blades, modelling knives or scalpel blades.

- Cigarette filters, cotton wool.

- Spoons discoloured by heat, often with a bent stem.

- Lemon juice, vinegar, ascorbic and citric acid.

- Tourniquets, syringes, needles, swabs, filters and water or drug ampoules.

- Folded five centimetre squares of paper (wraps or deals).

- Coloured powders, sets of scales

- Lighter fuel, lighter gas, hair sprays, spray deodorants, solvent glues, spray polishes, correcting fluids and dry cleaning fluids.

- Plastic bags, crisp packets, drink cans and clothing that smell of solvents.

- Use of strongly scented products.

- All pills, tablets, capsules, powders and dried plant material.

- Very small mushrooms, often dried.

- Very small stamp-like paper squares with coloured motifs printed on them (*trips* or *tabs*).

- Bottles with the bottom cut of and a plastic bag attached to the base (a *lung* for smoking cannabis).

NOTE: There may be perfectly rational explanations for possession of some of the above. You will need to check out your findings with an expert before making any assumptions or accusations.

CHAPTER 13

Managing Drug-Related Incidents

If the use of illegal drugs and other substances continues to grow in the way that it has in recent years, there can be little doubt that all those who are in positions of responsibility for other people, particularly young people, are potentially going to find themselves having to deal with an incident that is in some way related to that use. This could apply equally to a parent, teacher, social worker, youth leader or any other professional.

This chapter is not intended to lay down strict rules for the management of such incidents. What it is intended to provide is a set of guidelines that will help the person concerned approach and deal with the incident with a degree of confidence. Many professionals will already have a policy, laid down by their organization, that will outline an approved course of action, and they will have to give due regard to this policy when considering the guidance in this chapter. There may be times, however, when the incident is being dealt with by someone, such as a parent, relative or even a stranger, who has no official policy to guide them at all, or in circumstances to which an organization's policy does not apply. It is at these times that most people would feel at their most inadequate and when these guidelines may be of most help to them.

We have created a number of scenarios that describe typical drug-related incidents of the sort that readers could find themselves having to deal with. The guidelines for dealing with each scenario is outlined in some detail, and is accompanied by a simplified flow chart that takes the reader step by step through the action to be taken. The notes and the flow charts should be referred to together when considering each scenario.

Likely police action

The attitudes of different police forces towards drug matters may show some variation, but all will want to investigate the full circumstances of each case before deciding on a course of action. It is not the wish of today's police service to simply arrest and prosecute in every case. Police officers are able to exercise a great deal of discretion in the way that they carry out their duties, and will want to work in close co-operation with the person or organization that has brought a case to their attention. There will be cases where the offence is one of simple possession, and they may wish to leave the matter to be dealt with internally by the school or similar organization. In other possession cases, they may feel that the offender should receive a formal police caution in front of their parents, and in some serious cases they may wish the offender to appear before the courts. The courts have at their disposal many ways of dealing with such cases, and may feel that the offender should receive some supervision and guidance in a formal way through the probation services. The intention of such orders is not to punish but to help the offender to find a more positive way of life.

In cases where more serious offences, such the supplying or cultivation of drugs, have been brought to the attention of the police, then it is likely that the offender will find themselves in front of the courts, and will have to face the consequences of their actions, which may include a custodial sentence.

SCENARIO ONE
Displaying behavioural signs and symptoms of possible drug use

Note one

By reading through the chapter on behavioural signs and symptoms contained in this book, you will be familiar with most of the behavioural clues that drug users will display and the reasons for them. These are mostly the sort of clues that would only be noticed by someone having fairly regular contact with the person in question. They may see behavioural changes that could be very small at the beginning, but that will grow and accumulate until the observer begins to suspect that they are the result of drug or other substance use.

Note two

Having begun to suspect that someone is behaving in a way that could indicate drug use, an obvious first step to take is to talk to other people who have dealings with the person in question, and ascertain whether they have noticed anything out of the ordinary, and if they have similar suspicions to your own.

Note three

It may be that no one else has had the opportunity to observe the person closely, or if they have, has not noticed anything unusual. If this is the case, it would be a good plan to ask someone responsible to observe the person for a while, and give their opinion as to whether your suspicions are well founded or not. If that person is someone with previous experience of dealing with drug incidents then so much the better.

Note four

The observer may not agree with you, and reassure you that your suspicions are unfounded, in which case it will be up to you to decide whether to take further action. If you decide not to take it any further at this stage, then it would clearly be advisable to continue to monitor the situation.

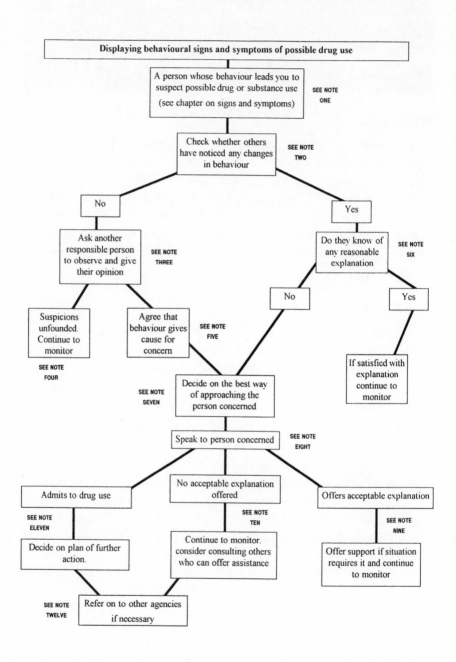

Scenario one

Note five

If the person you have asked to carry out the observations agrees with your assessment of the situation, then you are in a much better position to plan your course of action.

Note six

It may be that others have already noticed the behaviour that has aroused your suspicions, and indeed other signs that perhaps have not been apparent to you. There may be a non drug-related explanation for the behaviour, and others may be in possession of information not known to you that satisfactorily explains the matter. A case occurred recently where a teacher grew increasingly concerned at the bizarre behaviour being displayed by one of his pupils, and became convinced that it could be drug use related. On voicing his fears to another colleague, he was told that the pupil's father was dying of cancer, and that the boy was very distraught about the situation. If information is offered that appears to explain the behaviour, it will still be prudent to continue to monitor the person in question.

If others have noticed the behaviour and have no reasonable explanation for it, then it will be necessary to investigate further with an approach to the person in question.

Note seven

Having carried out all investigations that are possible to seek an explanation for the behavioural clues observed, if unsuccessful, there is little more that can be done except to approach the person concerned. Consideration needs to be given as to the best way of carrying this out. You will need to consider whether it would be best to see the person alone or whether it would be best to have somebody else present. It very much depends upon your relationship with the person concerned. You may judge that you are more likely to get to the truth if you speak to them alone, or it may be that you decide that it would be more prudent to have a witness or someone to provide a second opinion. Only you can be the judge in these cases. It is well worth trying to work out exactly what you are going to say to this person beforehand, and what are you hoping to achieve. What exactly is it that has led you to the suspicions that you have and what do you suspect the person of? You may need to seek some advice and support from someone with experience in these matters before you decide on the best method of dealing with this.

Note eight

Having decided upon the best way of approaching the person, it is worth taking a moment to consider how you will speak to them. It is never a good idea to adopt a accusatory or confrontational style, for it has been our experience that if a user is confronted too fiercely at this stage, then they may simply run off. Now, you not only have a drug user, but one who is missing. Therefore remaining calm is vital. Try to show by the tone and style of your conversation that it is your wish to help and not to provide the person with yet another problem. Explain the things that led to you forming the suspicions that you hold, and produce any evidence that you might have to back up your suspicions. Unless you have a clear grasp of drug slang, it is better to use only the correct terms when talking about drugs matters. Nothing makes a non drug user look more foolish than if they make mistakes with the use of drug slang. Remember the slang belongs to their world, and not yours, and they may react unfavourably if you try to use it and get it wrong.

Note nine

The person may offer a perfectly reasonable explanation at this point for the behaviour that you have noticed. This explanation may indicate that they have another, totally non drug-related problem that you can perhaps help with. You may be in a position to offer support, advice and practical help that will assist the person in coping with this problem. Even though you may be satisfied with their explanation it would be prudent to continue to monitor the situation.

Note ten

If the person denies all drug use but offers no satisfactory explanation for their behaviour you may not be in a position to substantiate your suspicions at this stage and may be unable to take it any further. You will clearly need to monitor the situation further, and may consider consulting with others who can advise you as to the steps available to you. It may be that you feel that you have done all that you can, and need to refer the matter on to others to deal with (see note twelve).

Note eleven

If your suspicions are well founded and your approach is well thought out, the person may admit to you that they are involved in the use of drugs or some other substance. It is especially important at this time to remain calm and to consider your next step carefully. It would be prudent for you to inform the person that you may find it necessary to pass on the details of your conversation to others, should you consider it the correct course of action. It will be very useful to gather some more vital information at this point. What drug or substance are they using? What method of administration are they using? How much and for how long have they been using? All this will help you to judge whether it is likely that they have become habituated to the drug, and what their debt position, if any, might be as a result. It will be useful to find out where they use their drug and with whom. This information may not be forthcoming, but if it is, it may enable you to take action to help bring such use to an end. The last, and perhaps most vital questions that you should seek answers to, are why they are using drugs in the first place, what they get out of it, and whether they require help. It may be that you can take steps that will help to eliminate their need to use drugs. You may be able to help bring about a change in their lives that will make drug use unnecessary. Most drug users in the early stages of use will not perceive that they have any sort of problem. They believe that they are in control of their drug use, not the drug controlling them. This may, of course be a fallacy, and it may be your task to bring them to an understanding of this. Invariably, you will not be able to provide any support or influence if the user does not accept that they have a problem. If they accept that they do need help, then it will then be necessary to work out with them a plan of action to resolve the situation.

Note twelve

It may be that after listening to all that the person has to say, you may decide that it is best if you refer the person on to another. This could be to your community drug service, who will offer confidential help and support to the person, or it may be that you feel the situation is such that you need to refer the matter to a higher authority, such as senior colleagues, parents or to the police. There will almost always be the need to refer the matter to a higher authority if the person will not co-operate with you.

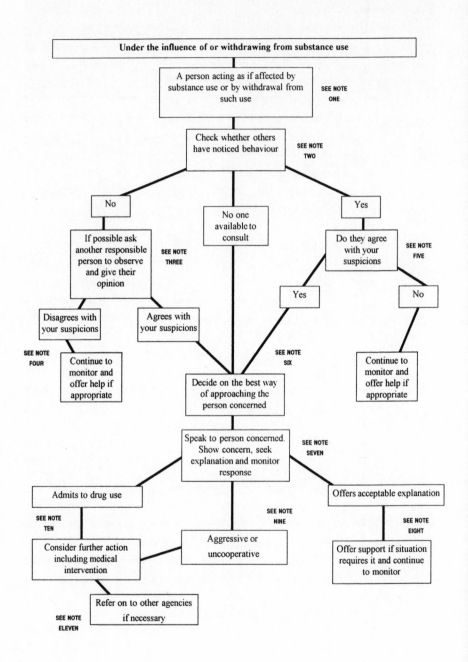

Under the influence of or withdrawing from substance use

A person acting as if affected by substance use or by withdrawal from such use — SEE NOTE ONE

Check whether others have noticed behaviour — SEE NOTE TWO

No

No one available to consult

Yes

If possible ask another responsible person to observe and give their opinion — SEE NOTE THREE

Do they agree with your suspicions — SEE NOTE FIVE

Yes

No

Disagrees with your suspicions

Agrees with your suspicions

SEE NOTE FOUR

Continue to monitor and offer help if appropriate

SEE NOTE SIX

Continue to monitor and offer help if appropriate

Decide on the best way of approaching the person concerned

Speak to person concerned. Show concern, seek explanation and monitor response — SEE NOTE SEVEN

Admits to drug use

SEE NOTE TEN

SEE NOTE NINE

Offers acceptable explanation

SEE NOTE EIGHT

Consider further action including medical intervention

Aggressive or uncooperative

Offer support if situation requires it and continue to monitor

Refer on to other agencies if necessary

SEE NOTE ELEVEN

Scenario two

SCENARIO TWO
Under the influence of, or withdrawing from substance use

Note one

The physical signs of drug or substance use vary considerably from person to person, and from drug to drug. It will also depend upon how much was taken, how recently and what previous experience the user has had of that drug or substance. For the non expert, it would be sufficient to be aware that a person who displays signs of intoxication, loss of control, unsteadiness, lethargy, hyperactivity, or is suffering from hallucinations, is possibly under the influence of a drug or other like substance. All of these signs could have another cause. They could be the symptoms of an illness, of accidental poisoning, or a side effect of a prescribed medicine. It is the responsibility of the observer to check out the reasons for the behaviour that they are witnessing. If the person is going through withdrawal from drug use, they are likely to display signs of disorientation, depression, mood swings, aggression, lethargy or tiredness. They may also, in extreme cases, show signs of suffering actual physical pain.

Note two

Having observed behaviour that leads you to suspect drug or substance use, the most useful thing that you can do is to consult with others to see if anyone else has noticed the same behaviour.

Note three

If no one has noticed anything out of the ordinary or has not had an opportunity to observe the person, it would be useful to ask someone to monitor the person and then give their opinion. Of course some discretion may need to be exercised here. It would not be wise to seek an opinion from an unreliable person or someone who is too closely connected with the person you are observing, for they may give you an incorrect answer in the belief that they are protecting their friend.

Note four

The person that you ask to monitor the situation may be able to satisfy you that the behaviour that aroused your suspicions is not drug related. If this is so, then there may be other forms of help that you can offer the person in question. Of course it will still be advisable to keep an eye on the situation in case it should reoccur.

Note five

The behaviour may have already been noticed by someone else and they may be of the opinion that it is not related to drug or substance use. If you are satisfied with that opinion, then proceed in the same way as at note four.

Note six

If there is no one available to give you an opinion, or if those that you have asked are of a similar opinion to yourself, then you have to decide on the best way to approach the person concerned. It is worth sounding a note of caution here. If the person is unknown to you, or if you are in any doubt about your own safety, then it will be essential to seek help from others before any approach is made, and it may be necessary to call in the police.

If you are satisfied that you are not at risk, then you need to decide on the best way to talk to the person. Dependent upon your previous relationship with them, it may be best to speak quietly to them away from others, or you may judge that it would be best to have someone with you. Only you can decide this.

Note seven

Having decided upon the best way of approaching the person concerned, it is worth spending a moment considering how you are going to speak to them. It is never a good idea to adopt an accusatory or confrontational style. It has been our experience that if a user is confronted too fiercely at this stage, then they may run off. Now you not only have a drug user but one who is missing. Keeping calm is vital. Try to show by the tone and style of your conversation that it is your wish to help and not to provide the person with yet another problem. Explain the things that led to you forming the suspicions that you have, and produce any evidence that you might have to back up your suspicions.

Closely monitor any responses, for this may enable to judge how deeply affected they are, and whether it is likely that they are going to need medical help.

Note eight

It may be that at this stage the person will offer an explanation of their behaviour that satisfies you that it is not connected with drug or substance misuse. By taking a non accusatory and helpful tone initially, it will be easier for the person to confide in you if they have some other problem. There may be some other form of help or support that you can offer.

Note nine

However carefully you plan your approach, the person may react badly to it and become unco-operative or even aggressive. If you are unable to calm them and gain their co-operation quickly, it will perhaps be best to withdraw from the situation and refer it on to others. It will depend on the circumstances of the individual case, but there may be someone in a position of authority that you can pass the matter on to or it may be necessary to inform the police.

Note ten

A careful and non confrontational approach may lead the person to admitting that they have been using drugs or similar substances. They may be experiencing very unpleasant feelings and be somewhat frightened by the situation they find themselves in, and want someone to help them. It will be important to ascertain, if you can, what they have been using, how much and how recently. You will need to decide whether it is necessary to seek medical assistance. If you are satisfied that immediate medical help is not needed, you can then consider what further action is called for. This will again depend upon your relationship with the person and circumstances of the case. It may be the very first time that they have ever tried drugs and will have been put off by the experience. If, on the other hand, it is part of an ongoing situation, then this will need careful handling. Only you can be the judge of this.

It will be worth referring to scenario one, note eleven, for further guidance.

Note eleven

If, after listening to all that the person has to say, you may decide that it is best if you refer the person on to someone else. That could be to your community drug service, who will offer help and support to the person in a confidential manner. You may feel that the situation is one that you need to refer on to a higher authority, such as senior colleagues, parents or to the police. There will almost always be the need to refer the matter to a higher authority if the person will not co-operate with your offers of help.

SCENARIO THREE
Person found unconscious

Note one

You may be the first person to come across someone who has lost consciousness as a result of their use of drugs or some other similar substance. Your actions at this stage can make the difference between full recovery or even death.

Note two

The first rule of all emergency aid is not to panic. That is easier to write than it is to carry out in real life, but somehow you must remain calm. By preparing yourself for such an eventuality you will make staying calm easier to achieve.

You will need to make an initial assessment of the situation, to check whether they are breathing and whether their heart is beating. Ensure that the airway is open, and clear it of any obvious obstructions. Unless it is necessary for you to perform immediate cardiac massage and or mouth to mouth resuscitation, you should place the person in the recovery position. This position will prevent the tongue from falling back and blocking the airway, and allows liquids such as vomit to drain freely from the mouth. Many people have had some level of first aid training, but it is worth repeating the instructions for placing an unconscious person in the recovery position. These instructions can be practised with a partner until both of you are familiar with them.

(1) Kneel on the ground alongside the person, straighten their legs and place them together. Put the person's arm that is nearest to you out at right angles to their body, and then bend it at the elbow laying it down with the palm uppermost.

(2) Take hold of the person's other arm, and draw it across their chest, bending the elbow so that the back of the person's hand is laid in contact with the side of their face nearest to you. Hold the hand in that position.

(3) With your other hand take hold of the person's leg that is furthest from you. Hold it above the knee and pull until the person rolls

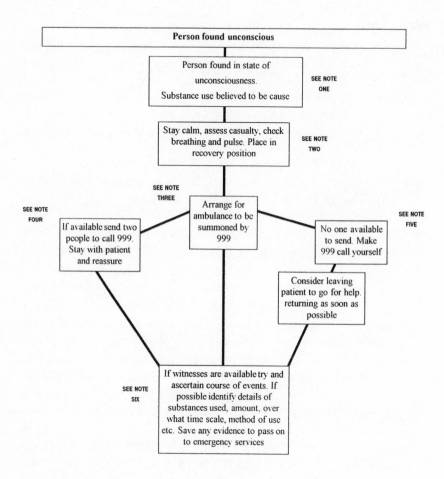

Scenario three

onto their side. They should now be lying on their side facing you, with their face supported on one hand, and with the upper leg sticking out at right angles with the knee bent to support the weight of the body.

(4) Tilt the person's head back to ensure that the airway stays clear and adjust the position of their hand if necessary. The person is now in a stable and safe position.

Note three

If a person is unconscious and you suspect that drug or substance use is the cause, you will always need to summon medical help as soon as possible. In circumstances such as these, it is never safe to wait and see if the person comes round of their own accord. Delay could have fatal consequences.

Note four

Once you have assessed the situation, if there is someone in the vicinity, then get them to summon help by dialling for an ambulance (999 in the UK). This can be being done while you are stabilizing the person in the recovery position. If possible, send two people to call the ambulance, for experience has shown that this ensures that it will be done. Nothing can be more frustrating for the person who is caring for the casualty than to wait in vain for an ambulance that has not been called, because the person sent to do it gave up when they could not immediately find a telephone. They may think that someone else has already done it by then. It happens all to often. If you send two people then there is more chance that the call will be made. As you wait for medical help, continue to monitor the person, as their condition may change and call for more first aid treatment from you. Their state of unconsciousness may lighten and you will need to reassure them that you have the situation under control. On the other hand it may deepen and they may cease breathing, in which case you will need to consider artificial respiration.

Note five

You may find yourself in the position of being the only person in the vicinity and have no one who you can send to summon help. In this case you may need to consider leaving the person to summon help yourself. Once you have put the person in the recovery position they should be fairly safe for you to leave for a short time. If you can further stabilize them, by placing cushions or something of a similar nature to prevent them rolling onto their back, then so much the better.

Note six

Once you are satisfied that help is on the way, you may have time to enquire as to whether anyone witnessed the course of events that led to the person becoming unconscious. Information of this nature could be invaluable to the doctors who will treat the casualty. Similarly, have a look around to see if there is any physical evidence that could help in the identification of the substances taken. Hand over anything found to the ambulance crew before the casualty is taken away.

SCENARIO FOUR
Self-disclosure of substance use

Note one

This scenario deals with a case in which a person discloses to you that they are using drugs or similar substances. Clearly there may be many reasons why a person will admit their substance use to you. It may be that they have become concerned about what they are doing, they may have been frightened by a bad experience, or feel that they are losing control and need help. It may simply be that they want to sound you out, to gauge your attitude to what they are doing. What ever the reason is, one thing is clear, they have chosen you to talk to, and that puts you in a very important and responsible position. If you respond in the right way you may be able to do a great deal of good. If you respond in the wrong way, you may make the situation worse.

Note two

The first thing that you must do is remain calm. This may depend upon your relationship with the person who has disclosed to you. If your relationship is very personal, then staying calm will not be as simple as it may be if your relationship is on a more professional level.

At this point you will need to consider whether you can keep confidentiality for this person. This will depend upon your relationship with them and the details that they have told you. You will need to make clear to them that you may find it necessary to relate to others what is said to you.

Note three

You must respond to the disclosure in such a way that the person feels able to go further and tell you exactly what they are involved in. You need to ascertain certain information if you are able to. This will include: what substances are they using, in what quantities, for how long and by what method. If you are going to help them to make the right decisions about their substance use, you will need as full a picture of what they are doing as you can.

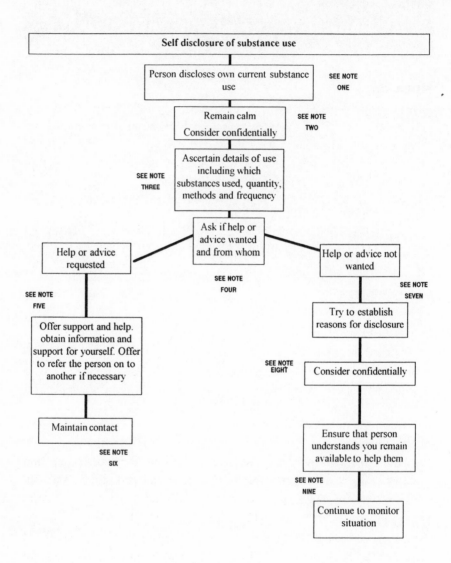

Scenario four

Note four

It may become clear very quickly that the person is seeking your help. You will need to find out exactly what sort of help they are looking for. Is it from you, or are they wanting you to refer them on elsewhere? You will need to gently explore with them the sort of help that might be the best for them (see Chapter 14 for details of treatment options).

Note five

If help is requested, it is vital that you do not try to promise more than you can deliver. It does no harm to say to the person that you are willing to support them but you feel that they need more help than you can provide. There is a whole range of other agencies who can offer confidential help and to which you can refer them.

If you are going to try and provide the help yourself, it is important that you get help and support for yourself before you become too involved. It is very easy to get into a position where you feel that you are out of your depth and failing to provide the help that you had promised.

Note six

If you do refer the person on to another agency it is important that you maintain contact with them if possible. They will greatly appreciate your continuing support, and it may help them to feel that they are not on their own as they try to deal with their problems.

Note seven

It may be that the person maintains that they do not require help, and refuses offers that you make. Now is the time that you need to find out exactly why the disclosure was made in the first place. In many cases disclosures are made to test out the person receiving the disclosure. It may even have been made to shock you or to show off. It could also be that the person does want help but cannot bring themselves to admit it. Careful questioning at this stage may make the reasons for the disclosure more clear.

Note eight

You may need to remind the person of the limits of confidentiality that you are able to offer them.

Note nine

Even if the person refuses all offers of help, it is important that they understand that you remain available, should they change their minds. The way in which you responded to them may lead them to return later to take up your offers of support and help.

SCENARIO FIVE
Third person disclosure

Note one

You are offered information that another person is misusing drugs or some other substance.

Note two

Clearly there will be implications of confidentiality in this situation. Information that is offered on the basis of 'don't tell anyone I told you' is often nothing more than gossip. You may need to make it clear right from the outset that whatever the person tells you may lead to some action on your part, or to you passing the information on to somebody else.

Note three

If the information is passed to you anonymously or is something that you have overheard, then consideration of confidentiality may not be necessary.

Note four

Whatever way the information reaches you it is important that you obtain as much detail as possible. Half a story is of little use. You need greater detail if you are to deal with the information in the best possible way.

Note five

There is a need for you to consider the reason why this information is being offered to you. What are the motives of the informant? They may be entirely genuine. The informant may be worried about what is happening, and want someone to help the person they are telling you about. On the other hand they may be trying to divert attention from themselves and perhaps their own drug use, or maybe they simply wish to cause trouble for the person they are naming. You will need to be satisfied that you are being given good information and not being used in some other way.

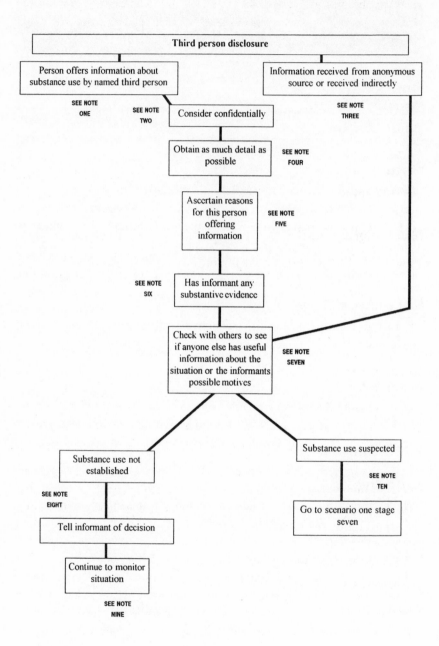

Third person disclosure

Person offers information about substance use by named third person

Information received from anonymous source or received indirectly

SEE NOTE ONE

SEE NOTE TWO

Consider confidentially

SEE NOTE THREE

Obtain as much detail as possible

SEE NOTE FOUR

Ascertain reasons for this person offering information

SEE NOTE FIVE

SEE NOTE SIX

Has informant any substantive evidence

Check with others to see if anyone else has useful information about the situation or the informants possible motives

SEE NOTE SEVEN

Substance use not established

Substance use suspected

SEE NOTE TEN

SEE NOTE EIGHT

Tell informant of decision

Go to scenario one stage seven

Continue to monitor situation

SEE NOTE NINE

Scenario five

Note six

Having obtained as much detail as possible, it would be wise to ask if the informant has any substantive evidence to back up what they are saying. Perhaps they know where the drugs or paraphernalia are kept by the person in question, or have something else that can back up their story.

Note seven

Whatever the level of information and back-up evidence, it is worth checking with others who know either the informant or the person being named, to see if they can add anything to what you have already been told. They may have information that will throw light on the possible motives of the informant or that will support or negate the information given.

Note eight

It may be that, having listened to all that the informant has to say, and gathered what other information is available, you are still not satisfied that this is a case of drug or substance misuse. If this is so, then you will need to tell the informant of your decision in whatever way seems appropriate to your reading of their motives.

Note nine

Even if you are satisfied that drugs are not involved it would be prudent to monitor the situation.

Note ten

If, on the other hand, you are satisfied that drugs or other substances are being misused, then you will need to think carefully about your next step. For more information on what approaches you can make see scenario one, starting at note seven.

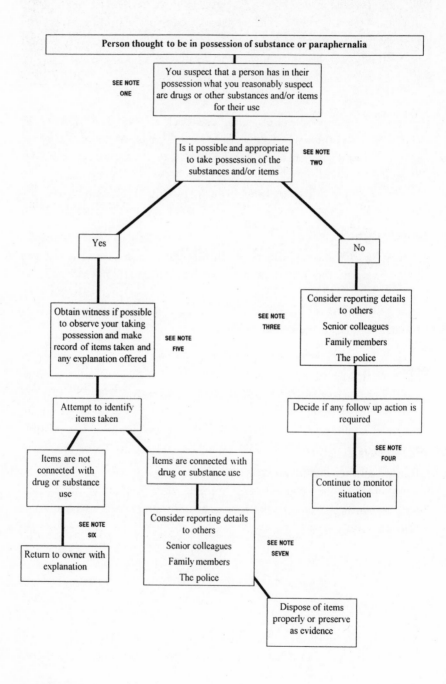

Scenario six

SCENARIO SIX
Person known to be in possession of substance or paraphernalia

Note one

This scenario deals with a situation in which you become aware that a person is in possession of what you have good cause to believe is an illegal drug or some other substance of misuse and/or items that are connected with their use. It may be that you have been given information that has led to this belief, or that you have actually seen the person using or handling something that has aroused your suspicion.

Note two

The first thing that you have to decide is whether it is possible for you to take possession of these items. This very much depends upon your relationship with the person. If that relationship is personal, such as a parent/child relationship, then you may decide that you are going to take possession of the items whether the person agrees or not. If, on the other hand, your relationship is on a more professional level, you will need to decide whether you can persuade the person to hand the items over. You have no right to search the person against their will, but there is nothing to stop you asking them to turn out their pockets or bags. It is often possible to persuade people to do what they would rather not do. This will depend on your confidence and skill.

Note three

If it is not possible to take possession of the items for whatever reason, then you will need to decide on what action you are going to take. You may feel that you have to do something, and it may be that you refer the matter to a higher authority. You can consider telling senior work colleagues and passing the responsibility on to them, or telling members of the person's family, or you can consider informing the police. The police have the power to carry out searches of persons and property, providing you can give them sufficient information to satisfy them that your suspicions are reasonable.

Note four

Depending upon the results of passing the situation on to others, you will need to consider whether there is any further action that you need to take. The situation may be taken out of your hands but, depending on your relationship with the person in question, there may be some follow-up action that you can usefully take. Whatever happens, it will be prudent to continue to monitor the situation.

Note five

If you are able to take possession of the items, it will be well worth obtaining a witness to your action if possible. This may prevent the person making unfounded allegations against you of assault or similar later on. Take note of any explanation that they offer for the items you have taken possession of. They may come clean with you and admit that the items are drugs or drug or substance related. On the other hand they may deny it flatly, leaving you to prove it.

It is worth at this stage covering two important points. Have you the right to take possession of an illegal substance, and how do you do it safely?

You are completely within your rights under common law in the UK to take possession of an illegal substance if you are doing so to prevent the commission of a criminal offence. In this case you are seizing the items to prevent them being possessed by the other person, and you are clearly acting within the law. Having seized the items, you now need to act in such a way that you stay within the law. In order to do so you need to do one of two things as soon as possible. You must either hand the items to the police, or destroy them. Destruction by fire may be appropriate in most cases, or small amounts of powder or tablet drugs can safely be disposed of by flushing them down the toilet. It would be wise to have a witness present at the destruction if possible. What you must not do is put the items away for safe keeping and then do nothing. You will then be in illegal possession of them.

Handling the items correctly is largely a matter of common sense. The following advice is intended to assist you to keep yourself safe and to preserve the evidential value of the items, if it is intended to pass them on to the police.

Drugs in solid, powder, tablet or capsule form

Such things may be found in wrapping or packaging that is either commercially produced or home made from folded paper, cooking foil, clear plastic film and so on. This wrapping should be preserved along with the substance as this could help in its identification.

When opening any suspect wrapper you should take care not to spill any of the contents. If any is spilled it should be carefully gathered up and placed in an envelope, not back into the original wrapping as this could contaminate the remains of the sample.

Great care should be taken to avoid spilling any of the contents on to the skin. Rubber gloves, even the disposal type, will provide adequate protection.

No attempt should be made to identify the substance by sniffing or tasting it. You are not a part of a detective film. This is real life, and such actions can be extremely dangerous.

LSD trips and tabs

The small paper squares that are impregnated with LSD called *trips* or *tabs* are commonly wrapped in clear plastic film to prevent deterioration. If this is the case, do not open the wrapping. If the wrapping is opaque, then open with care and do not touch the contents. It is possible for LSD to be absorbed through your skin if handled for a sufficiently long time. Re-wrap the LSD and dispose of it, or store in a safe place until handed over to the authorities.

Needles and syringes and 'cooking spoons'

These articles can present possible health risks to anyone handling them. If they have been used, then you are open to the risk of infections should the needle pierce your skin. They should be handled with great care and placed in a secure, puncture proof container to await disposal. If a suitable 'sharps' box is not available then a strong metal or plastic box will suffice.

Paraphernalia, bhongs, pipes, tin foil etc.

There are very few health risks if these articles are handled with care. They should be wrapped in clean paper and placed in a large envelope to await disposal.

If it is intended that the items will be handed on to the police, then they should be stored in sealed clean envelopes to await collection. If more than one item has been seized or found in different places, then they should be placed in separate envelopes. Details should be recorded of the circum-stances of each find or seizure.

Anyone who has handled an item that is suspected of being involved in drug use is advised to wash their hands thoroughly as soon as possible afterwards.

Note six

Having taken possession of the items it may become clear to you that they are not connected with drug or substance use. If this is the case then their is little you can do but return them to their owner with an explanation as to your actions.

Note seven

If, on the other hand, you are convinced that the items are connected with drug or substance use, then you have to decide what action you are going to take next. You may consider that you can deal with the incident yourself, in which case you should dispose of the items as detailed in note five. You may feel that the matter should be referred on to some higher authority than yourself, or to the police. If this is the case then you should preserve the items as evidence as detailed in note five.

SCENARIO SEVEN
Discovery of substance and/or paraphernalia

Note one

This scenario deals with the finding of drugs or other substances of misuse or the paraphernalia of their use. They could be found concealed, or simply abandoned.

Note two

In cases such as this, it is always worth making general enquiries to ascertain if anyone has any information that can give you a clearer picture of how the items got to be where you found them.

Note three

You are about to take into your possession something that could be an illegal drug (see note five, scenario six for rights to take possession of drugs). It would be as well to obtain a witness to your actions if at all possible. Having a good witness may well prevent anyone making allegations of wrong doing later.

Note four

Before you remove the items, give some consideration as to your own health and safety and the need to preserve the evidential value of the items, should you intend to involve the police. If the items are in a reasonably secure place, and you intend to refer the matter to the police, it would be best to leave them where they are, not to touch them or allow anyone else to do so, and call the police as soon as possible. If you intend to deal with the matter yourself, or wish first to consider your possible courses of action, it will be necessary for you to remove the items to a secure place. Take all necessary precautions for safety as detailed in note five, scenario six of this chapter.

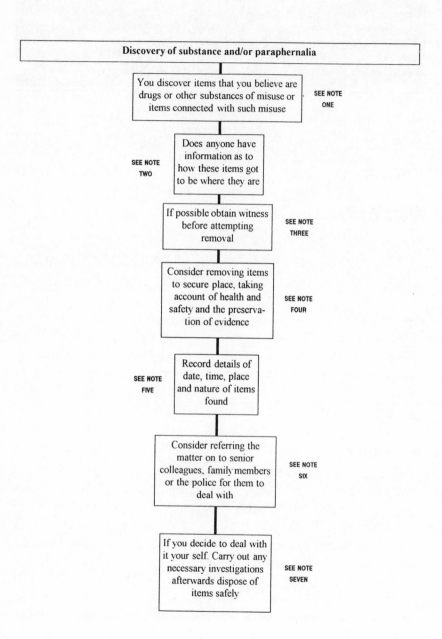

Discovery of substance and/or paraphernalia

You discover items that you believe are drugs or other substances of misuse or items connected with such misuse — **SEE NOTE ONE**

SEE NOTE TWO — Does anyone have information as to how these items got to be where they are

If possible obtain witness before attempting removal — **SEE NOTE THREE**

Consider removing items to secure place, taking account of health and safety and the preservation of evidence — **SEE NOTE FOUR**

SEE NOTE FIVE — Record details of date, time, place and nature of items found

Consider referring the matter on to senior colleagues, family members or the police for them to deal with — **SEE NOTE SIX**

If you decide to deal with it your self. Carry out any necessary investigations afterwards dispose of items safely — **SEE NOTE SEVEN**

Scenario seven

Note five

Having removed the items to a secure place make a record of the incident, including a description of what was found, location, time, witnesses etc.

Note six

Once the items are secure, you have to decide what to do next. In most cases you should consider referring the matter on to a higher authority for them to decide on what course of action to follow.

This higher authority could be senior colleagues, family members or the police.

Note seven

It may be that you intend to deal with the matter yourself. If this is the case then you will need to make as many enquiries as you can to establish the source of the items. The discovery of the items may be connected with enquiries that you are already involved in, and it may be possible to identify the person or persons responsible for them. If that is the case then you should refer to scenario one, starting at note seven, before approaching the person concerned.

CHAPTER 14

Common Reasons for Drug and Substance Misuse and Treatment Options

Common reasons for drug and substance misuse

There are almost as many reasons for using drugs as there are users, but many reoccur with great regularity. Dependent on what is being used, drugs can change or lift your mood, increase your energy levels, change your perspective, aid sleep, help you relax, remove emotional or physical pain, reduce your appetite and weight, lower inhibitions and increase libido, or give you feelings of great physical and mental prowess. Drugs can also be used in order to change your image, provide entry into certain groups, to rebel, or just to fill time and relieve boredom.

Substances may be used to mask a person's problems, but will only succeed temporarily. They are a short-term solution only, as they do not remove or resolve difficulties, but just change the user's perception of the immediate circumstances.

It is possible that some who use substances do so simply because of their availability, or for social reasons, and there may be no discernible underlying problems. Many however do have problems that even they themselves may be unaware of, and some are simply self-medicating these problems away. Problems may be of a complex and deep psychological nature, caused by earlier life traumas, for example abuse or bereavement, or they may be much simpler in nature such as, boredom or low self-esteem.

By using drugs to relieve these problems, the user can unwittingly be putting themselves into situations that actually increase and exacerbate them, for regular use may lead to other health, legal and social difficulties.

To keep things in perspective, most people will not use substances at all. Many who start out using drugs or other substances do so for only a short period in their lives, and of those, only a small percentage will go on to develop any medium or long-term problems as a direct result. But these users can cause damage to society well out of proportion to their numbers.

In a survey of tertiary college students, which we carried out in our local area, participants were asked to list all of the reasons that they were aware of as to why they or their peers had ever used drugs.

One surprising result came from a young man, who stated that almost every aspect of his life was controlled or manipulated by adults, and that he used drugs because it was one of the few areas of his life over which he felt he had complete control. So his stated reason for his own use of drugs were his feelings of powerlessness over his own actions and decisions.

The combined list of the students' responses is reproduced here.

- addiction
- to rebel
- attention seeking
- relieve boredom
- due to ignorance
- remove worries
- because they are available
- to look good
- because of insecurity
- to give confidence
- to relieve depression
- to escape reality
- to get high
- to be happy
- when drunk
- to self-medicate
- to lose weight
- to gain weight
- to make your hair grow
- because they are illegal
- to stay awake
- to increase strength and stamina
- to increase intelligence
- for experimentation
- enjoyment of experience
- out of curiosity
- out of choice
- to relieve stress
- to relax
- to get in the mood
- to get in with the right crowd
- peer pressure
- recommended by friends
- for nostalgia
- to relieve insomnia
- for research
- to commit suicide
- to cause trouble
- to remove inhibitions
- by mistake
- as a joke
- to forget
- for the experience
- because everyone does
- for fun
- for danger and excitement

- to change character and image
- culture and religion
- to increase self-esteem
- for enjoyment
- for convenience
- to be sociable
- for sexual purposes
- to expand horizons
- to relieve pain
- to mask illness
- for stimulation
- for inspiration
- to impress
- to remain alert
- as a reward
- for a dare
- to cope
- to increase performance
- to celebrate
- out of desperation
- because they are cheap
- instability
- a quick fix for problems
- because they are prescribed
- giving in to temptation
- why not?

Treatment options for people with drug problems

For some people, their use of drugs or other substances may not, in their eyes at least, constitute a problem. They may be using only recreationally, to be sociable, be easily able to afford what they use, may not be habituated either physically or psychologically, and not be suffering from any side effects or withdrawal symptoms. Indeed they may appear to have the entire situation under control, and for them it may remain this way. Certainly the majority of users start out like this. But situations have a tendency towards change after a time, and for many it may turn out to be quite a different story. Substance use for them may have reached a point where it is adversely affecting their physical and mental health, their finances, employment, relationships, education, their legal position and even accommodation. Also affected of course, will be many of the people around them, partners, family, friends, and the victims of any drug related crimes with which the users might be involved in order to fund their habits.

Even at this advanced stage, many users will still choose not to see their substance use as a problem, and may simply transfer any problem back onto others who may be affected, or who are showing concern, insisting that they are making something out of nothing. Even further along this road, the user may reach a point where, despite their wish to ignore the facts, there is no alternative but to admit to having a problem for which they may require help, support and understanding.

Depending on the degree and length of time of their usage, the particular drug or drugs being used, and any other life problems faced by the user, there are a range of services generally available in most countries for users and others who are also involved or affected in some way. However good these services are, they can only succeed in helping if the user is willing to co-operate and be totally honest with themselves and others.

If recognized at an early enough stage, some may well respond to simple interventions such as being spoken to by a parent, friend or partner who shows care and concern for them. Others may respond better after being spoken to by their Doctor, a social worker, teacher, police officer or some other authority figure who is respected by them.

But there will be those who require more than just a good talking or listening to. This is particularly true in cases where substance misuse is carried out in order to mask other problems in the user's life, whether consciously or not. The fear of having to cope without using substances as a psychological prop can be too great to contemplate.

Local Drug Services

Most major towns and cities will have drug and substance misuse services in them. These may be statutory or voluntary in nature, will be staffed or supported by trained personnel and offer a range of services to users and others alike. Many have trained counsellors, therapists and medical staff, any of whom may be assigned as key worker to the user, after an initial assessment interview to determine their needs. Counselling may be offered on a one-to-one basis or in groups and, in some cases, proves to be all that is needed to overcome the user's problems and help them to become substance free. Relapse prevention counselling may then follow to ensure that they remain substance free. Some agencies may even offer alternatives to counselling, such as acupuncture, stress management and relaxation classes, or even sport and exercise sessions.

Detoxification

Further help may be required in the form of prescribed medicines to help them cope with the possible withdrawal symptoms, or as a substitute for the original drug of choice. This may then be gradually reduced, over an agreed period of time, so that they are eventually able to become totally substance free.

This detoxification process, of clearing drugs from the user's system, and allowing the body to adjust accordingly, may be achieved quite quickly, especially if the user is committed to becoming 'clean'. This commitment may be due to the influence of other people, the desire to remain in a job, for travel or legal purposes, or even because of pregnancy or illness. The process however may take much much longer for others, and may never be totally achieved at all. This could be as result of relapse or panic as the end of the course of medication gets closer.

Detoxification can take place at home if necessary, especially where support is given by the user's family and friends, or where it would be impracticable for it to take place elsewhere, as in the case of a parent who is unable to leave their children. Many drug services will support this kind of venture, making frequent home visits to the user and enabling them to remain in the familiarity and safety of their own surroundings.

Other services will require the user to enter specialized residential detoxification units, sometimes located within psychiatric hospitals, for which they may first need to be referred by their Doctor.

If committed to prison, some users will have to detox against their will, and the regime may be unsympathetic, with the reducing period being rather short and painful with little back up or support. Happily this situation is becoming less common, as many prisons are now changing for the better with regard to making their new inmates drug and substance free.

If they are to work well, detoxification programmes have to be carefully planned. The pros and cons need to be discussed at length and questions such as 'why now?', 'is this the best time?', 'have I enough support services?' and 'what happens afterwards?' will have to be addressed. If, during this process, some of the user's other life problems, which may well have led to their substance misuse in the first place, are not dealt with, then they may simply be setting themselves up to fail. Such a failure will inevitably lead to the user going straight back to their usual way of coping, by using substances.

Similarly, large lifestyle changes may have to be considered. Changing one's circle of friends or even moving house may be thought of as necessary by some, in order to keep clear of familiar people, places and circumstances, any of which may trigger off thoughts of former drug use and lead again to a new bout of craving. It is therefore clear that detoxification is best carried out with professional and medical help in order for it to have a chance of success, although some brave souls have managed it on their own.

Rehabs

Residential rehabilitation facilities, known as 'rehabs', exist for users who seriously want to get away from substance misuse, and get their lives back together. But this option is time consuming, usually expensive and in great demand. There are four main types of rehabs, each with their own regime or working methods.

The first that we shall consider is the 'General Rehab' which acts rather like a small community. Its residents may well be able to decide on their own communal needs and rules, and counselling is carried out both individually and in group sessions. The average length of stay in this type of establishment is between six and eight months.

The second type of rehab is the Christian-based establishment which normally offers one-to-one counselling only, rather than group work. Residents here may be expected to adopt a Christian outlook in order to help them overcome their drug problems. This may involve regular bible study groups, prayer sessions and religious services. This may therefore be unacceptable to some users. Average length of stay in such establishments may be anything up to a year.

The third type of rehab, known as 'Concept Rehabs', are highly structured establishments where the residents time is filled to capacity. Therapeutic sessions here are both intense and somewhat confrontational, allowing users to get in touch with and express their feelings openly. Users' self-image and lifestyle may also be taken to pieces systematically in order to then rebuild them in a more acceptable way. As this way of working can prove to be too much for some residents, the drop out rate can be quite high, wasting precious resources. Average length of stay, for those who last the course, is between nine and eighteen months.

The last type of rehab utilizes something called the 'Minnesota Method' a programme based on the twelve steps to sobriety used by Alcoholics Anonymous. Substance misuse is considered by advocates of the Minnesota method to be a life long illness that requires constant counselling to avoid relapse. Residents' days here are very long and organized, with an individual's progress measured and assessed by both peers and rehab workers alike. The average length of stay at this type of establishment is quite short, being perhaps only between six and eight weeks. However, half way houses run by the rehab may then offer ongoing placement to former rehab residents, for anything up to a further twelve months. During this time they are offered further support before being totally integrated back into everyday society, where they must then fend for themselves.

Rehab is not for the faint hearted, and the different regimes must be studied carefully before the correct choice can be made. As residential establishments, they may well be situated far from the user's familiar haunts. This may be considered as an advantage by some who may want to get away from their previous lives. Others, however, may not wish to be so far from home due to commitments such as children, family or friends who they do not wish to leave too far behind.

Funding for referrals to rehab establishments is usually in the control of the local authority from their Community Care budgets, and therefore restrictions may be placed upon them at times of high demand. In some cases, dependent upon the financial circumstances of the user or their families, users could be asked to contribute towards the costs of their treatment.

Before being accepted to any rehab, all potential residents will first be assessed as to their suitability, and then interviewed to ensure that they have the right level of commitment. Similarly, it will be decided whether the particular rehab can meet their needs. These procedures, together with the issue of securing adequate funding, mean that there may be substantial delays between the user deciding to go to a rehab and them actually being admitted.

There are fewer rehabs catering specifically for women in the country than there are for men, possibly reflecting the greater use of drug and other substances by men than by women. There are even fewer establishments that can cater for pregnant women or women with dependent children.

Finally, it is worth stating that residential rehabilitation is not always totally successful. This may be because of many factors, not least the determination and co-operation of the users, and the degree of support available to them once they leave. Some may have to make several attempts before they can say that they have totally conquered their drug habits and dealt with the reasons that led to them being there in the first instance.

Prescribing

Amongst the substance using population, there is a percentage for whom drug taking has become simply a way of life, and one which they do not really have any wish to change.

Financial or medical considerations, or perhaps the threat of a gaol sentence, may for some of them be the only reason that they ever seek out agencies who can offer a prescribing service. A good number of users who are addicted to illegal heroin will be looking to obtain a daily maintenance dosage of legal methadone, a man-made opiate, as a substitute for their drug of choice. Others may be trying to obtain daily prescriptions for dexamphetamine to substitute for their use of street amphetamine. These two forms of medication have to be taken orally, usually on a daily basis. The amount prescribed is calculated by a doctor who equates it to match their current use of street drugs. Urine samples may be taken at this time in order to confirm that the user is actually using the substance that they claim to be.

In these days of HIV infection, these two forms of medication are especially useful, for much heroin and amphetamine is injected, and a daily dose of oral medication may well make this practice unnecessary. Prescribed drugs, unlike their street counterparts, are of a known strength and purity, and their effects may well last for much longer. For example, street heroin may produce an effect for the user that lasts six hours or so, whereas the corresponding dose of methadone may last for more than twenty-four hours, thus preventing the onset of withdrawal symptoms.

For many users, prescribed drugs are preferable and may keep at bay various medical, legal and social problems that otherwise may adversely affect their lives. Prescribing obviates the need for the criminal activities usually necessary to fund a drugs habit, and reduces the amount of physical and mental harm that can be caused by the use, especially intravenously, of street drugs.

Once a prescription is secured, the user will generally be in contact with a voluntary or statutory drugs worker, who in time may well be able to persuade them to consider changing their lifestyle for the better.

For those heroin users who would prefer to carry on injecting, perhaps due to a 'needle fixation' where they derive pleasure from the use of the needle itself, some services actually offer injectable forms of a synthetic opiate, called physeptone, as a substitute.

Cocaine, ecstasy and users of the hallucinogenic drug LSD are not so easily catered for, as there are no medical alternatives to them. Control of withdrawal symptoms and other side effects by using drugs such as tranquilizers, pain killers or sleeping pills, may be necessary in these cases. But because many tranquillizers, pain killers and sleeping pills can themselves lead to addiction problems, they are very carefully prescribed and their use monitored. In cases where users present with an addiction to these types of drug, alternatives can be offered, usually on a reducing basis, in order to break the dependence.

Needle and syringe schemes

For many years now we have been pro-active in the UK with regard to the prevention of HIV transmission within intravenous drug using populations, through the provision of needle and syringe schemes. The government's Advisory Committee on the Misuse of Drugs believed that HIV infection could prove to be a far more devastating problem for society than drug use itself could ever be, and this statement led to the setting up of a number of needle and syringe exchange schemes across the country. The schemes provide injecting users with free, clean injecting equipment such as needles, syringes, medical swabs, filters and safe disposal facilities, in order to greatly reduce or stem HIV transmission within the injecting population, and thus prevent wider transmission into the general population via sexual means.

The schemes reduce or remove the need to share or reuse dirty or contaminated injecting equipment, that may well contain HIV or one of the hepatitis viruses, if the original user was so infected.

In no way were the schemes intended to condone the injecting of drugs, but to simply be a means of safeguarding public health. At the same time they are saving much public money, money which the health service can ill afford to lose, for the low cost of needle and syringe provision to users is minimal compared with the cost of treating the many more cases of HIV, AIDS or viral hepatitis that would result if such schemes were withdrawn.

Needle and syringe schemes also provide a means of contacting those injecting users who would not normally access health-based services, including many nowadays who inject steroids in order to reshape their bodies.

As with local drug services, most areas of the country are covered by needle and syringe provision schemes that exist to facilitate easy collection and disposal of equipment, from pharmacies, surgeries, mobile and static drug services and other outlets.

For details of all the available services in your locality, it is only necessary to contact directory enquiries or look in the telephone book to obtain all of the information that you require. You may also get details from local doctors and hospitals, chemists, the police, social services, citizens advise bureaux or your local community health council (see Appendix 1).

CHAPTER 15

The Language of Drug and Substance Abuse

Slang abounds in drug using circles just as it does in any other exclusive area of society, and its purpose is just the same as anywhere else. The use of slang in the correct context can send to the listener important messages about the person speaking to them.

It may, for instance, give the speaker immediate credibility, inferring that they are familiar with and knowledgeable about the subject matter, that they are neither a spy in the camp nor a time waster. Their status then may rise further as the listener gains a degree of confidence and re-assurance from what he or she is hearing, being able to deduce from the information given, whether they are listening perhaps, to a seasoned or relatively new user of substances, a dealer, or simply a genuine customer looking for a supplier.

This process must obviously be able to work both ways before any real degree of trust can be built up and the conversation allowed to continue. Therefore if the correct and acceptable responses are forthcoming, the original speaker will also learn much about their conversation partner, and if they are not satisfied, then the conversation will be brought to an abrupt halt.

More important, the use of slang gives users the ability to exclude the uninitiated, non drug taking majority, keeping them ignorant of the true nature of conversations going on around them, whilst allowing those involved to get on with their dealings unhindered and without arousing any suspicion.

There are thousands of slang words in common usage around the various drug scenes today. Some may well be restricted to particular areas of the country or to particular types of user, whilst others are universally understood and accepted. New words appear from time to time, perhaps to introduce or advertise new substances, or to give old ones a new image. New paraphernalia also appears and will be given a new slang name.

The terminology currently in use is of a varied nature, some pieces of slang being quite obvious as to their origins, whilst others are more obscure. Slang can convey all of the aspects of drug and substance misuse, and may be indicative of colour, effect, place or country of manufacture, size, appearance, shape, weight, design, chemical composition, method of use, paraphernalia of use, trade name, quality or purity, associated danger, cost, historical usage or even be based simply on rhyming slang.

Examples of the above include:

Colour – Rhubarb and Custard (ecstasy – red and yellow)

Effect – Speed or Whiz (amphetamine)

Place of origin – Packi Baccy (Pakistani cannabis)

Size – Microdots (small pills of LSD)

Shape – Yellow Eggs, Rugby Balls (Temazepam capsules)

Weight – Louis (16th of an ounce), Henry (8th of an ounce)

Design – Doves (ecstasy tablet with dove imprint), Strawberry Fields (LSD 'tab' with Strawberry pictured upon it)

Chemical make up – Acid (LSD), Special K (ketamine)

Method of use – Puff, Blow, Draw (cannabis for smoking)

Paraphernalia – Spike (hypodermic needle), Barrel (syringe)

Trade names – Chewies (Tuinal), Moggies (Mogadon)

Quality or purity – Shit (poor quality heroin), Snideys (fake drug)

Associated danger – M25s (ecstasy)

Cost – Champagne (cocaine)

Historical – Hash or Hashish (cannabis – from Haschishin, a 19th century group of assassins who made use of the drug)

Rhyming slang – Bob Hope (dope – cannabis)

Slang terms may come and go. For instance, not many years ago *reefer* was the accepted term for a cannabis cigarette but this has long since been replaced by the terms *joint* or *spliff.*

It can therefore be quite difficult for the non user to fully understand how to use drug slang correctly, and it is therefore better to use it only if you are totally sure of the meaning, pronunciation, and the correct context in which it should be used. If not, then it is better to stick to known technical descriptions or commonly accepted terms to avoid losing face when dealing with users.

A list of the more common drug slang currently in use follows, to help you to understand this 'language'.

Word	Meaning
Acid	LSD
Acid head	LSD user
Adam & Eve	Ecstasy
Afghan black	Cannabis resin
Amp	Ampoule of drugs in liquid form
Amytal	Barbiturates
Artillery	Injecting equipment
Backtracking	To draw blood back into the syringe
Bad boy biscuit	Brown Ecstasy tablet similar to 'disco biscuit' but twice as large
Bad boy burger	Brown Ecstasy tablet similar to 'disco burger' but twice as large
Bad trip	A frightening or unpleasant LSD trip
Bag	A small quantity of drugs, usually powder drugs
Banging up	To inject drugs
Barrel	Ecstasy tablet or syringe for injecting
Batman	LSD 'tab' design showing Batman
Bennies	Benzedrine tablets
Bhang	Herbal cannabis
Bhong	Home made water pipe for smoking cannabis
Billy	Amphetamine
Billy whiz	Amphetamine
Bindle	A number of packages of drugs fastened together
Biscuits	A pale brown, rather coarse, grained ecstasy tablet
Black	Cannabis resin
Black knights	LSD 'tab' design showing a knight design
Blotters	LSD paper squares

Blousing	Sniffing solvents from a plastic bag
Blow	Herbal cannabis
Blue star	An LSD 'tab' design showing a blue star
Blue velvet	A mixture of amphetamine and heroin
Bolivian marching powder	Cocaine
Bombs	Small quantity of drugs wrapped in a cigarette paper for swallowing
Boot	A 'hit' of heroin
Bottling or **Hot bottling**	A version of hot knifing where a bottle with no bottom is used to concentrate the smoke
Brown	Heroin
Buddha	An LSD 'tab' design showing the Buddha
Buds	The flower tops of the female cannabis plant, added to tobacco to produce a high strength mixture.
Burger	A large brown ecstasy tablet
Bush	Herbal cannabis
Business	Injecting equipment
Busted	Searched (either a person or a house) or being arrested
Buzz	Amphetamine
Buzzing	Feelings after use of ecstasy
Champagne	Cocaine
Charlie	Cocaine
Chasing	Inhaling the fumes of burning heroin
Chasing the dragon	Smoking heroin on a piece of foil
Chewies	Tuinal tablets
Chi	Chinese heroin
Chill out	A period of cooling yourself down after overheating from ecstasy use

Chill room   A room provided at a rave o club for cooling down after ecstasy use

Chillum   Clay, glass or wooden pipe for smoking cannabis

China white   Heroin, particularly a synthetic form found in US known as fentanyl

City   Blue and white ecstasy capsules

Clean   Not using drugs

Clear caps   Colourless Ecstasy capsules

Cocktail   A mixture of drugs, often taken experimentally

Cog   Can of Liquid Petroleum Gas

Coke   Cocaine

Cold turkey   Withdrawing from drugs, particularly heroin, without medical help

Colombian   Cannabis resin

Come down   Withdrawing from the effects of drugs

Connection   A drug supplier

Cook up   To prepare a drug for injection

Crack   Freebase cocaine

Crack Baby   Baby born with an addiction to crack cocaine because of crack use by its mother during pregnancy

Crack head   User of crack cocaine

Crash   Coming down from amphetamine

Crystal splitter   A very strong ecstasy tablet with a crystalline coating

Cut   To mix other substances with a drug to add bulk and weight

Dabbing   Picking up a drug on a wet finger and licking it off

Deal   To sell drugs

Dealer   Supplier of drugs

Deck	A small package of drugs
Dennis the Menace	A red and black ecstasy capsule
Detox	To withdraw from drugs under medical supervision
Dex	Dexedrine
Dexies	Dexedrine, a form of amphetamine
DF 118s	Opiate pain killer in tablet form
DFs	DF118s an opiate pain killer in tablet form
Diesel	Cannabis oil
Dike	Diconal, a synthetic heroin
Disco biscuits	A brown, course grained, ecstasy tablet
Disco burgers	A brown, coarse grained, ecstasy tablet
Dollar white	Ecstasy tablet showing $ imprint
Doofs	Opiate pain killers in tablet form
Dope	Resin and herbal cannabis
Dopehead	Dealer who also uses drugs and deals to finance a habit
Dots	LSD in the form of small pills or tablets
Double Bart/Double Dutch Bart	A large LSD 'tab' design showing the cartoon character Bart Simpson
Double dove	An Ecstasy tablet showing imprint of dove which is double strength
Doves	Ecstasy tablets with dove imprint
Draw	Cannabis
Draw up	To load a syringe
Drop	Taking a drug by mouth
Drought	A local shortage of drugs
'E'	Ecstasy
Eggs	Temazepam capsules
Eighth	An eighth of an ounce of cannabis
Engine	A bhong for smoking cannabis

English	Pure medical heroin
Eve	Ecstasy
Five skinner	A cannabis cigarette made from five papers
Fix	An injection of drugs
Flashback	Tripping out again some time after LSD use. Can be days, months or even years later. Usually a bad trip.
Flintstones	LSD tab design showing the cartoon characters
Flushing	Drawing blood in and out of the syringe
Fold	A paper packaging for drugs
Freebase	Freebase cocaine
Galliano	A water pipe for smoking cannabis
Ganga	Cannabis
Ganja	Herbal cannabis
Gas	Liquid petroleum gas used for sniffing
Gasman/Gasboy	Liquid Petroleum Gas user
GBH	Gamma hydroxybutyrate or Sodium Oxybate, a liquid hallucinogenic stimulant
Gear	Any illegal drug, but most commonly heroin
GHB	Gamma hydroxybutyrate or Sodium Oxybate
Gorbies	LSD tab design showing the face of Mikhial Gorbachev
Gouching	Falling asleep while very stoned
Grass	Herbal cannabis
Gun	Hypodermic syringe
'H'	Heroin
Habit	An addiction
Half a barrel	An ecstasy tablet cut in half
Harry	Heroin
Hash	Cannabis resin
Hashcake	Cake containing cannabis

Hashish	Cannabis resin
Hash oil	Cannabis oil
Hay	Herbal cannabis
Head rush	Sensation of injected drugs reaching the brain or sometimes loss of sensation or mini black out lasting a few seconds while dancing
Hemp	Herbal cannabis
Henry	An 1/8th ounce of cannabis (Henry the 8th)
Herb	Herbal cannabis
High	The feeling of being up while under influence of drug
Hit	To buy or to inject drugs
Home grown	Herbal cannabis, grown in the UK
Honey	Cannabis oil
Hookah	Water pipe for smoking cannabis
Hooked	Addicted
Horse	Heroin
Hot knifing	Smoking a drug by touching it with a heated knife blade and inhaling the resultant smoke
Hubble bubble	Water pipe for smoking cannabis
Indian hemp	Cannabis
Indians	White ecstasy tablet showing peace pipe or totem pole imprint
Indica	A variety of cannabis plant, grown mostly in countries away from the tropics, but with warm climates. It needs less light than sativa but grows more slowly
Iranian	Heroin
Jack up	To inject drugs
Jellies	Temazepam in capsule form
Joint	A hand rolled cannabis cigarette

Joker	A type of cannabis joint, using five papers arranged and cut into a large triangle shape to produce a cone shaped joint
Junk	Heroin
Junkie	Drug user
'K'	Ketamine
Karma	The state of being high on drugs
Khat	Leafs of the plant Catha Edulis a mild stimulant that is chewed in some African cultures
Kicking	To stop taking drugs
Kit e kat	Ketamine
Kulfi	Sweets containing cannabis. Very rare in UK
Leaf	Cocaine
Lebanese	Cannabis resin
Liberty cap	A species of hallucinogenic mushroom
Lid poppers	Amphetamine
Lines	Narrow lines of cocaine arranged for snorting
Liquid ecstasy	Gamma Hydroxybutyrate or Sodium Oxybate
Liquid gold	Amyl and Butyl Nitrite
Locker room	Amyl and Butyl Nitrite
Lose it	To become detached from reality through drug use
Losing the plot	Becoming disorientated after repeated or long term drug use
Louis	A 1/16th ounce of cannabis (Louis the 16th)
Love dove	Ecstasy tablet with dove imprint
Lung	A device for smoking cannabis using a small bottle and a plastic bag
M25	Ecstasy
Magic mushrooms	Any of the species of hallucinogenic mushrooms

Main lining	Injecting drugs
Marijuana	Herbal cannabis
Mary Jane	Herbal cannabis
Mesc	Mescaline
Meth	Methamphetamine or methadone
Micro dots	LSD in the form of small pills or tablets
Microfines	1ml syringes with a very fine needle
Micro's	LSD in the form of small pills or tablets
Mikes	Microfine syringes
M&Ms	Ecstasy in various colours with hard shiny coating
Moggies	Mogadon sleeping pills
Monged out	Being heavily under the influence of drugs, usually cannabis
Moroccan	Cannabis resin
Moroccan gold	Cannabis resin
Mouth organ (playing the)	Using a match box to collect the smoke of burning drugs and direct it into the mouth
Mule	A person who smuggles drugs into a country for a third party
Munchies	An eating binge whilst on cannabis
Mushies	Hallucinogenic mushrooms
Nederweed	A hybrid cannabis variety grown in northern climates with a high THC level.
Needle fixation	Obsession with needle and syringe use
New Yorkers	Ecstasy tablets
Oil	Cannabis oil
Om	LSD tab design showing Hindu word Om. A mystic word regarded as summing up all truth
Packi black	Cannabis resin
Phy-amps	Methadone in ampoules (physeptone)

Pink panther	An LSD 'tab' design showing the cartoon character The Pink Panther
Playboys	Ecstasy tablet with rabbit imprint
Poppers	Amyl/Alkyl/Butyl nitrite
Pot	Cannabis resin
Pot head	Cannabis user
Puff	Herbal cannabis
Purple om	LSD tab design showing the Hindu word Om in purple
Push	To encourage others to use drugs
Quarter	A quarter ounce of cannabis
Red & blacks	Red and black ecstasy capsules
Red leb	Cannabis resin
Red seal	Cannabis resin
Resin	Cannabis resin
Rhubarb and custard	A red and yellow ecstasy capsule
Rizla	A brand of cigarette rolling paper. Common brand used for rolling cannabis cigarettes. Also available in king size
Roach	A cardboard tube inserted in the mouth end of a cannabis cigarette, often made from a piece of the cigarette paper packet
Roasting	Heating resin cannabis to make it easier to crumble
Rock	Freebase cocaine
Rocky	Cannabis resin
Roid Rage	Aggression following steroid use
Ruderalis	A variety of cannabis plant, grown mostly in European countries. Needs only low light levels and will tolerate cool climates. Produces low levels of THC
Rugby balls	Temazepam capsules

Runner	A person who acts as a go between between the user and the supplier
Rush	A rapid onset of the drug effect
Saddam Hussein	An LSD 'tab' design showing the face of Saddam Hussein
Sativa	Herbal cannabis
Scag	Heroin
Scat	Heroin
Score	To purchase drugs
Script	Prescription for drugs given as an alternative to illegal drug use or for the management or treatment of withdrawal symptoms
Sense	Sinsemilla. The flower of the cannabis plant
Sensi	Sinsemilla. The flower of the cannabis plant
Set	The state of mind of the user prior to taking their drugs
Shit	Cannabis resin or heroin
Shoot up	To inject drugs
Shrooms	Hallucinogenic mushrooms
Silver dollar	LSD 'tab' design with $ emblem
Sinsemilla	The flower of the cannabis plant. High THC content. High cost
Sitting duck	Ecstasy tablet
Skag	Heroin
Skagging	Smoking heroin on a piece of foil
Skin	Paper used for making cannabis cigarettes
Skinning up	Making a cannabis cigarette
Skin popping	Injecting subcutaneously
Skunk/Skunk weed	Herbal cannabis
Slate	Cannabis resin
Smack	Heroin
Smiley	LSD 'tab' design showing the smiley face

Smiley blue eyes	An LSD 'tab' design showing the smiley face but with blue eyes
Snidey	Substances sold falsely as a particular drug
Sniffer	Solvent abuser
Snorting	Sniffing cocaine or other drug up the nose
Snow	Cocaine
Snowball	Heroin mixed with cocaine
Spacey	Feeling calm whilst under influence of drugs
Sparking up	Lighting a cannabis joint
Special K	Ketamine
Speckled dove	A speckled ecstasy tablet with dove imprint
Speed	Amphetamine
Speedball	Heroin/cocaine mix
Speed freak	User of amphetamine
Spike	Hypodermic needle
Spliff/Splith	Hand rolled cannabis cigarette
Splitters	Various forms of very powerful ecstasy tablets
Spotting	Smoking cannabis without using tobacco by burning small quantities on the end of a pin and inhaling smoke
Stacking	Combining the shorter acting oral steroids with longer acting injectable steroids
Stag	Amyl and butyl nitrite
Stash	An amount of drugs, usually hidden
Strawberry	Ecstasy or an LSD 'tab' design showing strawberries
Strung out	Coming down from drugs
Sucking	Inhaling LPG gas or aerosols
Sulphate	Amphetamine
Swab	An alcohol pad used to clean skin prior to injecting

Swallower	A person who carries drugs through customs in condoms that have been swallowed
Tabs	LSD paper squares
Teenth	16th oz of cannabis
Temazies	Temazepam capsules
Ten pound bag	A deal of heroin costing ten pounds, approx. 1 / 8th of a gram
Thai sticks	Herbal cannabis wound around a stick and secured with thread
THC	Tetrahydrocannabinol, the active ingredient of cannabis
Three skinner	A cannabis cigarette made from three papers
Toke	A puff of cannabis, usually from someone else's joint
Toke can	A home made smoking pipe made from a drinks can
Track marks	Injection scars
Trip	A hallucinogenic experience under LSD
Trips	LSD paper squares
United	Red and white ecstasy capsules
Vitamin K	Ketamine
Wacky bacci	Herbal cannabis
Wash	Crack cocaine
Washing	Using amphetamine by rubbing it into the gums or on to the teeth
Weed	Herbal cannabis
Weight	A substantial quantity of a drug
White	Cocaine or heroin
White callys	White ecstasy tablets
White dove	LSD 'tab' design showing a white dove
White robin	Ecstasy tablet with bird imprint
White stuff	Morphine

Whiz	Amphetamine
Whiz bombs	Ecstasy tablets or amphetamine wrapped in a cigarette paper
Windows	LSD gelatine squares approx. 5mm x 5mm
Wired up	Being tense as a result of drug use
Works	Syringes and needles
Wrap	5 cm square of paper folded to hold drugs
Yellow callies	Yellow ecstasy tablets
Yellow eggs	Temazepam
Zoom	A mixture of cocaine, heroin and amphetamine, sniffed or injected

CHAPTER 16
The Legalization Debate

Increasingly in recent times, the question of whether certain drugs should be legalized or not has raised its head. Currently it is cannabis that is the subject of much debate. This debate is largely being led by those who would wish to see a change in the present law. This would include current and prospective users, those who stand to make profits from the sale of the drug, and those who feel that it is a question of freedom of choice.

We, the authors, have been engaged in considering this question in great detail over a number of years, yet despite the many arguments put to us in favour of legalization, we are still firmly of the opinion that a change in the current legal position of cannabis would be a grave, highly damaging and irretrievable blunder, for which future generations would not thank us.

Our work has brought us into contact with many admitted users of the drug and countless others who believe that cannabis is an innocuous, natural and indeed beneficial substance. Yet despite the arguments and opinions put forward, we have heard nothing to date that convinces us that we should change our stance.

Many of you will also become involved in discussions of this issue, and you will need to be fully aware of all aspects of the debate, in order that you may be able to participate fully and come to your own informed decisions.

To assist you in this, it is the purpose of this chapter to set out those arguments which are commonly put forward by those in favour of legalization, and to follow this with counter arguments that are based on our knowledge and experience of the drug scene.

Is cannabis a harmless natural substance?

Statements that cannabis is a harmless, natural substance are often made, especially by young people. During a presentation on the subject to a group of 'A' level biology students, one of them said to us, 'How can cannabis be harmful? It is a naturally occurring herb. God would not have put it on the earth if it was harmful.' We would not presume to speak for God, but the earth contains many natural 'herbs' that are not just harmful but that can be deadly. Tobacco, deadly nightshade and the death cap mushroom are just three examples. Such a statement from an 'A' level student may seem to the reader to be ludicrous, but it is backed up by all sorts of literature aimed at young people. There is even a 'T' shirt available that has a superb picture of a cannabis leaf on the front with the slogan 'God doesn't make mistakes'.

All such statements are unfortunately made from a lack of any real knowledge or understanding of the drug. Cannabis is a very complex substance, and one that we are only just beginning to understand. The reader is advised to study the chapter on cannabis contained within this book, especially the section on adverse effects.

Is cannabis good for people with certain medical conditions?

Statements are often made in support of the argument that cannabis is harmless and has many uses in medicine. There are a number of pieces of research going on in this country and abroad into the use of cannabis in the treatment of certain conditions. The main areas of research concern the use of the drug to alleviate the eye disease glaucoma, the nauseous effects of chemotherapy, muscle spasm in sufferers from multiple sclerosis, and to encourage appetite in patients suffering certain wasting diseases such as AIDS. None of this research is complete and is unlikely to be so for some time. Many drugs have appeared useful at first only to have disastrous consequences later, Thalidomide being only one example. There do appear to be some beneficial properties of cannabis, and it may be that some medical uses will be found, but that is not a reason to believe that it is harmless to all. Many illegal drugs have medical uses. Heroin in pharmaceutical form is used to treat extreme pain, often in the cases of certain terminal illnesses. Cocaine is still used in small quantities as an anaesthetic, whilst amphetamine is used in the treatment of sleep disorders and for hyperactivity in children. None of this means that they are harmless drugs for all to use.

Is cannabis addictive?

It all depends upon what you mean by the word 'addictive'. If you mean a solely physical dependence upon the drug, where the user's body has undergone physical changes that will necessitate further doses of the drug in order to keep going, then the statement has some truth in it. It is very rare for a user to develop a true physical dependence, but it is extremely common for regular users to develop a profound psychological dependence. We have worked with an enormous number of cannabis users over many years, and many of them live their entire lives around their cannabis use. We have known users who could not get out of bed in the morning and face the world without first using the drug. One user we have seen kept a fully charged bhong alongside his bed, and lit up as soon as he woke. Regular users often get themselves into a position where they are afraid to face life without cannabis.

People have been using cannabis for thousands of years

While it is certainly true that people have grown cannabis for many thousands of years, most of that growing has been to produce plants for use as a source of fibre for cloth, rope etc. Examples exist of the use of cannabis as a mood altering drug going back throughout recorded history, but its use in this way is very patchy. There has never been wide spread use of the drug even in countries where the plant occurs naturally. Its use as a drug has occurred within fairly restricted groups and never seems to last for a long period. Its use fades and then reoccurs in other groups years later. Unlike opium and coca, there exists no long-term history of mass use, merely a series of separate examples of small scale usage. Today's generation of users are the first in the history of the world to use cannabis on a large scale. They have volunteered to take part in the largest field trial of an unknown drug ever held. We have no idea what the result will be.

Has cannabis many non medical uses?

The figure that is always quoted in publications that support the legalization of cannabis is that there are fifty thousand non medical uses for the plant. We have been unable to discover how this figure is arrived at and who first quoted it. It seems to have become part of the mythology that surrounds cannabis. We would suggest that it is unlikely that there are fifty thousand different uses for wood or plastic, let alone cannabis. It is certainly true that cannabis fibre can be turned into cloth and rope. Hemp based ropes are still produced and have a valued use in many industries. Hemp cloth is vary rare and has almost disappeared from the normal clothing trade. Other than these two examples, there is very little use made of the plant anywhere in the world.

With over three million regular users should it be made legal?

This is a curious question. It is being suggested that if enough people do something illegal then it ought to be allowed. We would suggest that there are many examples of laws that are broken constantly by people without anyone suggesting that they ought to be repealed because of such non-compliance. It is likely that considerably more than three million people in the country drive at speeds above the legal speed limit at some time during the day. This is not a reason to do away with speed limits. Given a chance to, a large number of people would chose not to pay their income tax, but no one suggests that is a reason to scrap the income tax laws. Something may remain undesirable however many people chose to do it. The counter argument to this is that cannabis use is a victimless crime. Users are not hurting anyone but themselves and so it should be allowed. That is a common argument and provides a glimpse of the essentially selfish nature of all drug use. Drug users refuse to recognize the validity of the feelings of those around them, particularly those who care about them. They refuse to accept that their families and friends have any right to be concerned, frightened, angry or ashamed of their drug use. It is their business and no one else's. They are going to do it what ever others think.

Why do we criminalize an accepted social activity?

The first thing to say is that this cannot be an accepted social activity because it is an illegal act. It turns logic on its head to suggest otherwise. Even if there are some three million users in the UK, that still leaves over 55 million others to whom it is anathema. We live in a democracy, and society has the right to decide what is acceptable and what is not. Just because a small minority wish to do something that most do not, that is not a reason to suggest that society has to change its views in order to accept theirs.

Is cannabis attractive to people just because of its illegality?

There is no doubt that many people, especially young people, are attracted to cannabis use precisely because it is forbidden. There is an extra attraction to doing something that is against the rules. That much is true, but to think that by legalizing it you will stop the problem is to misunderstand what drug use is all about. If cannabis is legalized, all that you will have dealt with is the drug, not the users. They will still have the desire to break the rules, to do something risky and illegal. With cannabis legalized, they will not be able to exercise that desire with cannabis. What then? Perhaps they will move on to break the law with other drugs, amphetamine being the obvious choice. Much as we feel that cannabis is a harmful drug, it is clear that young people breaking the law by using cannabis is preferable to them doing it with amphetamine or other drugs.

If you legalize cannabis will you get rid of the dealers?

First of all we will need to decide how cannabis is to be marketed if it is legalized. Some have suggested that it should be sold at local pharmacies to those over a certain age. Suggested ages vary, but sixteen, the same as tobacco, or eighteen, the same as alcohol, are two favourites. With this model of marketing you still leave the dealer to satisfy the needs of those under age, or for those for whom the pharmacy is too far away or open at inconvenient times. Another suggested model is to sell cannabis at the same places where tobacco is available, such as newsagents, public houses, convenience stores, garages and so on, but still only to those over a certain age. This still fails to remove the dealer, who will still serve the needs of the young user.

If we legalize cannabis totally and allow it to be sold to anyone, of any age, and through any retail outlet including vending machines, then the dealer will have little trade available to them for cannabis. What will the dealer do then? Will he or she give up and sign on at the job centre. We doubt it. We suggest that they will carry on doing what they know best. They will carry on dealing drugs.

This is exactly what has happened in Amsterdam since cannabis became available from cafes. The dealers simply switched to selling other drugs, particularly amphetamine, which has seen a massive increase in its use in Holland.

The only way in which the dealer could be taken completely out of the picture is to legalize all drugs and sell them everywhere and to anybody. Are we really ready to contemplate that? Does anyone really believe that such a move would result in less drugs being used?

Would there be less crime committed if cannabis was legalized?

If cannabis was legalized it would be left to the private sector to supply and market it. It is hardly likely that the government would consider becoming involved in the production and supply of cannabis for street use.

Private enterprise would set the price at what the market would bear. When the sale of alcohol was legalized in America, following the ending of prohibition in 1933, the new breweries set their prices to match what the public had been used to paying for their illegal liquor in the 'speakeasies'. That is what is likely to happen here. Perhaps competition between suppliers would bring the price down a little, but that can only happen if sales rise because more people are using the drug. On top of that, it is likely that the government would place a tax on cannabis in the same way as they do with alcohol and tobacco. This may mean an overall rise in the price, with the potential for more crime taking place to pay for it.

At the moment tobacco and alcohol products are common targets during burglaries and similar crimes. That targeting will simply switch to cannabis also.

Will legalizing cannabis save Police and Customs resources?

If cannabis is made legal, then clearly that will mean that police and customs officers will save valuable time investigating the importation, supply and use of the drug. If that then leads on to a rise in the use of other drugs for the reasons that we have outlined earlier in this chapter, then it is likely that no overall saving will be made. On top of that we need to consider what effect mass use of cannabis will have on public safety and order. There is already a problem on our streets caused by large numbers of people affected by alcohol. Are we ready to add cannabis to this situation?

Some other things to think about

It is our view that to change the law in relation to cannabis so that it is more freely available would lead inevitably to an increase in its use, and that of other drugs. Such an increase in drug use would lead to the same level of increase in the calls upon our already over stretched health service. Who is going to pay for that? Not the regular drug users, that is for sure. A large percentage of them will not be in gainful employment and not making any sort of contribution to the Treasury.

And where are we going to get enough cannabis to meet this increase in demand? It is likely that growers will try to produce as much as they can in this country, but there can be little doubt that the majority will have to be imported at large cost to our balance of payments situation. Production in this country will displace the cultivation of other crops, and replacements for these will have to imported, compounding the problem. We will need to think about where we are going to import cannabis from. It is highly unlikely that any other countries would follow us in legalizing the drug, and would be very unhappy about supplies travelling through their territory to reach us. It may even be necessary for our government to make arrangements with organized international criminals in order to obtain the necessary supplies and then to become involved in smuggling it through other countries to reach ours.

What will happen to educational standards if the majority of our young people, and indeed those educating them are using cannabis regularly? We know that it affects short-term memory and long-term motivation, and it is difficult to see how standards can do anything else but decline sharply. The same may happen to production in industry and commerce, with workers at all levels suffering from the affects of cannabis use.

If cannabis was available freely in the UK we could become the centre for massive drug tourism, with many thousands of foreign nationals being attracted here to obtain their supplies and to take quantities of the drug back to their home countries. We would also see the arrival of foreign suppliers trying to muscle in on the trade. What would happen to the reputation of this country? To catch a glimpse of what would happen it is only necessary to look at the situation in Holland. If you ask the average man in the street what comes to mind when they think of Amsterdam, they will not talk of tulips, canals, windmills, clogs or Anne Frank, but will talk of drugs, especially cannabis and cannabis using. Is that really the sort of reputation that we want for our country?

If we decide to go down the road of legalizing cannabis, it needs to be clearly understood that it is a one way road. Once legalized, its use will, in our view, increase to such an extent that it will become impossible to try and return to the present position. This is not something that can be experimented with in order to see what would happen. If we do take that step it will be forever. There will be no going back.

Once the legalization of cannabis is secured, what will be next? To think that some of the supporters of cannabis will be satisfied then is to show a degree of naiveté that defies belief. Some will not be satisfied until all drugs are legalized. And where will that leave us?

Formulation of a Substance Misuse Policy
Guidance Notes

The following notes are intended to provide a check list for all those who are attempting to formulate a school, or similar institution's, substance misuse policy. It is recognized that schools and other institutions vary greatly, and may face different problems, but each point in the check list will need to be considered if the policy is to be comprehensive.

1. A statement of the school's philosophy towards the use of illegal substances, the misuse of legal substances and the provision of substance misuse education.

   Points to consider

   - Possession and or use of illegal drugs, solvents, tobacco, alcohol, prescribed medicines or legal but undesirable substances.

2. A clear definition of where, when, and to whom the policy applies.

   Points to consider

   - Limits of school site
   - School trips, including foreign trips
   - Application to pupils, staff, ancillaries etc.
   - Application to visitors to the school
   - Application when pupils revisit the site out of school hours, either authorized or unauthorized
   - Application out of school but in uniform or still identifiable as part of the school
   - Application when not connected with the school, i.e. in own time.

3. Statement of disciplinary sanctions that can be applied to breaches of the policy.

Points to consider

- Exclusion, first or last option
- Possession for own use
- Encouragement of others to join in substance misuse
- Supply or possession with intent to supply.

4. Contact with parents.

Points to consider

- Providing an opportunity for parents to comment on the proposed policy
- Involvement of parents when substance misuse is suspected
- Feedback to parents on implementation of the policy
- Provision of awareness raising sessions for parents.

5. Liaison with the police. Will the police be called in to deal with incidents and in what circumstances.

6. Liaison with other bodies who use the school premises.

7. The circumstances in which members of staff will carry out searches of school premises, lockers, desks and cupboards, pupils' possessions and person.

8. Will the school admit pupils who have been excluded from another school following an incident of substance misuse.

9. The appointment of a 'key person' who will co-ordinate all enquiries into substance related incidents.

10. Training of staff in the recognition and management of substance related incidents.

11. Liaison with the media.

Points to consider

Should all media enquiries be dealt with by named person or persons. The school's position with regard to reporters who may wish to interview staff or pupils either in school or 'at the school gate'. Parents may make comments to the press that call for a response from the school.

12. Liaison with other agencies, such as drug misuse services, local doctors, hospitals, health promotion units, etc.

National Agencies and Help Lines Concerned with Substance Misuse

The following are national organizations that may be of help to anyone seeking further information, help or support due to a drug or substance problem.

AUSTRALIA

The National Drug Strategy Committee
GPO Box 9848, Canberra ACT2601
Tel. 6 289 7731
Fax. 6 282 5430
(Information and advice concerning substance abuse)

CANADA

Canadian Centre on Substance Abuse / National Clearing House on Substance Abuse
112 Kent Street, Suite 480, Ottawa, Ontario KIP 5P2
Tel. 613 235 4048
(Information and advice concerning substance abuse)

REPUBLIC OF IRELAND

The Department of Health
Hawkins House, Dublin 2, Republic of Ireland
(Provides details of services available)

Irish National Drugs Help Line
Tel. 1850 70 1850
(Provides free confidential advice to drug users, families and friends.
Line open 10.00 am to 10.00 pm)

NETHERLANDS

Netherlands Institute for Alcohol and Drugs
PO. Box 725, 3500 AS Utrecht, The Netherlands.
Tel. 0 30 34 13 00
(Provides advice and literature on drug matters)

Association of Committees for the Care of Drug Addicts
PO. Box 1447, 3500 BK Utrecht, The Netherlands
Tel. 0 30 33 10 65
(Provides advice regarding facilities for those addicted to drugs)

Netherlands Association of Advice Bureaus Against Alcohol and Drugs
Chr. Krammlaan 8, 3571 AX Utrecht, The Netherlands
Tel. 0 30 72 04 94
(Has 16 regional offices who provide advice and referral)

NEW ZEALAND

National Society on Alcoholism and Drug Dependence (NSAD)
20 Parumoana Street, Ponrua, New Zealand
Tel. 42370273
(Provides advice and literature on drug matters)

New Zealand Drug Foundation
PO. Box 3082, Thorndon, Wellington, New Zealand
Tel. 44992920
Fax. 44992925
(Provides advice and literature on drug matters)

UK

SCODA – Standing Conference on Drug Abuse
32–36 Loman Street, London SE1 0EE
Tel. 0171 928 9500
(National co-ordinating body for agencies and organizations working in the drugs field)

ISDD – Institute for the Study of Drug Dependence
1 Hatton Place, London EC1N 8ND
Tel. 0171 430 1991
(For up to date material on various aspects of substance misuse)

Release
388 Old Street, London EC1V 8LT
Tel. 0171 729 9904 or 0171 603 8654
(Advice, information and referral on legal and drug related problems for users, their families and friends)

RE-SOLV
30a High Street, Stone, Staffordshire ST15 8AW
Tel. 01785 817885
(Works to reduce and prevent solvent abuse)

National Drugs Helpline
Tel. 0800 77 66 00
(free, confidential, 24 hour service to users, their families and friends)

National Aids Helpline
Tel. 0800 567 123
(free, confidential, 24 hour service)

Welsh Committee on Drug Misuse
Secretariat, c/o HSSPIA, Welsh Office, Cathays Park,
Cardiff CF1 3NQ
Tel. 01222 823925
(Details of local services and literature on substance misuse)

Scottish Drugs Forum
5 Waterloo Street, Glasgow G2 6AY
Tel. 0141 221 1175

Northern Ireland Council for Voluntary Action
127 Ormeau Road, Belfast BT7 1SH
Tel. 01232 321224
(Details of drug services in Northern Ireland)

UNITED STATES OF AMERICA

National Clearinghouse for Alcohol and Drug Information
PO Box 2345, Rockville, MD 20852
(Information and advice concerning substance abuse)

Cocaine Helpline
Tel. 1 800 C.O.C.A.I.N.E.
(24 hour free and confidential help regarding cocaine use)

National Institute On Drug Abuse Hotline
Tel. 1 800 662 H.E.L.P.
(24 hour free and confidential help and referral for those with drug problems)

Index